RENOVATION

LESLIE ABNER

RENOVATION

A NOVEL

atmosphere press

chapter
one

On our first anniversary, my husband reserved a table at an upscale restaurant in midtown Manhattan where a salad cost twenty-five dollars and the waiters wore designer suits. We had cut back on takeout for a few months, saving up for the celebratory dinner. Neil had spent days researching and identifying the perfect spot, and he called precisely thirty days in advance to secure a table. He stood a little taller, showing his pride in planning an overpriced dinner, even though we'd had to save up. The restaurant was miles away from his childhood of home-cooked meals with few dinners out.

I let Neil take the lead. Truth is, he enjoyed the planning, the decision-making. I appreciated his assertiveness after my childhood filled with too many responsibilities. Besides, my previous boyfriend had thought a romantic evening consisted of a barstool and a Corona.

"Just confirming our plan, I'll meet you back home after work. Then we can head over to the restaurant together," Neil said.

"Yup, I told Francine I had to be out on time tonight. I was very clear. Don't worry," I promised, placing my hands on his narrow shoulders, leaning so close that our noses almost kissed. Neil tucked my hair behind my ear and pecked my forehead before pulling away and pouring his coffee.

I didn't find my part-time job as an assistant interior designer demanding, but Francine, my boss, frequently assigned "imperative" tasks as I began packing up for the day. If they were truly important, I wouldn't have minded, but it was usually something like sharpening pencils or vacuuming the office. It was my first experience working for a designer while I finished design school and a stepping stone to greater things. Despite Neil's judgment, jeopardizing my career over an extra hour of busy work didn't seem constructive.

I planned to go home, get ready for dinner, and surprise Neil with the sexy lingerie I'd squirreled away from a shop near Francine's office. I'd bought the hottest black negligee I could find during their sale after Valentine's Day and saved it for our one-year anniversary.

As I should have expected, Francine insisted I refold an entire closet's worth of fabric samples at exactly five forty-five. I overtly checked my watch, hoping she would notice.

"This whole closet needs work, Skylar. Organize by color, then by style," she instructed.

"I need to leave in fifteen minutes, remember? My anniversary dinner," I said sheepishly.

"Oh. Yeah. Well, you can stay a little later, right? What time is the reservation?" she asked.

"I think it's seven thirty, but I wanted—"

"Oh, so you're fine; you have plenty of time."

"Well, I wanted to go home first. It's a nice restaurant. I don't think I can go like this." I glanced down at my jeans covered in lint and strings.

"You look adorable. Try to get through the whole closet by seven fifteen, and you won't be late."

I wanted to burn every last sample in that closet and dump the ashes on Francine's pristine desk. When I left a voice message for Neil, I made sure I spoke loud enough, demanding Francine's attention. I would have quit if I didn't need a part-time job while finishing my graduate degree in design. Francine could push me, but quitting symbolized failure, and my parents would not live in disappointment again due to Francine's inconsideration. My parents never let my sister quit her fight to live; quitting was a certain failure in my family.

I could barely pronounce the word Rhabdomyosarcoma when my sister had been diagnosed. I had jotted down phonetic notes while eavesdropping on phone calls to gather information. By the time I turned twenty, I spoke medical jargon with ease, but it hadn't helped. Chrissy closed her eyes for the last time, and it had devastated me. I lost so much of myself when I lost her. There's the Skylar with Chrissy in this world and the broken version of myself after she disappeared. A sadness hovered over my family after that, but if I established my own design firm, I imagined the softening of my parents' worry lines, relieved that at least one daughter achieved her dreams.

Francine didn't lift an eye off her paperwork. I sneered in her direction and quickly looked away. Maybe I would save the lingerie for after dinner. Would Neil even notice or appreciate my efforts? I practiced in my head the conversation I would have with Neil, smoothing over another late night at work. He chided me that my softhearted nature never served me well, but my pacifist nature had developed when my sister became ill, courageously ensuring a calm home even at my own expense. Consoling my parents and jumping at every painful task in my sister's caretaking made me feel useful; anything easing my parents' anguish was worth the sacrifice.

I flew into the restaurant at seven fifty. Neil sat at the bar with a stiffened back and a blank look on his face, but I could smell his concealed agitation permeating the air like an overly perfumed woman in an elevator. I planted a long, passionate kiss on his lips, hoping he would forget my tardiness. I knew he despised sitting alone. Neil's body tensed as I kissed him, and the pang in my gut lingered.

"I'm sorry. It's Francine. She's so pushy. The most insensitive woman on the planet," I said.

Climbing toward my career goals drove me. Neil felt the

same about his career, and he excused his frequent travel, yet never my inconsistent hours. I wanted Francine's approval, and I yearned for more responsibility in her business, but balancing the needs of Neil and Francine was exhausting. For the moment, work was my top priority.

"Really, Sky? I can't believe you couldn't get out of there earlier. Just get up and leave," Neil said.

I pulled air deeply into my lungs, searching for relief from the stress of his disapproval. I wasn't in the mood to argue. Neil didn't appreciate unpredictability, and I had learned how to restore equilibrium when I set him off-kilter.

"I'm sorry. I wanted to, but she insisted, and I didn't want to have a big thing with her. Let's focus on having a great night together. I may even have a surprise for you later." I wrapped my arms around him, smothering any opportunity for an argument. Our marriage had taught me tricks for diffusing his temper, and my awareness of Neil's mood often dictated my buoyant attitude in overcompensation.

"It's so beautiful in here. And the flowers. I've never seen anything like it," I gushed as soon as we were seated in the serene dining room.

"Yeah. Nice," Neil said, burying his head in the oversized menu. "What are you going to order? Maybe you should order the fish. That would be good for you. It has shallots. Your favorite."

I smiled. Neil remembered the little things, reminding me how well he knew me.

I silently analyzed the space, tilting my head back to observe the ceiling. The cloud-like, all-white interiors of Narcissus made me nervous about ordering red wine. I swear I heard an elongated hush when we entered the vast dining room.

"Sky? What?" Neil asked.

"No, nothing," I said.

"C'mon. I see those eyes. What's happening in that creative little head of yours?"

"It's just the lighting—I think they're not using uniform lightbulbs in the fixtures. It's nothing, you know, it's just me." My eyes scanned rooms with robot-like precision, identifying fine designs and overlooked details.

"Don't be so judgmental, Sky. Not everyone can live up to your design standards." Neil shook his head and changed the subject, going on about the new project his technology firm recently acquired. As the lead programmer and developer on the job, Neil had secured a hearty promotion.

While I was proud of his accomplishments, Neil's quick advancement had catapulted him into a frenzy for success. I listened carefully, trying to comprehend the complex programming he had developed, and drenched him with accolades even when the concepts evaded me. I occasionally interjected tidbits of my own day, and Neil praised me like a puppy retrieving a stick for the first time. I heard my mother's voice rewarding me for taking out empty trash cans filled with gauze pads and surgical tape. My heart had warmed when I pleased my mother and made her daily life easier, and I felt the same tingle of pleasure in taking care of Neil before myself.

On our walk home, I reached for Neil's hand and fiddled with his fingers. He stroked my thumb three or four times before loosening my grip and placing his hand in his pocket. He demonstrated love through romantic dinner reservations and quiet Sunday afternoons reading the paper together. He rarely showed his love for me with gestures, but I knew Neil loved me, and that was enough.

After our normal bedtime rituals, we slid into bed from opposite sides, meeting in the middle beneath the sheets. Neil wrapped his arms around me, and his hands wandered beneath my new negligee without noticing the unfamiliar lace. Our routine of expected caresses, kisses, and positions satisfied us both. For a few moments, Neil's body lay close behind me, molding to my curves until he turned toward the window, and his heavy breathing escalated and morphed into a snore.

I lay in the dark room thinking about how quickly our first year of marriage had passed. Neil had whisked me away from the trauma and turmoil that had stayed with me after my sister died. His insistence on picking the restaurant and every other detail in our lives at times seemed overbearing, but his strength and decision-making proved how much he cared for me. Nursing and grieving had consumed my parents, and I often felt invisible and then guilty for having such selfish thoughts. Neil had stepped into my life, doting on me and taking control when decisions were overwhelmed by grief. The days when Chrissy's memory felt like weights in my shoes, Neil had pressed his lips to my forehead and let me loaf on the sofa while he folded the laundry and picked up the groceries. I'll always be grateful for his taking care of me.

chapter
two

"233, 235, 239," I mumbled to myself. *Where is 237?*

Francine had requested I pick up the prints of professionally photographed projects for her portfolio. She treated me more like a servant than a part-time design assistant. Normally, she kept me captive in her SoHo office like a Disney princess for the sole purpose of answering occasional client phone calls. I sat for hours honing my doodling skills, thankful for the array of colored pencils in the supply closet.

"My clients need me, Skylar. They must always know I'm there for them," she said.

Her palpable fear that a client might suffer the unthinkable consequence of receiving her voicemail seemed ironic as her recorded message repeated in my ear for the fourth time. I hung up after I heard the "*au revoir*" in an authentic French accent at the conclusion of her message.

Francine's dire need for professional photographs for a new client meeting the next day forced her into her last resort. In her desperation, she had given me a task out of the office, and my determination to impress my boss dominated my day. I twirled my hair as I approached the clerk in a bodega on the block. "Excuse me, I'm looking for 237 West 22nd Street?"

He shook his head. "No 237."

My mind betrayed me, convincing me it was my fault, even though Francine had never provided the name of the photo lab. It reminded me of the nights I had tossed in bed, wondering if my sister's cancer was my fault. If there was something I could have, should have, done differently. Despite the chilly December twilight, sweat pooled in my armpits. I speculated that the lab's operating hours were nearly ending, as was my patience. My lengthy message for Francine begged for guidance as my simple task morphed into a scavenger hunt. I bounced with relief when my phone rang in my overcoat pocket.

"Hey, what's up?" Neil said.

Neil expected me at our tiny Upper East Side apartment for dinner. I could visualize his bouncing knee speeding its pace.

"I'm just searching aimlessly in the West Twenties for a photo lab that doesn't seem to exist." Sarcasm filled my words.

"What do you mean?" he asked.

As we talked, my feet pounded the frigid concrete. I dug my exposed hand deep in my pocket, searching for a trace of warmth.

"Francine must have written down the wrong address, and I can't get in touch with her, so here I am." I gazed up at the delicate flakes falling from a sliver of sky framed by the reaching pre-war buildings.

"How long have you been down there?" Neil sounded annoyed, as if he were the one inconvenienced. He had little patience for incompetence. Even in preparation for our wedding, Neil had compiled detailed lists and drawings for each vendor, then scoured over the menu, choosing the vegetable based on color, preferring the green string beans over the orange carrots, and contemplating whether the beef should be placed to the left or the right. Of course, it had turned out perfectly. Everything Neil orchestrated followed a well-thought-out plan. His military father had demanded precision in every facet of his life, and that explained Neil's success in the exacting science of computer programming. As we'd recited our vows, a perfect pink sunset had glistened around us precisely at dusk in the simple, non-denominational ceremony that Neil's best friend had officiated. Sixty friends and family had encircled us as Neil's thumb stroked my hand and I whispered "I do" into his icy blue eyes.

"Magical, just magical!" my aunt had repeated over and over again.

The snowflakes picked up speed, and one landed in my eye, pulling me back to the frigid sidewalk blanketed in snow. "I don't know, maybe thirty or forty minutes. I'm hoping Francine will call me back."

"Skylar, that's insane. Can't you just come home? I'm starving. It was her mistake, right? So, forget it, her problem, not yours."

Anxiety crept into my chest, and I longed for Neil's tolerance of my unpredictable work schedule. Normally, his mathematical mind created solvable equations for any situation, so my stomach never twisted into knots and my palms remained cool and dry, knowing his control resulted in success. His confidence and eloquence charmed those he encountered, but he couldn't hide his moodiness from me, especially when my career interfered with his agenda.

"Neil, I can't just—oh shoot, this might be her; I gotta go." I clicked the line over.

"Hi, Skylar. What's the problem? I wrote everything down for you. I really can't be disturbed when I'm with clients. It's very unprofessional."

The shoulds slipped into my head. I should have called in advance. I should have noticed the lab's name was missing from the scrap of paper. I crumbled under her dissatisfaction. Maybe her disappointment was justified. My confidence waned, and it weighed me down, dragged me under. I longed to feel courageous and large, but Francine shrunk me. I envied her gumption in starting her own business and wished someday I would discover that faith in myself. My parents didn't have the luxury of encouraging my dreams, and I always wondered if my goals were realistic or simply fantasies.

"I'm sorry, I didn't know what to do. I can't find the lab. It seems there's no 237 on 22nd Street."

"I don't know what the problem is, Skylar. It's really a simple task," she huffed.

"I'm sorry. I've walked up and down the block several times. What's the name of the lab? Maybe I can call them," I stammered.

"Ugh, no, it's 24th Street," Francine grumbled.

"Oh, okay, that explains it. I'll go now. I'm sorry." My palms felt slick within my clenched fists.

"Skylar, you really need to think before you call. Try to use your head and figure it out. All you twenty-somethings are too needy."

A sharp, twisting pain lingered in my chest.

"Francine, I had the wrong address, and you didn't give me the name of the lab, so—"

"Skylar, I can't do this right now. I'll see you tomorrow . . . with the photographs."

Francine hung up, and I kept moving.

chapter
three

The next morning, I opened the door to Francine Heger Bosck's design studio. The three-name thing struck me as a bit affected, but when I met her, she'd hidden her venti-sized ego.

Many designers offered internships, but paying jobs were a challenge. Although Neil never pressured me about our finances, my contributions, even if small, lit my pride. He had a secure job at an established technology firm that aided dozens of small start-ups struggling to build their programs. Their successes translated into decent bonuses. As the firm had expanded, Neil had earned his place as an integral part of the team. When Francine had offered me a paying position, I'd hoped for the same job satisfaction Neil had found.

Unaware of Francine's reputation and design style when I began my job search, I'd relished her office location in the heart of SoHo. I'd jumped when she offered me the job.

Manhattan's downtown vibe made my spine grow taller and my strides longer. Uptown felt like coloring neatly within the lines, while downtown's abstract scribble defied the rules in pursuit of artistic freedom. Situated in a former textile factory, Francine divided her office space with her husband Scott, who owned a start-up gourmet food business. I could feel him perk up as I stepped through the door. He undressed me with a squint.

"Hi, Skylar! How are you today?" he purred.

I immediately rolled my shoulders forward, as if I could hide. Ten years my senior, Francine and Scott had an aloof downtown aura. They were artistic and creative in their business approach as well as their lifestyle. Francine wore outfits with cascading fabrics in vibrant colors that concealed her hefty figure. Scott's chalky skin, floppy gray hair, and lanky frame were diametrically opposed to Francine's appearance. I was tempted to slip a business card for a local orthodontist on his desk.

My dreams of a fantastic job in design had faded quickly. I wasted hours in her cramped office space, wondering why she hired me. My nerves around her caused a stream of aimless words to flood faster than my brain could provide direction. In a botched effort to fill the space and acquire her friendship, I had asked too many questions and watched helplessly at my rambling.

It was clear she had no intention of relinquishing any responsibilities or mentoring me. Francine tended to clients on job sites while I passed the time in her office with her creepy husband lurking nearby.

"So, Sky, whatcha up to today?" Scott asked as he circled my desk.

He placed one hand on my shoulder, then the other, and began a forced massage. I froze as if demonstrating tonic immobility.

"Doesn't that feel good?" he moaned.

My shoulders grazed my earlobes, preventing his wandering hands from exploring any further. I imagined myself standing up and planting an open palm across his bony face, but the pacifist within me hijacked my nerve.

"I'm good, Scott." I squeezed my shoulder blades tightly together, cocking my neck sideways with a slight shake.

"Awww, c'mon, Skylar. You just need to relax." His words poured out smoothly like melted chocolate.

"No. Really. I'm good. You can stop now. Thanks. Please stop, Scott." As the words slipped out, I berated myself. Please? Why would I say please?

Was I that desperate to keep this crappy job? I imagined Neil's impatience if I shared the office dynamics, and I tamed my jitters by inhaling deeply. His anger would be justified, but finding my own strong voice kept me from sharing certain details with him. Scott smiled, peering down at me, then bowed, aligning his face with mine. My fingers quivered as I grasped my water bottle. I tilted my head back and gulped water as my eyes avoided contact with his. My inner voice repeated, "Please go away" about ten times, as if silent prayers could influence his behavior.

"Okay, sweetie, but you are really missing out. I give a killer massage. I would have you relaxed in no time," he whispered so close to my ear that his lips brushed my earlobe.

I jerked my body away from him.

A thousand questions went through my head in only seconds. Is this really happening? Will I get fired if I tell off my boss's husband? Why aren't I doing something? I berated myself but remained motionless.

He slowly removed his hands from my shoulders, dragging his fingers along my neck and back before completely removing them from my body. My stomach thrashed, and nausea settled in my throat. I grabbed my phone to call Neil. After entering the first few digits, I paused.

Neil would persuade me to quit or insist I quit. He might be right. My proximity to Scott grossed me out, but showing Neil and my family that I could save myself guided my actions. I longed for my own decisions and consequences. Sharing my experience with Neil would complicate the already twisted situation.

Neil and I were like a comfortable, worn-in pair of jeans. Evoking a smile and hearing his laugh was worth the extra effort to keep our marriage smooth, and in return, I appreciated his intelligence and ambition. When we had met, Neil wanted my devotion and all my time. My sister's illness had left little room for indulgent nurturing at home, and Neil's love had cloaked me in the attention and security that didn't exist in my childhood.

As I'd slid the silk gown over my narrow hips the morning of our wedding, I had pictured a beautiful, unwrinkled life with Neil. I had placed him at the center of my world, and he had made me the center of his. He didn't need to be burdened with a warped sleaze like Scott. I could handle it.

———

chapter
four

My days of interior design school were almost over, and each morning after my classes ended, I ignored my watch. I delayed my journey downtown to Francine's office, where an afternoon of useless filing and a dash of sexual harassment awaited me. I engaged in social conversations in the school lobby or feigned an important question for a professor. Francine wasn't teaching me much, and my anxiety, mixed with boredom, tested my emotional endurance. Only her downtown location coaxed me to stay.

One cold day, I arrived at a scene of Francine obsessing over holiday gifts. She'd settled on boxes of hand-printed stationery and consumed herself with selecting the perfect wrapping paper. My eye rolls grew more frequent, and I heard Neil's voice in my head warning me of my passive-aggressive tendencies.

Francine placed the tape, scissors, coveted wrapping paper, and ribbon on the table next to Scott's desk. I began the meticulous process of cutting the delicate paper and covering the boxes with precision.

"How's it going?" Francine's billowy skirt puffed as she bounded across the room. "You must match the pattern. This looks sloppy. Can't you see the pattern is not aligning?"

My cell phone vibrated on the desk, with Neil's number scrolling across the screen. "That's my husband; I'll just be a minute."

She uttered a loud sigh as she turned away from the table.

"Hey, I only have a minute. What's up?"

"Just found out I need to fly out to San Francisco tonight. Some jerk over there rebooted the system before making a backup. Can you believe—"

I had to interrupt him, or Francine's stare might have burned a hole in my forehead. "That sucks. When do you think you'll be back?"

I pictured Neil inspecting his fingers and biting at the cuticles, a symptom of his stress.

"Hard to say. Need to see when I get there. I hope two or three days, but I'll let you know."

"Okay. I'm sorry, but Francine is waiting for me, so . . ."

"Oh, please. She can wait. She's barely paying you, for God's sake. I have to run anyway. Go ahead. Call me later."

Regardless of my pay, or lack thereof, I dressed professionally, folded fabrics neatly, and kept the office well organized. Neil equated compensation with value, but the interior design business didn't operate that way. The margins weren't large enough to pay rookies well, but I understood how an outsider might view this luxurious business, servicing an exorbitantly rich clientele, as lucrative. Interior design could never generate income like Neil's employer, Giotto Technologies.

More influential than money, the power of designing a space for someone's life to unfold within appealed to me. I remembered my childhood surroundings as gray, and I would close my eyes and imagine a new, happier backdrop for my family's suffering. My mother hadn't had the luxury of choosing drapes or pillows. Instead, she had chosen hospitals for my sister, all with matching green scrubs, faded gowns, and rigid vinyl furniture. Her choices had been between the day shift or night shift based on doctor's appointments. My sister and I had spent afternoons painting with watercolors, covering hospital rooms with the pages like wallpaper. A mélange of checks, stripes, and swirls had surrounded her bed, and even during her final days, she had been able to push out a remnant of laughter gazing at the hodgepodge of papers barely hanging onto the ceiling above her. My fantasy of a brighter, happier space for my sister had come alive with her help.

I imagined responding to Francine's request with a booming and distinct, "Hey, crazy lady, your clients don't care about aligned wrapping paper!" But I wilted and stepped away from the table, observing Francine executing the task as she envisioned.

"Really?" Scott asked. "I think it looks great. Do you really think anyone will notice perfectly matched wrapping paper? It's Christmas! People care about the gift, not the wrapping."

Francine glared at him as if he were a disrespectful child talking back to his mother. "Scott, this has nothing to do with you, and why are you defending her?" Icicles hung from her words.

"She's young. She's doing a great job, Francine. You're being too hard on her," Scott cajoled.

I sat between the awkward exchange, biting my lower lip, feigning preoccupation with the stupid wrapping paper. I silently prayed Scott's defensive babble would end.

"Scott, outside. Now." Francine motioned with her hands for Scott to follow.

Francine peered over her shoulder, sending a scowl my way as she entered the vestibule. I balanced my forehead on the heel of my hand and shook it back and forth. I knew the urgency of getting out of this mess, but I didn't want to be a quitter. I wanted to prove my resolve to Neil. Although he never uttered the words, Neil obviously viewed my career more like a hobby. He categorized design as a mere artistic whim, a fun job, unlike my vision of a serious career filled with goals I strove toward. I hadn't shared my work's offensive details with Neil, and I dreaded explaining a brisk exit.

They made no attempt to hush their screaming. Francine accused him of wanting to "screw her," which I assumed referred to me, and he called her "frigid" twice. The words became less recognizable, not based on volume or distance but because their roars folded over one another.

Intuition and self-preservation took over before I could give it more thought. I collected my bag, threw my shoulders back, and stomped through the boxing match.

"Skylar, where are you going? The gifts aren't done," Francine barked.

I paused and granted myself a moment to compose effective words. "We're done here." I controlled my words and annunciated each syllable for effect. "You should put a leash on your husband before you hire a new assistant. And, for the record, there's no chance I would ever, in a million years, 'screw' him. He's all yours."

I rushed through the space between Francine and Scott, eliminating any possibility of a rebuttal.

As I stood on the northbound 6 Train, I was filled with disgust and hot tears pushed forward, burning my cheeks. I should have left months ago. I should have told Scott off. Why hadn't I told Scott off? I had taken pride in improving the situation by avoiding Scott and disengaging. I had thought the circumstances would just improve if I removed myself from the harassment, but perhaps an uncomfortable confrontation had been necessary. In the end, people are who they are, and I learned I would be better served trusting my gut instinct.

How would I explain leaving to Neil? I hoped blaming Francine's controlling behavior would suffice. I couldn't bear Neil's reaction to Scott's inappropriate behavior or being seen as a quitter.

chapter
five

Fortunately, I quit just as show house season began, where the trendiest designers transform spectacular townhomes and invite the public in for a viewing. Throughout the hand-painted, art-strewn halls of New York City's premier show house, each room precisely furnished by a different designer, I overheard cosmopolitan women raving about wallpaper for their Long Island beach retreats. I visited the various show houses each spring, gathering inspiration and contacts in the industry.

Upscale women from the city and surrounding areas donned their designer ensembles, grabbed their Hermes leather goods, and pilgrimaged to show houses. Elite interior designers exhibited their talents for high society while simultaneously supporting a local charity.

Attendees modeled perfectly coiffed hair and diamonds like ice cubes. It would be easy to sneer at these entitled breeds, but I found them entertaining. Their behaviors and conversations were an alternate universe to my simple life. Although I would never be a member of that species, I'd watched Francine's clients deliver gifts from their luxurious vacations and include her in extravagant dinner parties. Not in a condescending, you-work-for-me kind of way, but surprisingly genuine. I mean, as genuine as one can get in a working relationship with the privileged. I hoped one day, I would have clients that did the same.

I woke up early to get ready, allowing plenty of time to

linger in the show house.

"Neil, you almost ready?" I called into the bedroom from the kitchen.

Silence.

This time, louder: "Neil?"

I strode into our bedroom, where the pillows propped Neil up and his legs were outstretched and crossed at his ankles. His green-and-white flannel pajama pants were stained with toothpaste. Neil stared at the television even as I entered the room.

"I thought we were going to leave soon?"

"Huh?"

"The show house?"

"Oh, that. Do we really have to go?"

I tugged at the lone string hanging from my jeans pocket, winding it around my finger, then unwinding and repeating. My gaze met the floor.

"We don't have to, but I really want to go. I mean, it would be good for me to start getting into the interior design world."

"This guy's an idiot. How could he not know that answer? And it was the three-hundred-dollar question. That's the easiest one." He stared at the TV, clearly more interested in it than me or my career.

"So, you're not coming?"

The string ripped from my jeans.

"Come here." Neil patted the empty space on the bed beside him. I approached the side of the bed, fiddling with the denim string. Neil reached for my hand, but I was too far away.

"Can't we just relax? Do you really need to go to this thing? It's just looking at fancy real estate. *Lifestyles of the Rich and Famous*. I just want to chill with you here. And I know you're dying to see who wins *Jeopardy!*."

I couldn't lift my eyes from the frayed string in my fingers. "I'd really like to go. I thought we were going together."

"Okay, okay, if you feel that strongly about it, just go."

"Well, I don't want to have a big fight . . ."

"Just go. It's fine," Neil said, staring back into the light of the television.

The edge in his tone left no room for interpretation. Neil didn't want me at that show house; he wanted me home next to him watching *Jeopardy!* for the hundredth time. I felt shards of eggshells beneath my feet, and I shuffled out of the room with my shoulders rolled forward in disappointment.

I counted my steps when walking to the show house to distract myself from the ick in my stomach from being blown off. My conversation with Neil repeated in my ears for nine blocks, but then I remembered when he encouraged me to apply to an interior design school. He surprised me with piles of supplies and pressed his hands against my sweaty palm on the steps of the school, calming my first-day nerves. It was the first time I could remember, or at least the first time since my sister died, that someone had been fully focused on me and what I wanted in life. Two days later, he slid the silver-and-diamond ring over my knuckle, securing his place in my life. I smiled, recalling his enthusiasm, and my stomach settled. The counting faded, and I regained my excitement about the show house.

Meandering through the lush first floor, then climbing the curved regal staircase, I imagined designing a room for a show house. First, I would need a sophisticated company name, and on cue, they sped across my thoughts like the NASDAQ ticker tape: Interiors by SP, Skylar Pearce Studio, S Interiors, Pearce Home Design. My excitement swelled at the thought of achieving such an accomplishment, then quickly deflated like a balloon pierced with a pin. I needed much more experience, and how would I obtain clients? How would Neil feel about it? I filed the thought under pipe dreams.

The impressive lady's primary bathroom flaunted hues of pink, highlighting the hand-crafted silver wallpaper that set the room aglow. Silver leaf frames containing Botticelli-inspired artwork accessorized the art deco space like jewelry on a fashion runway. Polished chrome faucets covered with intricate carvings sat upon the onyx countertop. I lifted my chin and hung my head back as my eyes absorbed the hand-painted metallic ceiling.

"Hi!" a voice said. "Please let me know if you have any questions."

I was pulled from my trance by a woman with curly blond hair and an adorable grin. Her pedestrian outfit dismissed any possibility of blending with the chichi women parading through the show house.

"These drapes are beautiful," I said. "What showroom is the fabric from?"

During my first job, as a showroom employee in the Decoration and Design building, I'd studied the various fabric showrooms and had a particular interest in designers' selections. The Decoration and Design building, affectionately called the D&D building to anyone in the know, housed seventeen floors of showrooms representing exclusive brands in an architecturally uninspired building.

"Let me see . . ." She pulled out a sheet of paper from a drawer in the bathroom vanity. "Ah, here it is. It looks like the fabric is from Osborne and Little," she replied.

"No way!" I said, "I used to work there."

"Really? That's so funny," she asked.

"I worked at the sample desk, but now I'm looking for a job with a designer. I'm Skylar, Skylar Pearce. I just love this design. It's beautiful."

"The designer will be thrilled to hear that. Andrew is great. Such a nice guy and so talented, too. I've known him for years," she said.

Memories flashed through my head, reliving my dreadful experience with Francine. I'd jumped at the job Francine offered, but this time around, I assured myself I would choose carefully. Gaining knowledge about design and running a business in a more desirable work environment became paramount.

The résumés resting in my tote begged to be released. My mind drifted from the woman's chatter as I devised a tactful way to pass one along. I wanted to at least meet this Andrew she continued to rave about.

"... and this is the fourth time he's been invited to do this show house, which really is unheard of," she continued.

I sheepishly reached into my bag, feeling for my résumé. "Would it be possible, would it be okay, if I, um, just gave you my résumé to pass along to the designer?"

I braced myself for a resounding no.

"Of course. Andrew hires a lot of young kids like you." As my résumé transferred hands, I couldn't contain a smile, encouraged by the first step yet realizing the process could be long. With minimal experience, I assumed finding a position at a reputable design firm would take some time.

I continued through the home, marveling at the talent and creativity displayed at the extraordinary Upper West Side townhouse. The primary bedroom, adjacent to Andrew's space, featured African influences and primitive carved sculptures of wood adorning the walls. Its design was dark, and the room dimly lit. A musk-scented candle on the night table flickered as a group of women beside me dragged their fingers across the textured wallpaper consisting of woven dried grasses.

"What is this? It's wonderful!" said a redhead.

Her friend agreed, "Oh, my God. This is amazing. Go look and see who makes this. I could use this in the Aspen house."

I pressed on through the zebra-wood library, garden-themed dressing room, jazz-inspired music room, and neon-green teenage bedroom. Descending the stairs to the main floor, I recognized a few guys from design school in the kitchen and hoped they weren't handing out their résumés as well. I used to think guys couldn't see the details and beauty in the world like I could, until I enrolled in design school. That was probably because of the way Neil cocked his head when I marveled at gargoyles perched upon a prewar building or his simple nods as I explained Jackson Pollock's genius while we were strolling through the Museum of Modern Art. His eyes always lost focus as his brain seemed to drift.

The transitional kitchen was incredible, featuring cabinetry adorned with hand-forged hardware mimicking twigs and branches. I closed my eyes, stroking the bumpy, asymmetrical texture. White marble countertops highlighted with brown veining reflected glimmers of light from the antique pendants and created a delicate, star-like pattern.

In my gut, I believed I could have my own design firm someday. I visualized it perfectly, but the road would be uphill. These magnificent rooms inspired me, lifted me above the darkness of my past, and pushed me toward achieving a goal my parents and Neil would be proud of.

chapter
six

When Neil and I had moved in together, I only had one more project left: finalizing my postgraduate interior design degree. The two years of working on my degree had transformed our apartment into a maze of presentation boards and drafting materials.

"Sky, how long before I can see the floor again?" Neil had quipped.

"Soon. I want these boards to be perfect," I had said as I twirled around Neil, searching for his smile.

"Okay, well, how about our apartment being perfect? Our real apartment, not the imaginary projects you're working on. Can that be a priority as well, maybe?" Neil had asked at the end of each semester.

Although I had felt the bite, I had brushed off his comments. Still, I had acquiesced and organized my supplies. Assuring Neil our lives would soon return to a normal schedule and that our floor would reappear never stopped his complaining. Navigating the pressures of school and Neil's irritation burdened me. Typically, marriage flowed with Neil, but disruptions I caused in our patterns tangled our relationship.

Anxiety over embarking on a full-time job caused sleepless mornings filled with dreams of forming my own design firm. I swam amid my thoughts and lay still, trying not to disturb Neil's peaceful slumber. I treasured the rare moment of private introspection. The fear of failure haunted me, so I wasn't ready to share my dreams with anyone, but I strategized in my head like a general composing a long-term military operation. Finish final project. Graduate. Find a full-time job as a designer.

The next time Neil headed to San Francisco, I used my extra time to plan for the future. I pored over design magazines, searching for inspiration. The pages flipped by, and suddenly, the image of a magnificent dining room grabbed me. A tiny photo in the corner of a larger layout pulled me from the monotony of images and sparkled with creativity. The white monochromatic room highlighted the designer's skills, where he'd layered textures and various shades of white for a fresh and creative design. I fanned the pages of the magazine, locating the designer and his sources. "Well, I'll be . . ." I muttered to myself.

DESIGNER: ANDREW THORNE

My mouth dropped at the coincidence. It had been almost three weeks since I visited the show house, and I still hadn't found a full-time position.

Maybe he had never received my résumé. I hopped on my computer and drafted a cover letter. Stamped and sealed, I kissed the envelope and lowered it into the blue metal mailbox.

"So, I have news," I said to Neil. It was eleven in the evening in New York but eight in San Francisco.

"Lay it on me."

"Well, remember that designer I loved from the show house I just went to?"

"What show house?"

"You know, the one on the West Side. A few weeks ago, you were supposed to go with me? Remember I told you about the cool branch hardware in the kitchen?"

I hid my agitation, but blood heated through my veins, and beads of sweat formed on my forehead with anger from Neil's disinterest.

"Uh, I guess, I mean, kind of. Anyway, yeah, so there's a designer you like ..."

"I sent a résumé to him today. I happened to see a photograph of his work in a magazine, and I decided to follow up."

"That's great, Sky. I'm sure he gets a million résumés a day, but hey, maybe you'll get lucky."

"Well, I think it's a small firm, so maybe not a million, but ..."

"All you can do is wait and see."

I wasn't a wait-and-see kind of girl. Taking every step possible was the only way I would find a job soon, so I ignored Neil's advice despite my discomfort in going against him. A week later, I followed up and called Andrew's office, and it completely shocked me when he accepted my call. During our brief phone conversation, he suggested we meet in his downtown office. When he uttered the word "downtown," the hairs on my forearms rose like seedlings from soil.

Neil preferred the unblemished, coordinated grid of uptown streets, which complemented his orderly life. Although living uptown was not my dream neighborhood, it was a small concession I was willing to make. The one-bedroom apartment was minuscule. Our queen-size bed filled the bedroom completely, and I could brush my teeth while sitting on the toilet, but it was home. We'd painted the walls the first Sunday we moved in, or I had painted the walls, I should say. Neil had held up his hand, indicating he'd be back in one minute after his office called, and three hours later, he had still been solving coding issues. I had sewed panels of fabric for window draperies, and I'd wake early on weekends, scouring the Chelsea flea market for furniture. Luckily, the apartment had limited space, which kept our spending in check.

On the day of my meeting with Andrew, I darted to the subway and dug deep in my bag, confirming I had packed my résumé. I suffer from a disorder where the first symptom is the conviction that I've forgotten something important, followed by intense panic, and concluding with swelling relief, amazed that I remembered the item in question. I pulled the résumé from the bag and laughed.

It was unclear if Andrew Thorne's firm was big or small. I had tried to do some research but found only the office address and a few publications of his work.

As I descended into the subway, the stench of sour milk rose from the depths of the hot tracks, shocking my olfactory glands. It was putrid. I traveled south, transferring trains and walking the remaining few blocks. Even with the foul-smelling subway ride, my creativity ratcheted up with my first steps into the downtown neighborhoods. Although I hadn't traveled very far, downtown felt like a hundred miles from my uptown existence.

I passed a fancy, well-known apartment building and turned right after the grocery store. Nortrom Street was a charming block connected to a highway. It possessed a peacefulness despite its coordinates. I glanced at the tiny scrap of paper where I'd scribbled the address. 175 was at the end of the block, one small building away from the freeway. The attached townhouse built in the '80s was nothing fancy but clean, with minimal charm. I approached the door, and my gut reassured me that this was a step closer to achieving my dreams.

A short, red-haired woman in her thirties revealed herself upon pulling the door open. Her faded jeans, sneakers, and T-shirt made me doubt my wardrobe choice until I heard Neil's voice in my head. "Look the part." He had a thing for appropriate personal presentation. I wore my trendy black pantsuit with a crisp, white menswear shirt and a silk scarf.

"Andrew will be down in a minute." Her thick New York accent sliced the air.

I sat in the mid-century suede chair with my back erect and eyes at attention. She tapped away on the computer and opened a green folder filled with invoices. I heard voices from upstairs and the adjoining rooms.

Andrew breezed into the office space wearing a lilac shirt and black pleated slacks. He'd cinched his narrow waist with a smooth black leather belt crowned with a silver monogrammed buckle. He balanced a folio on his hip.

"Hiiiiii, Skylar!" Andrew drew out the long I sound. "How are you? Thanks for coming down! Did you find it okay?" he said as he flicked his wrist in perfect time with his words.

"Yes. It was fine, thanks."

My hands quivered, and I hid my nervousness by clasping them behind my back and popping my palms together.

Andrew's hair showed signs of gray near his temples and sideburns, and his lean frame with muscular arms pushed at the seams of his clothes.

"So, tell me, did you enjoy the show house?" Andrew inquired.

"Yes, it was great! Your room was beautiful."

"Thanks. Thanks so much. Wasn't it fabulous? It was fun but lots of work. You know, *House Beautiful* plans to feature it in their annual show house issue. Did you happen to see the write-up in the *New York Times* Style section?" His voice deepened and eyebrows raised, crowing about his publication accomplishments. "I don't even work with a PR firm; I just let it happen." Andrew flung his arms wide open.

"That's amazing," I said. My mind drifted, imagining what it would feel like to see my work featured in a magazine. I marveled at Andrew's success and immediately knew I wanted to be a part of his world.

"So, Skylar. I have Sandy and Dawn running the office, but I could really use an assistant. Mine abandoned me last week without any notice. Suddenly, she's moving to Connecticut, and I'm scrambling. I have a young girl organizing and such in the office, but I can tell by the letter you sent me you're beyond filing finish samples. Basically, you would be doing a little bit of everything. I need someone to return fabrics, pick up samples, take notes in client meetings, organize the office, and shop for furniture. That's my story. Tell me what you're thinking?" he asked, making direct eye contact with me.

"Well," I said as I fidgeted in my seat and twirled my smooth wedding band as if it was a wind-up toy, "I just completed design school, and I'm looking for a full-time position."

"Tell me more."

A level of comfort set in, and I shared my prior experience with Francine. "It was a good experience—I mean, not great, I learned a bit, but the designer really preferred doing everything on her own, and I'm eager to work. I like getting my hands in it all, if that makes sense."

His warm smile eased my nerves enough for an easy conversation.

"Well, Skylar Pearce, we certainly could use someone who rolls up their sleeves and jumps right in. I'll tell you what. I like you, and I can see you have a great work ethic, so let's do this. I'll pay you twenty dollars an hour, and trust me, I will keep you busy. Sound good?"

I'd earned a bachelor's degree in science from a competitive college and a graduate degree from the top interior design school in the city. A meager hourly salary with no benefits should have been insulting. Despite the measly pay, I happily accepted his proposal like an inequitable lunch swap of carrot sticks for a bag of Oreos. I worried about paying the balance of my design school tuition, but Neil's career was plowing ahead, and we no longer had the same intense financial worries we'd endured in the past.

"I got the job!" I screamed as soon as I opened the apartment door. "Neil? Are you here?"

I bounded through the tiny apartment and found Neil's feet dangling off the recliner he'd insisted on moving into our apartment. I had been plotting the demise of his worn-out brown leather recliner from the moment I laid eyes on it. It reminded me of a piece of burned wood. His eyes fluttered as I approached. Neil's traveling to the West Coast had steadily increased, and the red-eye flight never got any easier.

"Ooooo, sorry! I didn't know you were asleep," I whispered and tiptoed out of the room.

I grabbed the phone, immediately calling my biggest cheerleader, my best friend, Charlie.

"I got the job!"

chapter
seven

Andrew launched me into the design process, entrusting me with selecting fabrics and furniture, coordinating color schemes, and handling client phone calls. I puffed with pride when he displayed confidence in my work. I had visualized this moment for years and reveled in his belief in my skills as a designer. My certainty in my abilities swelled with each task Andrew assigned.

My previous part-time experience in the D&D building had taught me which showroom supplied the best leather, traditional trim, or whatever specific item Andrew required for a project. I recalled where to find complimentary coffee or tea in the morning, who offered the best candy selection, and which bathrooms were the cleanest—all important information when checking off long shopping lists in limited amounts of time.

Shopping in the Decoration and Design building brought me back to my first job in the industry, working for a popular showroom. Design showrooms posted available positions on the job board at the design school, and I had applied after completing my first semester. I had needed the experience, and even a tiny salary could help pay for some expenses.

My position in a showroom on the tenth floor had been as the boss lady of the sample room. Fabric showrooms exhibited large boards hinged to walls that flipped like pages in a book. Designers had thumbed through these "wings," selecting fabrics while recording style numbers on a small notepad pro-vided by the showroom. Lists had been submitted, and I had retrieved fabrics from a large stock room. Some lists had been short, just two or three selections; others had been lengthy, like a numeric novella.

"Should be about ten minutes. I'll be right back with your samples," had become my automated message throughout each day. Designers had often retorted with a curled lip.

"Can you get them any faster? I'm in a rush." Designers were perpetually rushing.

"Of course," I had said, donning a massive grin.

My posture grew tall as I remembered, and my purpose-ful strides led me to all the familiar showrooms, where I was greeted by the salespeople and showroom managers. The Decoration and Design building was Manhattan's nerve cen-ter for interior design, and creativity swirled through the halls like wafts of cinnamon from a bakery. Designers shopped for furniture, lighting, wallpaper, fabric, paints . . . Almost any-thing could be found in the D&D building. Designers escorted clients through a maze of showrooms and encouraged them to stroke fabrics and lounge in sofas.

Back then, I had promised myself that someday, when requesting samples as a designer, I would empathize with the lowly sample room runner. I ignored their stresses and ven-tured to engage them in conversation.

"Working on a big project?" or "Have you seen our new line?"

My former coworker had been about thirty-five and kind enough to show me the ropes when I had first arrived as an employee. As he had taken a generous bite of his donut, my stomach made a simultaneous twist and growl. Neil's morn-ing schedule had allowed little time for breakfast. He insisted I choose his shirt and tie for the day and preferred I prepare his toast while he dressed, claiming I browned the bread the perfect amount. Tech firm employees wore a uniform of jeans and T-shirts, but Neil favored jeans, Converse All Stars, and a button-down shirt complete with a tie.

My coworker used to entertain me with his Monday morning replay of the weekend's festivities. I had envied his free spirit and courage to speak his mind with lovers and boyfriends, unlike my whispering inner voice as I struggled with interpreting messages from my gut.

His morning story would go silent when we had heard the screaming and frantic energy thundering from the showroom's customer service office next door. My arm hair had bristled. Time to duck and cover.

Scraped tables, unrecoverable upholstered chairs, shattered chandeliers, and sofas set adrift in a warehouse abyss had been the daily tsunami in customer service. Numerous hands touched a single order, commencing with the salesperson, followed by customer service representatives, truckers, warehouses, and, of course, the artisans creating the furniture, leaving vast room for error. Deals had been cut after nasty fights ensued, and visions of the department head clutching her chest and keeling over from a heart attack plagued me still. Her epitaph would someday read, "Here lies our client service manager, killed by a designer's wrath."

When the showroom had been quiet, we had eavesdropped on the drama unfolding behind us. "I told you, we scoured the warehouse! It's not there!"

"So, are you going to call the client and break the news? No, I didn't think so!" This side of interior design was not as pretty as the cascading fabrics in the showroom. While the combative interactions with designers had frightened me, it hadn't deterred me. I had felt prepared for the problems I would navigate when I was the designer, but I had made a clear mental note: avoid a career in customer service.

I had preferred helping designers and dreaming about the future. Once, I had spied a rookie design assistant nervously looking down at a long list in his hand.

"Excuse me, do you know where I could, umm, where can I find leather samples?" he had asked.

In those moments, I had reveled in my knowledge of the showrooms within the building.

"Well, we have a few selections here, but it's very limited. I would first try Edelman on three, but Donghia on six has an excellent selection as well. If you still need more choices, there's always Kravet."

He had looked at me with glazed-over eyes and stood perfectly still in his navy blue peacoat and tartan plaid scarf. "Want me to jot it down for you?" I had asked.

"If that's okay, if you don't mind. It's kind of, you know, a lot. The building, I mean," the rookie had said.

I had sighed while watching him leave the showroom. Could that be me someday? Would I ever achieve the same success as the designers I pulled fabrics for? Even then, Neil's questioning voice had filled my head, replacing dreams with doubts.

chapter
eight

I loved being back in the D&D building working for a design firm. All day, I wandered the hallways of the design building, looking for inspiration for one of Andrew's projects. When I arrived home, I found Neil with his limbs sprawled across the sofa in front of the television, wrapped in a navy blue blanket.

"Where were you?" Neil asked.

"Oh, just shopping around the D&D building. I saw some of my old friends from when I worked there. They've all been promoted and have serious clout now, running showrooms and hiring assistants. Has me dreaming again. You think I could ever have my own firm like Andrew's?"

"Where's this coming from?"

"I don't know. I've been thinking maybe that could be me. I could start with a small home office."

"Huh. I guess I never thought about it. I mean, it's a little premature, don't you think?"

My stomach made an unfamiliar gurgle. His doubt snaked around my gut and tightened enough that I couldn't ignore the twinge. I assumed his pragmatic mind wasn't an indication of his belief in me, but rather a precise calculation of how my career should unfold.

"I mean, I guess. But it's fun to think about. Dream about something to work toward."

"I guess. But what's the rush? You love Andrew. You're happy. You're learning a lot. Don't get ahead of yourself, Sky. Opening your own gig is a huge commitment."

"No, of course. I realize that. I know. It's just important to have a goal. You could help me set up a home office, and I would have all my own clients, creating all my own designs. Maybe it's just a daydream."

Neil untwisted the blanket and sidled up next to me. He lifted my chin and kissed me. "Oh, Skylar. You can be so naive. You can't just snap your fingers and suddenly be a successful designer with your own clients. Working for Andrew is just fine for you. You can help all those rich people during the day, then come home to me. There's no need to stress yourself out with a whole new business that would occupy much more of your time. Your nights and weekends would be filled with work. Being Andrew's assistant is a perfect fit. With me traveling so much and my career getting serious, it's better for our life right now with you as an assistant. I'd hate to see you stressing about your own firm with all I have going on in my life."

I wished Neil understood that designing spaces was more than just picking pretty fabrics. In a strange way, designing a client's space felt like caretaking, creating an environment in which intimate moments were shared, family secrets were divulged, and privileged information between spouses was revealed. It was a place where clients could twist the pillow fringe during a breakup, leap onto the sofa when reporting a coveted job offer, or settle in dining chairs that would catch the sauce off grandma's homemade spaghetti. My designs invaded their lives whether they realized it or not, and my choices formed the backdrop for their life story to unfold. While staging someone's background for these moments drove my desire for my own design firm, perhaps Neil had a point. I needed more time to develop as a designer and learn from the best before I could create impactful designs and manage a business.

My bags overflowed with fabrics and heavy finish samples as I plodded to the subway. When I arrived at Andrew's office, I proudly spread the samples across the glass table, evaluating their merit.

This is too busy. This blue isn't working, too many checks. I fearlessly settled into a rhythm of assembling the design for a primary bedroom in Gramercy Park. Andrew walked by and looked over my shoulder.

"I love how that's looking, Sky." Andrew praised my efforts, and my confidence grew with each project. As my responsibilities increased, I yearned to report back to Neil with the small triumphs. Unfortunately, he didn't have time to entertain my daily recaps since his travel to San Francisco had gradually increased to full weeks on the opposite coast.

"Maybe just add this for drapery? What do you think?" Andrew asked.

Andrew had a keen eye, and I immediately agreed, thrilled that my opinion mattered.

"Looking good, Skylar. Why don't you come with me to the client presentation? I think you're ready."

I swiftly lifted my gaze from the fabrics and stared at Andrew in disbelief. My heart sped, and my cheeks hurt from the massive smile I couldn't contain.

"Really? Wow. Of course, I would love to. That would be amazing." I began planning my most professional outfit in my head for this huge next step in my career.

Anthony Geno's curly brown hair was trimmed short, drawing attention to his high cheekbones and full lower lip. His light green eyes sat deep in their sockets, and a well-maintained gray goatee had speckles of brown shaken throughout. He seemed intimidating. Anne Marie, his wife, was a waif of a woman with platinum blond hair like cotton candy set upon a flimsy paper cone. I pondered the myriad of salon equipment necessary to achieve this defiance of gravity. Her ice-blue eyes appeared much too large for her face, and I could identify every bone in her frail body.

The Genos' excessive home had an intricate marble-encrusted foyer reminiscent of a large corporate bank. A drapery of lush velvets and delicate silks cascaded from the windows, and Corinthian columns lined the edge of the great room.

"Okay, guys," Anthony said, taking charge of the meeting in his thick New York accent. "What you got to show me?"

Andrew spread the drawings and samples for the library across a vast dining room table. Tony held the green-and-gold multi-stripe fabric.

"I dig this. For the couch, right?"

I cringed. For those of us in the industry, it's a sofa, not a couch. A sofa is more formal, typically elegant and refined, whereas a couch is a casual and less structured piece of furniture. Clients never knew the difference. "Sofa" and "couch" were interchangeable to them.

Up next, cream damask wallpaper with beige and green accents to coordinate with the sofa and a custom wool carpet that boasted massive green and gold vines meandering across a cream background with a large green G in script featured in the center.

"Oh, man!" Tony got excited. "Now this, this is something. Oh. Drew, you hit it outta the park, buddy."

My pen swiftly danced across the page, keeping up with Tony's feedback. Delighted with his rave reviews, I hoped Andrew would recognize my contributions to the design.

"The wallpaper looks a little, well, boring, don't you think?" Anne Marie commented.

"Are you kidding?" Tony asked. "This is classy stuff, Anne Marie."

"I don't know, Tone; seems a little boring to me."

"Babe, why don't you go back to your meatballs and let me

handle this." Tony laughed. "Boring, phhh; she kiddin'?" Tony mumbled to himself.

"I'm just sayin', Tone. You don't gotta get so . . ."

"You know what? Just go. Seriously. Just go," he instructed her.

I felt sorry for Anne Marie, but kept my tongue still. I thought about Neil. His neatly gelled hair and boyish face flashed in my head. He would never dismiss me like Anthony had Anne Marie. I wondered how women tolerated men like Tony. Anne Marie dutifully accepted Anthony's treatment without uttering a word of rebuttal. A wash of appreciation rolled through me, thinking about Neil.

"I have other options. Maybe Anne Marie would like to look." Andrew navigated between the husband and wife. He deftly pacified both parties, avoiding an explosion while moving the Genos toward final decisions.

On our way out, my shoes click-clacked on the marble like long, manicured nails pecking at a keyboard. I imagined the warmth our fabrics and furniture would bring to the space, knowing it would change it from a cold cavern to an inviting, elegant home. Tony paused at the massive carved mahogany doors. "Hold up just a sec."

He returned with a large brown paper bag. The top portion was rolled and scrunched, forming a handle like a school kid's lunch. He shook Andrew's hand as he passed off the oversized lunch bag and whispered in his ear.

I wondered what was in the bag. Fabric samples? Leftovers? In the car, Andrew unrolled the brown bag, tilting it toward me. Green. All green. Stacks and stacks of green as if we'd completed a bank heist. I worried this guy was in the mafia. Was this dirty money? I began to freak out. But I trusted Andrew, and his composure kept me balanced.

Neil would have piously blown the whistle on such an infraction. But I fantasized Tony was the Godfather and put my trust in Andrew. I was in the inner circle, part of the team.

Wads of hundred-dollar bills packed neatly in banker piles stared back at me. There must have been fifteen, maybe twenty stacks. Five figures' worth, for sure. I gave a nervous laugh, and Andrew joined.

"We need to get to my safety deposit box," Andrew said. "Tony only pays in cash. I don't even know if they have a bank account."

On the drive back to Manhattan, Andrew returned calls and guided the office staff through billing questions. He was stressed out about his boyfriend, Jorge, and had been ignoring his calls throughout the day. As we entered the midtown tunnel, Andrew dialed Jorge's number just as his service cut out.

"Jorge is going to kill me if I don't have dinner with him tonight," Andrew said of the man I had yet to meet. Andrew, like my friends, acquaintances, and complete strangers, regularly divulged their guarded secrets as if I held the key to their vault of classified information.

"He's very needy. I mean, I love him, but I'm also trying to build a business here. And to get published, I need those big-budget jobs," Andrew said.

I nodded and listened, recalling Neil's worry about starting my own business. It would be long hours and sacrifices, but what was wrong with working hard? Andrew pushed himself, and I pictured myself following in his footsteps, happily grinding toward a goal with purpose and meaning. Lofty goals meant late nights, early mornings, and networking. He went to dial Jorge's number again, then remembered there would be no service until we exited the tunnel.

"I know he supports me," Andrew said. "But if anything gets in the way of his attention, there's hell to pay."

"I can relate to that. How long have you two been together?" I asked.

"Forever!" Andrew joked. "I think it will be twelve years in September."

I thought about twelve years with Neil. I tried imagining what our life might look like in another nine years. In my head, Neil would achieve executive-level status at Giotto Technologies, and I would have a fully staffed office with exciting projects rolling in daily. A dynamic duo of success.

"I'm sure Jorge understands. Neil certainly struggles with my work schedule, and I worry he misunderstands the level of dedication necessary in a creative job. It's not all fun and games."

"I'm not so sure Jorge understands either. It's like his work-day is over, so mine should be. It's not that simple. Especially since I've been out of the office all day. So much catching up when I get back in the office."

"I can stay late. Is there anything I can do to help?" I offered, despite knowing Neil preferred having me home for dinner when he was in New York.

"What's Neil like? Do you like being married?" Andrew asked.

"It's nice having a forever someone. You know, comfort, security."

"Let me see what awaits when I get back. I just need him to understand. If I want to be considered a top-ten designer in New York, I need more publications. I need to be on those lists of elite designers, and that won't happen if I'm not pushing for more." Andrew's drive toward notoriety was as strong as a bull's when chasing a red cape.

"Andrew, you are so talented. You just need the right project, and magazines will feature you on the cover."

"I'll call the bank and see when they close," Andrew said. "If they're open, let's stop in on our way back to the office."

Alone in the sterile bank vault, we pushed and shoved the stacks of cash into the box. Just like trying to wrap a queen-size fitted sheet around a king-size bed, we knew it wasn't happening.

"We need the largest box available," Andrew requested.

"Is this normal?" I whispered.

Andrew chuckled. "For Anthony, it is!"

"How are you ever going to spend all of this cash?" I asked.

Andrew shrugged.

The guard and the bank representative both arrived with a copious vault box. Other than in the movies, I had never seen so many Benjamin Franklins in my life. We filled the large metal box with stacks of hundred-dollar bills.

Andrew's trust in me was proven during the meeting, and in return, I wanted to help him obtain his goals. I'd be looking for a way to be a valuable part of Andrew's team and raise his firm to an elite group of designers in Manhattan.

chapter
nine

The cramped cafe where I met my friend Amy bustled with a vibrant crowd. She had generously treated me to numerous lunches here, as she was fully aware of my budget, thanks to my complaining. The tables, inches apart, afforded zero privacy, but the hum was exactly what I loved about the place. Amy and I had bonded over study sessions and group projects throughout interior design school. She squeezed into the seat in her designer ensemble and Italian handbag.

"Hey, Sky!" she chirped as she wrapped her arms around my shoulders.

Amy had an interest in design, but no intention of pursuing a career in it. She was married to a successful Wall Street type, and her school projects reflected personal dreams of nurseries and playrooms.

"I love that we have a lunch spot," I joked.

"Yes, this is definitely our spot." She laughed.

Amy's petite frame and luxurious dark skin turned heads as we entered the restaurant. Her dark eyes contrasted with her full bubble gum lips, and her voluptuous figure was soft like Botticelli's muse. I envied her alluring beauty and loathed my ordinary blond hair.

I settled in and ordered a sauvignon blanc.

"None for me," Amy said.

"No wine?" I asked.

"So, I have some news." Amy smiled. "Well, it's more like two pieces of good news."

I leaned in, clasping my hands across the miniature table. "First, we just signed the contract for raw space in Chelsea. We're going to build it out."

I lurched over the table, grabbing her. "Amy! That's fantastic!" I was edging a yell, drawing attention in the pint-sized cafe. The corners of her lips almost met the crooks of her eyes.

"I know. I can't believe it's all happening so fast."

"That's great! I'm so happy for you. It's going to be great. I can't wait to see the space. Have you hired an architect yet?" I asked.

"Yes. Architect is all set and working on the plans."

As Amy explained the details of the space, I wondered if I could arrange for Andrew to design Amy's new apartment. What if I made the connection? I knew—well, I hoped—that attracting clients for my own firm would be necessary someday, and this was the perfect opportunity to gain some experience.

"So, there is one more small thing," she said. "Michael and I, we're expecting. I'm pregnant!"

I gasped with delight because this had been Amy's dream since we met. "That's amazing! I know how long you have wanted this."

I patiently listened to Amy's endless babble about baby names, baby strollers, baby cribs, and parenting techniques. I tried steering the conversation back to design and her plans for construction, but her obsession with babies prevailed.

It wasn't that I didn't want kids someday, but my head was in a different space. With my career finally taking off, the thought of being tied down petrified me. Neil and I had agreed we wouldn't discuss starting a family until his career solidified and our finances were dependable. As my career emerged, that would be a consideration as well. The image of me cradling a newborn in my arms felt uncomfortable and far-fetched. Staring across the table at Amy, I wondered if I would ever share her feelings about babies.

Having watched my mother suffer a loss she could only pretend to recover from, I wasn't sure I could allow myself to love someone so deeply. My mother had insisted my sister keep up her schoolwork, demanding I read the classics aloud to her and show her my math worksheets while she stroked her hand, ignoring the inevitable. I placed my hand on my chest and inhaled a deep breath, relieved Neil never discussed a baby timeline.

"How's Neil?" Amy asked.

"He's good. Still at the tech firm. Busy with a big project in California. Lots of weekend and evening conference calls. He's been traveling to the West Coast a lot, but all good stuff."

I welcomed Neil's travel for work. His intensity bordered on exhausting, and didn't any good wife need a break from the daily grind of married life? Andrew appreciated my extra hours at work when Neil was out of town, and not worrying about being late for Neil was a relief.

"And how's your job going?"

I was thrilled when Amy asked. Here was my opportunity.

"It's great. I'm learning so much. So much more than we learned in design school. Andrew is very talented, and his business is growing. He's asked to design show houses all the time, and word is spreading about his talent. *Elle Decor* just called yesterday. They want him to be in a piece they're calling 'Ask the Designer.' We're waiting on details. I'd love for you to meet him sometime. Maybe he could even help you with the new apartment when you're ready," I gently suggested.

"I would love that. I would love to meet Andrew, and honestly, Skylar, you always did have the best designs in school."

My racing mind slowed, and I took a deep breath of relief after hearing her confidence in me.

We dined on gourmet, overpriced salads, and I noticed Amy placed her fork on the table after a few stingy bites. I sipped my sauvignon blanc.

"Well, this was great!" Amy said as we gathered our bags to leave.

"I know. When can I come see your new apartment? I know it's raw, but I can't wait to see it. Maybe I'll bring Andrew," I said.

"Yes, of course. That sounds great. Let's talk next week."

A few weeks later, Amy, Andrew, and I toured the raw space in Chelsea. He charmed Amy with innovative design ideas for the apartment. Andrew and I knew the finished product would be spectacular. Construction continued for several months, and when completed, I marveled at the beauty of the apartment, which featured the exposed brick walls and enormous arched windows typical of the neighborhood. The rooms were generous, boasting long, gracious hallways adjoining the spaces. The secluded primary bedroom suite on the second floor was particularly difficult due to the misplaced spiral staircase leading to a massive roof terrace that ran the entire length of the building. I spent evenings reworking the floor plan over and over, eventually solving the challenging layout. The minimal light worried me, but with the right wallpaper and paint in the bedroom, it could be exquisite.

Manhattan's bustle seemed miles away from the oasis Amy had created on her roof. Large cedar planters with full-size trees lined the perimeter and protected their privacy. Areas of gravel interspersed natural stone pathways. Fountains at either end produced the soothing sound of running water and diluted any noise from street level. Few apartments in Manhattan included fifteen hundred square feet of outdoor space. Now that the construction was complete, Amy was prepared to tackle the interiors.

After the meeting, I glanced at my wrist, calculating West Coast time. Mid-afternoon seemed like a good time to catch Neil, even accounting for his unpredictable schedule.

"Hey," I said.

"Hey, how are you?"

"I'm good. Actually, I'm great."

"Okay. Stop biting the inside of your cheek and tell me," Neil said.

"Andrew and I just walked through Amy's new apartment. It's amazing. I think there's a good chance Amy will hire Andrew for the interior design."

"Wow. Are you sure you want that pressure? She's your friend. What if something goes wrong? I would hate for you to be in the middle of that and jeopardize your friendship." I hadn't thought about the risks involved with Amy hiring Andrew, and Neil's opinion ignited apprehension within me.

"I just thought if I can bring in new clients, I would contribute to the firm in a real way and make a difference in the success of the business. And you know Amy; this will be a no-expense-spared project."

"That's all true, but maybe you're better off just being the best assistant you can be. Leave the rest to Andrew." Neil's words hijacked my excitement, and I wished he shared in my successes rather than highlighting roadblocks.

"Really? I can't believe you're saying this."

"It's nice of you to introduce them and all, but this isn't your place, Sky. Just focus on being the best assistant you can be. You do that so well. You are a fantastic assistant, and sometimes you get ahead of yourself with all this dreaming."

My lip quivered and my brow furrowed as I struggled to understand Neil's comments. Was he trying to keep me in the small box of being an assistant forever? I knew I was capable of so much more, but did he believe in me? Maybe I misread his intent. It had to be. But maybe he was right; maybe this was asking for trouble. I hated how Neil clipped my wings as I was about to take flight, but as my husband, I trusted his perspective.

"If Amy does come to the firm, Andrew needs to pay you a percentage of the commission or a finder's fee. You know that, Sky, right? Don't let your boss walk all over you. Don't let your soft heart get in the way again."

Neil liked protecting me, but a wave of insecurity washed through me. Had I been naive to think bringing Amy in as a client would be a positive for everyone? I just wanted to add value and have Andrew see my commitment to the firm. I struggled to understand Neil's point of view. I didn't agree, but I refused to have a cross-country argument.

Our phone call lingered with me throughout the day. My mind replayed the conversation, igniting doubt regarding my new venture with Amy. Had I made the right decision?

chapter
ten

After little Heather was born, I connected Amy and Andrew so she could inquire about designing the interiors of her newly renovated loft-like apartment. Referring a juicy project would help Andrew view me as more than just a design assistant. Amy would be an excellent client with a great design sense and a healthy budget.

"I think you're ready," Andrew casually said as I was packing up to head home.

My arms tingled with goosebumps in excitement.

"Yes, my dear, I believe it's time. Don't pack up those bags so fast. You need to get working on Amy's project."

"Me? You want me to design Amy's apartment?"

Andrew giggled at my shock, surprised that I hadn't expected his request. I couldn't believe he released control, asking me to lead a project for the first time. I quieted my nagging worries about taking on such a large project and began envisioning how I would design the empty space.

"I know your style represents mine perfectly, and my clients adore you. This is a no-brainer for me, Skylar."

"I know I can make this apartment stunning, even worthy of a magazine spread. Maybe we'll even get your name across a magazine headline," I said.

"Well, that would sure be a relief for me," Andrew said as he made himself a cocktail with a very generous pour. "Cheers to us." He raised his glass, followed by a double gulp, draining half of the crystal glass.

"Guess who's the lead designer for Amy's new apartment?" I said, batting my eyelashes at Neil.

"Let me take a wild guess. You?"

"ME! I'm so excited. I've dreamed about this moment forever. I can picture the whole thing in my head."

I immediately envisioned Amy's large family room with two transitional-style seating areas. One with a gray-tone sofa and coordinating club chairs, the other with cream swivel chairs.

I pictured antique rugs grounding each area with hues of blue, rust, and gold, tying the color scheme together. At the far end of the room, a gas-burning fireplace would sit within a custom-designed unit that would house a television and audio equipment. The dining area was open to the family room, providing a unique opportunity to showcase a spectacular, one-of-a-kind crotch-mahogany table.

"It's a lot of work, but I don't really care. If it means I'm creating the design, I'll gladly do whatever it takes."

Neil shook his head in irritation. "You really think it's worth all the extra time? It's not like you're getting paid for all the extra work. If you're the assistant, you get to have the fun yet can leave and come home at a decent time. What am I supposed to do when you're working all those extra hours?"

I wished Neil understood how the power of designing someone's home provided a self-assurance greater than money. I hadn't felt a rush like this since I worked for my first boss out of college, Johnny Tithler. Even though Johnny had held tight control over his fashion empire, he had believed in my abilities and trusted my design sense. Johnny had never needed convincing; he had seen the skills I saw in myself.

Andrew's trust gave me a similar feeling, even though I still needed his approval for my selections. He spent most days intent on securing magazines' commitments to his project. He hoped schmoozing editors, writers, and photographers over long lunches would accelerate the process. I preferred focusing on the design rather than the notoriety, but I assumed Andrew knew more about the path to a successful interior design business than most.

With the design completed and approved, our clients often chose to have their new furniture, accessories, and lighting delivered to a warehouse until all purchased items arrived, and Amy was no exception. Andrew called this the "voila" effect, allowing us to install everything in one or two days. Clients returned home to a dazzling transformation.

I watched Amy and her family stuff their SUV with baby gear and duffel bags as we prepared for the magical transformation. My nerves stepped forward in anticipation of the weekend ahead. I was acutely aware of the high stakes—how Andrew would view me and, of course, as Neil often reminded me, my friendship with Amy. They headed upstate for a long weekend while we braced ourselves for the arduous installation we had prepped for all week.

Other tasks and worries vanished in my drive to perfect Amy's apartment. My focus was sharp. Personal calls and to-do lists would wait. Neil had protested when I told him there would be no weekend for me. He had played every angle of persuading me to opt out and leave it to Andrew, but that had never been an option. My heart was in Amy's apartment, and barring death, I would not back away at the final stage.

Moments after their departure, antique chandeliers, custom upholstery, area rugs, beds, and bedding settled in their new home. The dining room table had been delayed several times throughout the design process. It had never made it to the warehouse, but would arrive directly from the wood shop. On the final day of installation, the table still hadn't arrived.

I called Amy and gave her an update. I estimated the countdown until her return, hoping to gain some extra hours.

"Hey, Amy!" I feigned an upbeat tone despite my worry about the dining table. "Everything is going great. Just wanted to check in and see what time you will be arriving home."

"We're running late. Is that okay?"

"That works for us. See you tonight."

I took a deep breath and pressed the call button for the elevator. It creaked and shook as I entered. The delivery truck hauling the massive custom dining table had just arrived. At $37,500, I marveled at the workmanship. After weeks of delays and excuses, the table was finally on site. Three delivery guys, one husky and two visually unfit for the task, followed me into the building, evaluating the musty elevator.

"If I bring it in this way, on its side," the delivery man said as he measured the opening, "then can we turn it this way?"

Our dissection of the forty-inch-wide by twenty-foot-long table's route unfolded. Most dining tables were manufactured in pieces, but not this one. The center of a crotch-mahogany tree trunk is split open, creating a mirror image of the wood grain, resulting in a rare, one-of-a-kind tabletop. This extraordinary design can only be achieved if the wood veneer is in one solid piece, making the table enormous and difficult to move.

I had designed a pair of table bases, flaunting ornate carvings with gilded accents. Thankfully, their size didn't pose an issue for the cramped elevator.

"Honey." One of the guys motioned to me. "This ain't never gonna fit in here." He gestured toward the elevator.

"Well, I guess you need to walk it up," I replied without a pause.

I knew he was annoyed, but that's the business. Whatever the client wants or needs, they get. Personally, I had spent the afternoon moving clothing into a new armoire, and there is nothing worse than touching a client's socks and underwear.

Glamorous work, it was not.

"What floor they on?" he asked.

"Eleven." I would not acknowledge his hesitation. He stared back for a moment, and eventually, our eyes connected in a staring contest I would win.

"Okay, let's go walk those steps and see what we got," he said.

Andrew remained up in the apartment, and I called with an update.

"Yes, they're walking up now. Checking out the stairs as an option. Can you open the door to the stairwell so they'll have access to the apartment?"

Andrew grunted at me, clearly distracted.

I tilted my head in confusion. What was his problem? Although his indifferent behavior annoyed me, I concentrated on Amy and my design becoming a reality.

They spent forty-five minutes scouting the stairwell and recruited two additional delivery guys before the table emerged from the truck.

"Grab them bases. We gotta get them up first," said a delivery guy.

The table bases arrived on the eleventh floor, and I meticulously positioned them in anticipation of the colossal table's arrival. Andrew watched as I took control and measured the exact placement.

I looked over as Andrew swished his brown drink and wondered what was in the glass. I leaned close, feigning a look at the clock behind him, and inhaled the scent of scotch. Recently, I had noticed the aroma of alcohol replacing his usual cologne but dismissed it. If this continued, what would it mean for me? My job? My career? I had invested and trusted in Andrew and his reputation. I needed him.

I pushed my thoughts aside and pretended it wasn't happening. I prayed Andrew didn't have an alcohol problem, and if he did, I would snap him out of it. I would keep this amazing journey going as planned.

Focusing on the problem table took precedence.

It was an exercise in determination from the onset. The snake-like stairwell taunted the elongated, straight-angled table. Beads of sweat formed on foreheads and descended across the cheeks of the delivery guys. Every so often, I could not contain myself, belting out, "Watch the corner!" or "The side! Watch the side!"

I cringed as the table approached each curve and wished Andrew would step in to assist. Exposed pipes and beams loomed like daggers and filled my head with visions of scrapes like an angry lover's key marks across Amy's beautiful, expensive table. Six months to create and a second to destroy. A Xanax would have been helpful.

On the final set of steps, a pipe hung lower than the others. My heart filled my chest and throat. It took two attempts to maneuver the table gingerly around the final obstacle. Three hours after its arrival, the beautiful table settled unscathed in the dining area of its new home.

"I must admit, that was some serious skill you used. I'm impressed," I said, giving each delivery guy a high five and a generous tip in appreciation.

Adding the finishing touches to the apartment was the final step before Amy and her family arrived home. I searched the apartment for Andrew and found him passed out in the guest bedroom. *How is this happening to me? My first successful job as a designer on my own, and now this.*

Why couldn't anything be easy? I just wanted a good job with a nice boss, a sober boss, something I'd thought I had until this moment in Amy's beautiful, nearly completed apartment. Maybe that's why Andrew wanted me to take the lead on the project. I hoped he gave me this opportunity because he trusted me and my design sense, but maybe he knew his drinking had taken over, preventing him from fulfilling the demands of work.

I gently placed my hands on his shoulders and shook him. My eyes passed over the nearby clock. "Oh, my God!" I screamed. "They're going to be here any minute!"

I speed-dialed Amy's cell to check in.

Andrew flew out of the bed and stormed out of the apartment. I rolled my eyes in disgust as the door slammed behind him.

"Hi. Just checking in on your timing."

"We decided to drive back in the morning. It just got too late, and with Heather . . ."

I dialed Andrew's number, but no one answered. I hit redial over and over until I could waste no more time. I spent the next two hours wiping down every surface in the apartment, removing any evidence of dust or foot traffic. I dashed out to the bodega on the corner, collecting a bouquet of flowers. Adding small details like fresh flowers throughout the apartment was a luxurious detail we provided for all our clients. I arranged them in vases I found in the kitchen cabinets, distributing them throughout each room in the apartment while carefully scanning the contents of each space.

It had been a long, annoying, exhausting day. As I adjusted the final florals and pillows, a whir came from the kitchen. Turning the corner, I saw water surging from the dishwasher and pooling in the kitchen.

I darted to the laundry room, returning with towels and frantically mopping up the continuous stream of water. After throwing the towels down, I called the superintendent.

"How do I—where do I turn off the water for the kitchen? It's everywhere. It's not stopping."

The water began to creep out of the kitchen and into the hallway area rug. I screamed to the super over the phone.

"I'm coming up."

"Hurry! Please hurry."

I watched helplessly as the water spewed and drifted near the area rug and down the hall toward the bedrooms. I closed the doors, splaying towels across the floor, slowing the water from invading the bedrooms. The super arrived in moments.

"Where do we turn it off? Just turn it off!"

"Okay, I'm going."

He disappeared into the stairwell, and although it felt like hours, the stream of water slowed to a stop within minutes. I leaned my forehead against the freshly papered wall and inhaled deeply, tears pushing their way out.

"You, okay?" he asked.

"Not really. Now what am I going to do? What the hell happened?"

"I dunno, hon. Need to get a plumber up here tomorrow. Want me to call?"

"Yes, please."

He stood staring at me, and I glared at him, hoping he would go away.

"Uh, you have anything else for me?" he asked.

Then I got it. "Just a minute. I went to my bag and retrieved the only money in my wallet, a crumpled ten-dollar bill, and handed it to him.

"Thanks."

He looked at me and then looked at the ten-dollar bill in disgust.

"Sorry, it's all I have."

He turned away, grumbling under his breath. I slumped in one of the dining chairs, fighting searing tears. The stench of the water from the kitchen swept by me, triggering more tears. I began the mopping up of the water and started a load of laundry with the towels.

"Hey," I said after Neil picked up the phone.

I pictured him in his Sunday night sweats and T-shirt and messy hair. I envied his leisurely day, where he likely slept late, read a book about some major historical event, dozed off for a few hours, and snacked on chips and salsa or whatever else was hanging around the kitchen. I'd invited this responsibility, but I had never expected the chaos of this job.

"Hey. How's it going, babe?" he asked.

I sighed. "Well, minor disaster at Amy's. Seems there was some plumbing malfunction, and I'm just cleaning it up now."

"What happened?" he asked.

"I don't really know, but I need to make it right by noon tomorrow."

"Where's Andrew? Can't he deal with it?"

"He's gone. Long gone. He basically passed out on the job and disappeared." I needed to be strong and professional, proving I could handle the pressure. If Neil heard me cry, he might think I couldn't run my own interior design firm some-day.

"Skylar, that's crazy. Screw that. It's his company. What the hell? See, this is exactly what I was afraid of with taking Amy on as a client," he practically snarled through the phone. His forceful voice escalated, and I could still hear his words even when I pulled the phone away from my ear. I cowered from Neil's anger.

"I know. This is the first job where Andrew gave me real responsibility." I defended my decision but wondered why proving myself to Neil was necessary.

"Yeah, but you're not getting paid more or earning a commission even though you brought in the business."

"I know. But everyone's got to pay their dues."

I never envisioned the journey toward my dream of running my own design firm would be easy or without mishaps. How could Neil expect a perfect, unfettered path?

"This is a bit more than paying dues, don't you think? It's kind of ridiculous, Sky. Just come home; call it a night. You can deal with it tomorrow."

"I can't, Neil. It's Amy."

"She'll understand."

"Just forget it," I finally said.

Neil changed the subject and rambled on about his projects at work. "Look, Sky, I get you're having some bumps on the design road, but if you only knew what real hard work and problems were, you'd have some perspective. I just had to deal with a major technical problem, and now it's taking longer than we expected to develop our product, but it's going to be incredible. Problems are all relative, and trust me, yours is a one out of ten, so you need to stop sweating it."

Neil's excitement mounted as he relayed the details of his project. I listened, but the disarray in Amy's apartment and the late hour distracted me.

"Are you listening, Sky?"

"Yes. Of course."

"Oh, okay. Good. I thought you were tuning me out."

"Nope. I'm here."

I squirmed in my seat from my unrest, but I didn't want Neil's anger escalating, so I feigned interest, keeping him calm.

Amy's family returned Monday afternoon. Somehow, I managed to put the apartment back together before they arrived, except the water remained off in some of the rooms. I inhaled a deep breath as the satisfaction of accomplishment settled in. This was hard work, bordering on chaos, but the process ignited my passion for creativity and brought out my ability to stay focused, organized, and calm in the eye of a storm. I quietly acknowledged my achievement, regardless of Neil or Andrew's opinion. First job down; hopefully, many more to come.

The apartment's interiors were gorgeous. Amy arrived exhausted, but a smile consumed her face the moment she entered her apartment.

"It's gorgeous!" she said.

"Of course it is," I replied. "You spared no expense, and every item was custom-designed."

"Unlimited budgets don't always produce the best design,

but you made it happen, Skylar. This is just incredible."

The more a client pays, the more they expect, and Amy was no different. I'd been waiting for "the" call a few days after the installation when, sure enough, the office manager let me know Amy was on the line.

"Hey, Skylar, Michael and I were talking. We think the sofa is not that comfortable. He's concerned."

And there it was. No job is complete without complaints. Dissatisfaction was expected, but Amy's upset made the muscles in my back tense and cramp. I swallowed hard and blocked out the small pulsating throb at my temples. Conflict was not my friend, and escaping it had become a life goal.

"I'm so sorry to hear that. Let's set up a meeting." I tried to sound effortless and unflustered.

"That would be great."

A week later, I arrived at their apartment to review the sofa issue. Michael was unhappy with the pitch of the sofa, claiming it did not "cradle his body" as he expected. We explored possible solutions, which included changing the fill of the sofa, adding additional lumbar pillows, or sending the sofa back to the upholstery workroom, where it would be taken apart and reconfigured.

"I'm thinking we start by adding extra throw pillows," Michael said.

Relief set in. It would have been a massive effort to rebuild the sofa. Arranging deliveries and ordering replacement fabric, not to mention the cost incurred by the firm. Client dissatisfaction was routine. Designers expected it, and working through it was part of the job, but the stakes felt much higher this time.

Amy's file was moved to the completed jobs bookcase, and our newest client submitted their signed contract. It was time to start the process again, but this time, I had more clout with Andrew. Even with the complaints, Andrew and I viewed Amy's project as a success.

chapter
eleven

I inhaled a full chest of oxygen in preparation for Christine's intensity before ringing the apartment bell. With Christine at a petite five feet tall, even her bedroom slippers boasted six-inch heels, elevating her stature and elongating her tiny frame.

She and Ivan were in a May-December marriage in which his finances had clearly factored into her decision. The twenty-one-year age difference was not uncommon in our client profiles.

During our initial consultation, Ivan's presence had taken up space. He was built like a football player: tall, broad, and thick in the middle. His career required that he travel between Russia and the United States every ten days. You could detect a trace of his Russian accent, which had diminished over his many years living in the United States.

Ivan looked weathered compared to Christine's taut face and body. She was the perfect accessory for him. I imagined their life and pictured Christine lunching with women at the top of the social ladder and securing dinner reservations at the newest and most expensive restaurants in New York.

During the hours I spent in their home waiting for deliveries, I saw loneliness settle on her shoulders in the privacy of her own home. My job let me become a fixture in homes, and clients often forgot my presence. Like a lamp in the corner or a painting on the wall, I observed families in their natural habitat. At times, Christine seemed more like Ivan's mother than a wife. She laid out his clothes each evening, booked his doctor's appointments, and stroked his back throughout our meetings. Christine perfected her makeup and smoothed her skirt with some anxiety before Ivan entered a room.

The pressure to guarantee Ivan's happiness looked exhausting, but I understood it. Neil had his quirks, too. I never shared the details of our clients' personalities or their demands, thus circumventing Neil's judgmental speech from his oversized soap box.

The few times I had spoken to him about clients, Neil had ridiculed the money they spent on impractical accent pillows and decorative candle sticks, but I focused on the design rather than the cost. Neil didn't see the power bestowed upon designers. Yes, clients would thrash, asserting their power occasionally, but they handed over their surroundings to me. I cringed as he dissected and judged Andrew's clients, completely ignoring the description of the designs we created. I could never sort out if he found it boring, unvaluable, or both. Either way, when he dismissed my excitement, it stung. So, I avoided detailed conversations about my work. Without wealthy clients, I would be out of a job. I never longed for wealth after witnessing the underbelly of their lives. Life with or without money provided the same issues.

Except I knew that, with money, my sister could have received better care, and it would have freed my mother from her work schedule. That would have allowed her to focus on the gut-wrenching task of nursing my sister through her slow and painful death. Money would have allowed us to simply love her through her final months without obsessing about dosages, calibrating oxygen tanks, or daily trips to the pharmacy. Caring for my sister left my mother hollow, and the sacrifices left me longing for the undivided attention I wanted but felt too guilty to even dream about. When Neil stepped into the empty space in my heart, his devotion and attentiveness healed me day by day.

Hollow. That's what I saw when I looked at Christine. I would never allow myself to be that vacant woman who catered to a man and abandoned her own goals. I feared what I witnessed in her. I saw glimpses of Neil in Ivan's behavior, triggering a pang in my belly and drawing attention to my buried resentment. I sighed, pushing away the slightest thought that Neil could possibly act like Ivan. Our marriage was good, without the damage my parents had endured from caring for a dying child. If my parents' marriage had survived, we'd be fine.

Neil's lack of understanding of my passion for interior design impacted me more than I admitted. I relished the surge of creativity that came with drafting floor plans and assembling coordinating fabrics for clients. Whenever Neil minimized my work, I reminded myself that Andrew and the clients entrusted me with choosing their surroundings. I created spaces where they would eat, sleep, and invite their families for Christmas dinner and birthdays, where they would console crying children and make love to their spouses.

Neil's programming career might someday be lucrative, and I reminded him that perhaps he would seek out an interior designer's expertise if he had the means and desire.

"Skylar, let's be clear. I will never be one of them. I would never pay five hundred dollars for a pillow even if I had five hundred million in the bank."

And that was Neil. Evan Ivan saw the value in making his apartment a home.

Christine and Ivan's new apartment faced north on Central Park South. It had a spectacular view but was not as large as I might have expected at only thirty-two hundred square feet. The layout could have been improved, too. But the view, combined with a great outdoor space, explained why they rented the apartment. Yes, rent. Complete with an astronomical price tag of $21,400 per month.

When they had hired Andrew, the couple had been relocating from a ten-thousand-square-foot estate in Long Island. Our first assignment had been an evaluation of antiques, selecting those to be auctioned and those to accompany them to Central Park South. Christine had overnighted photographs so we could review the antiques and submit our recommendations. The following morning, a package arrived containing a three-ring binder filled with thirty pages of photographs. As I flipped through the novel of antiques, yellow Post-its appeared on pages denoting Christine's favorites.

One Post-it highlighted a four-panel eighteenth-century decoupage screen. After learning about the technique in design school, I appreciated how it enhanced accessories with paper cutouts glued to various objects. I found it fascinating that decoupage originated from art in Siberia. "Keep the screens" had been scribbled in black ink across the Post-it stuck to the photograph. While I didn't have an aversion to decoupage, these screens didn't coordinate with the aesthetic they requested we design for their apartment, and I needed to explain this to Christine.

"I just love the dogs on the screens! They look exactly like mine," Christine squealed.

"They seem a bit large for the apartment, Christine. I'm sure they were wonderful in the house, but maybe we should pass on them for the apartment," I gently nudged.

"Skylar, the dogs look exactly like my dogs. How could you not love the dogs?"

Pictures of dogs can't dictate design, except when you're working with Christine. I hung my head in defeat. I tried to lead clients to good taste, but many times, conceding was necessary.

We continued paging through the binder, and it was a case

study in emotional attachment, as if each piece were an over-priced family member and Christine was bidding them fare-well.

"Now this one, this one has quite a story. Ivan and I were in Palm Beach ..."

I patiently sat with her, listening to details about each antique in question—how it was acquired, how much she paid for it, and what meaning it had for her personally. I consumed bottomless cups of caffeinated drinks and concentrated on her babble. It would have been an easy task for us to choose the antiques, but in the end, we blended Christine's emotional ties with our design. Painstakingly, she made her final deci-sions so the project could move forward.

Christine's daily activities included shopping, working out, and lunching with friends. The couple employed a lovely Spanish woman, Diana, who cleaned, cooked, and shopped for them. With the project underway, most days, I stopped by to check the progress or meet workers on site. Typically, Diana chopped vegetables, folded laundry, or mopped the floors. When I found her organizing bags of frozen peas on the counter, I thought it was a bit odd, but I continued my rounds. Then Christine emerged, wobbling on her four-inch designer heels and hiding behind oversized Chanel sunglasses even though we were indoors.

"Bring me the peas!" she barked, immediately retreating to her bedroom.

I looked to Diana for answers, but she simply smiled and said, "Hello, Miss Skylar." Then she ran into the bedroom, fro-zen peas in hand. Christine hid from me and didn't reemerge until the following Monday.

I guess it wasn't only a new apartment she had been searching for. Her face suddenly seemed new, too. I smiled and said hello, acting as if the bruises on her face were not visible. I realized it was her eyes and lips that had been improved. I had never noticed her lack of youthful eyes but clearly, she had.

Confidentiality as an interior designer proved to be equally as important as creating a stellar design. Learning privileged information from clients was commonplace. It became a psychological study of emotions, relationships, and secrets. And enough dirt to write a novel.

Christine and Ivan's job was in the final phase of installations. As I climbed the steps to the second floor of the apartment, sunlight drenched the rooms. The second floor had been designed to be a copious primary bedroom with two large roof terraces flanking the space, but Ivan preferred it be transformed into a billiard room.

Reupholstering a Chesterfield sofa from the Long Island house, we redesigned the space with an English billiard room feel. The wall-to-wall carpet had been selected and approved by both Christine and Ivan. I was certain this design element would make a huge impact. The carpet had a black background, adding to the drama of the room. Installers were just finishing as I arrived at the top of the stairs. Another twenty minutes to completion. The carpet was lush and as transformational as I had anticipated. I was pleased with the result, and I knew that the additional wallpaper, drapery, sconces, and throw pillows would be exactly what Andrew envisioned. Just as the installers were packing up their equipment, Christine crossed through the doorway with a friend.

"Hey, how's it going?" She motioned to me with a gentle wave.

"Great!" I replied. "Carpet looks fantastic." I smiled.

I felt her hesitation. She tilted her head to the side, pondering. She turned to look at her friend. Her friend turned to Christine and gave her a disapproving look. I quickly thought of an exit strategy.

"Sorry to run, ladies. We have a huge presentation this evening that I need to prepare."

Always good to let them know our business is thriving. When I arrived by elevator at street level, I immediately dialed Andrew.

"I'm just leaving the Vetrov apartment," I reported.

"Great! How does the carpet look? Everything go smoothly?" he inquired.

"Well, the carpet looks great, but Christine seemed lukewarm about it. May be hard for her to visualize at this point."

Andrew agreed and asked me to cab it back to the office.

The next day, we received "the" call. Christine's frantic, out-of-her-mind call. Andrew looked over at me.

"We are not curing cancer here. It's decorating," he said before he took the call. Andrew didn't know about my sister, but I immediately thought of her and the paintings wallpapering her hospital room. I wondered what she would think if she could see me now, choosing real wallpaper. Andrew put Christine on speakerphone, and I knew what was about to come.

"Andrew," she spoke firmly and louder than her normal tone of voice, "I hate the billiard room carpet. It is absolutely UGLY! I mean, my friend came over last night and . . ."

That's all Andrew needed to hear. The friends mess it up every time. They all listen to their friends, and every interior designer throughout the world cringes. These friends hold so much weight that one would think they have a substantial design background.

Andrew patiently and politely dealt with her twenty-five-minute rant, calming her little by little. He gently reassured her that it would all come together. She was screaming so loudly the entire office could hear at one point. I think Andrew had an involuntary chuckle during the conversation. We both shared the unfortunate reaction of nervous laughter, and we used it as a coping mechanism during highly stressful moments. I gave him a silly face to show my solidarity.

"I want this carpet ripped out immediately! I did not agree to this. Ivan will never go for this. I had no idea . . ." Blah, blah, blah.

She wanted to be heard, and we were paid to listen. Her improved lips were coming in handy. At some point, all you heard was a nasal voice of nonsense like the teacher on Charlie Brown cartoons: "Whonk, wha whonk, whonk." Eventually, Christine's tone mellowed.

"Fine. I will live with the horrible carpet for now. But if I'm not happy when the room is finished, I want it out!"

Three weeks later, the billiard room was fully assembled, including the custom billiard table, antique sconces, and blue stripe wallpaper.

"Andrew, it's Christine. I just have to say, Ivan and I think the billiard room looks outstanding," she conceded.

"I am so happy you're pleased," Andrew replied.

"It really did come together as you promised. I just sent out the invitations for our holiday party. You and Skylar must be there!"

Christine was used to getting her way, and knowing she wanted me at the party gave me a boost of confidence. The invitation was a seal of approval, an indication she appreciated our work. I heard the little voice in my head encouraging me. With each successful project with Andrew, I moved closer to my ultimate dream of establishing my own firm and creating my own designs.

chapter twelve

The elaborate party invitation arrived at Andrew's office on a Tuesday. It was on oversized, thick, shiny red card stock. Red glitter dusted the table as I removed it from the envelope, and gold ribbons draped from the corners. It was a holiday and housewarming party combined. Andrew and I would, of course, attend. Clients enjoyed gloating about their newly renovated or furnished homes, and our presence was required. Frequently, we received new clients from these house parties and inevitably met interesting people.

"I'm heading home to get ready for the party. I'll meet you there," I told Andrew.

Andrew poured himself a drink, which was becoming routine. The volume of my inner voice, which I had muted, avoiding any confrontation, began to rise. This job boosted my sense of self to a crescendo. I always thought I was capable, but now I knew I was capable. Andrew's lips on the edge of that designer, cut-crystal lowball glass jeopardized my trajectory. One sip, two sips, a gulp. He swallowed my path to success.

"I'm sure they'll have a fabulous bar at the party; no need to fill up early," I said on the way out.

"Oh, don't you worry about me," Andrew sang back.

Andrew feigned happy-go-lucky, but I could see drinking was becoming necessary for his daily functions.

Choosing an outfit for these types of events gave me stress. I had to balance being cool and creative with being professional.

"You're home early. I'm not used to seeing you home during daylight," Neil quipped, leaning against the closet door.

His comment was a jab at his unhappiness with my long hours.

"Yeah, I know. I brought some work home. Just needed a change of scenery. I didn't even get lunch today."

"So, since I'm home," Neil said, wrapping his arms around my waist, "why don't you skip that boring client party and come out with me?"

"Very funny," I said.

"What's funny? I'm serious. I'm rarely in New York on a weeknight. Besides, it's a silly Christmas party. It's not like it's real work, Sky." Neil began backing away, frustrated by my failure to comply.

"But it is work, Neil. Listen, you know I'd love to hang with you, but I told Andrew I would be there. The clients want me to be there."

"Skylar, it's Andrew's firm, and *he* needs to go. You don't need to go."

I felt a quiver of guilt in my chest. Christine's party wasn't just a regular party, and receiving accolades after the long design process was rewarding. I was concerned about Andrew's excessive drinking, so there was no way I could blow it off. Maybe I could water down his drinks or make them disappear when he put his glass down for a moment. Maybe I could be home in time to make Neil happy.

"I wish I could stay," I said, rubbing his shoulder and giving my best compassionate face.

Neil shuffled away from me into the kitchen without a word. Like stones being assembled on the center of my chest, I felt the weight of his disappointment. My eyelids closed for a moment. I paused, seeking strength to hopefully shake off the heavy guilt he placed upon me. Neil continually made me responsible for his happiness, and I tiptoed across eggshells in these moments.

Focus. Back to wardrobe selection. I settled on a black pencil skirt and a white blouse. I added a blue silk scarf just to add a splash of color. I grabbed a pair of high black leather boots and freshened up my makeup for the evening.

The apartment was drenched in Christmas. Large evergreen trees encrusted with massive globes in jewel tones anchored the corners of the room. Delicate silver and white powder resembling seasonal snow dusted the floors. Evergreen wreaths dotted with acorn-sized twinkling lights and sparkling gold butterflies hung in place of their artwork. Waiters resembling Ford models roamed the apartment, identifiable by their ruby-red bowties, fluffy Santa hats, and million-dollar smiles.

"Skylar!" Christine's sing-song tone was festive. "I am so thrilled to have you, darling. Come. There are some guests I'd love you to meet."

I saw Andrew out of the corner of my eye, clasping a nearly empty lowball, eyes searching for a waiter like a hound for a bird. He entertained a plump brunette in a short leopard dress. I couldn't catch his attention and needed to acquiesce to the numerous introductions.

"This is Skylar. Isn't she just adorable?" Christine cooed. "She's Andrew's assistant. So talented!"

She had her hand around my waist, intensely steering me through the room as if I were a celebrity. She clearly had certain people she needed me to meet. This was not unusual.

Potential clients filled the room, and we hoped to find them between their clinking glasses and air kisses.

"Matthew," she said as she tapped a tall gentleman from behind to relieve him from his current conversation. "Matthew," she repeated, "I want you to meet Skylar."

Matthew swiveled to face us. Ignoring his cute, boyish looks challenged my composure. Something about his crooked smile tugged at me. He was handsome but unconventional. Not a poster boy by any means. Not like Neil. I could feel women looking at Neil when he walked into a room, but Matthew was understated and unique-looking. Something drew me in. My eyes registered the interesting yet handsome look, but I didn't expect the jitters in my knees.

"Skylar, this is Matthew Cherning. Skylar is Andrew's design assistant. Isn't she adorable? Skylar is from Pennsylvania and attended design school here in New York. She's going to be the next big thing in design. Matthew is an old friend who does a ton of business with Ivan now. If I can brag for a moment, Matthew, don't kill me, but he's quietly made quite a name for himself. Okay, I'm off, you two enjoy." Christine fluttered into the crowd.

I awkwardly extended my hand to Matthew. My engagement ring caught the light, and I could see the sparkle landing on his lapel. Good reminder.

"Pleasure to meet you," said Matthew.

An unexpected fever sizzled across my skin as he touched my hand. My inner voice spoke up, telling me to breathe and think about Neil. I pulled a memory of Neil in my head, a photograph taken of Neil and me on the beach.

I could barely hear Matthew's words over my internal reprimands. Why did he affect me this way?

He was about six feet tall, and his frame was thicker than any of the men in the circle of conversation. I watched his sandy blond hair bounce when he turned toward me, ignoring the group. When I caught a glimpse of his chiseled jawline, my lips froze. Matthew cocked his head, slipped his hand in his pocket, and boyishly smiled into my eyes.

"So, how does a girl from Pennsylvania end up as a design assistant in New York?" he asked.

"It's a long story," I said, trying to think of a way to reference Neil.

"I have time," he replied, staring with intensity and flashing his comforting smile.

I wondered why he cared. I'd tried avoiding a detailed conversation, but he wasn't letting me skirt the topic.

"I studied design in college and dabbled in the fashion industry for a few years."

Matthew barged in on my words. "Wait, I knew you looked familiar!" He extended his finger toward me, shaking it up and down like a teacher reprimanding a child. "Did you work for Johnny Tithler?

I laughed like an unabashed teenager. "Yes. Yes, I did. Wait, I'm so confused. I thought you're in the real estate business with Ivan?"

"I am, but I was working on a deal with Johnny, and your desk was just outside his office, right? I must have walked by you a hundred times!"

Matthew's strong eye contact throughout our conversation couldn't hide his genuine interest. There was a comfort in his attention and enthusiasm that I couldn't help but compare to my interactions with Neil. This felt different.

"Really?" I asked.

"Yes! I thought you looked familiar."

"Wow. I can't believe you remembered. I'm sorry I didn't recognize you."

"No, no need for an apology. I guess I'm pretty good at recalling faces. I used to entertain a lot for work, and you get used to keeping a lookout after a while. So, do you still talk to Johnny?"

Stunned by his interest, it took me a moment to respond.

"Yes, I do. I loved working for Johnny."

"Tell me more. What did you do at his firm?"

Matthew and I ended up in a conversation that muted the noise of the party. His questions were specific, and his eyes were eager for responses about my life. He told me how he met Ivan and how he used to love the client-relationship aspect of real estate but recently began structuring contracts and deals instead. Our conversation flowed, and my nerves vanished as we laughed about Johnny's habits. Talking with Matthew left me full.

"Sky?" I heard Andrew's voice from behind me.

I had no choice. Turning away from Matthew was my only option. The scent of alcohol wafting off Andrew was as strong as coffee in Dunkin' Donuts. I'd completely forgotten babysitting Andrew was on my agenda for the evening.

"How's it going? Did you see that woman I was speaking with?" His words slurred as he gestured with his left thumb. I reached for his glass as we spoke, removing it from his grasp while maintaining direct eye contact and pretending the separation of glass from hand was not occurring. I tried chalking it up to holiday stress, but I knew my excuses couldn't hold up against his emerging pattern of heavy drinking.

"Yeah, big-haired leopard-clad lady?" I whispered.

"Yes. She's renovating a townhouse on East 63rd Street. I think you should go chat her up. She hasn't hired a designer yet." He spoke a little louder than I would have liked.

"Okay, will do. I'm on it," I confirmed and prepared for possible damage control after Andrew's boozy conversation with Leopard Lady.

"Where's my drink? Where'd you put my drink?" His voice grew louder.

Shoot.

"Let me get you a glass of water." As I spun in search of water, Matthew's gaze caught my eye, and I watched in slow motion as he tilted his head to the side with an inquisitive squint at my panic mode.

"Water? Why would I drink water? Sky, where's my drink?"

"Listen, Andrew, you know there are so many potential clients here, and—"

"Skylar, where's the damn drink?"

"Maybe have a water and just, you know, pace yourself."

"Pace myself? I'm not sixteen, Skylar."

Andrew stormed away. I turned toward Matthew, but he was already engaged in another conversation. Just as I looked away, our eyes snapped together for an extended gaze, sending pinpricks down my legs.

I set off to hunt Leopard Lady. Time to pull out the charm.

"Hi. I'm Skylar, Andrew's assistant. I just wanted to introduce myself."

"Oh, Andrew was telling me about you. He seems like such a doll!" Her voice was high-pitched yet powerful. "Yes. We recently purchased a townhouse. We just closed last week. I guess you could call it a Christmas gift." Her gruff laughter caused a few partygoers to turn their heads. I joined in her laughter, feigning interest.

"Wow. Indeed. That sounds like a perfect Christmas gift. It will be a busy and exciting year ahead. Have you chosen a general contractor yet?"

Rope tossed.

"Well, I have a list of names, but perhaps you can recommend someone. Christine raves about you even more than Andrew, so I bet you have connections with the best in the city."

A tingle of excitement trickled down my back at hearing her praise. I felt an unexpected nudge of my elbow as Andrew sidled up next to me. I silently prayed he hadn't heard her comment.

"Absolutely! We have excellent connections. I would be happy to put you in touch with some of our top contractors. Just ring our office anytime." Andrew slurred his words.

Andrew slammed his already empty cut-crystal glass on the dining table and gave me a side glare as he walked toward the bartender. I chased behind him, taking quick baby steps so as not to draw any extra attention.

"Andrew," I whispered, "can we talk before you get a drink?"

"No, Skylar. We cannot talk before I get a drink."

"I-I'm helping you. Getting drunk isn't going to solve anything."

"Drunk? I'm not drunk. What are you talking about? I don't need a babysitter, Skylar. Just do your assistant job and let me do the rest."

I wanted to close my eyes, twitch my nose, and magically start the evening over. I could have done a better job counting Andrew's cocktails, and I certainly could have spent less time wondering why I craved more conversation with Matthew Cherning. How long could I tolerate Andrew's dysfunction? More importantly, how long before I could work for myself?

chapter
thirteen

Andrew insisted we start the week with a clean slate and proper scheduling. Monday's rituals usually helped me feel organized, but lately, it just highlighted his drinking and created a pit in my stomach on Sunday evenings.

"Okay. We have a hectic week ahead." Andrew stumbled through his words, and hectic sounded like "haytuck."

"Let's review the schedule. Give an overview, will you? First, deliveries scheduled, orders being placed, presentations scheduled, then necessary site visits."

Normally on point and exacting in these meetings, today Andrew seemed unable to focus and made a speedy exit up the stairs. All eyes followed, but mouths stayed firmly closed. The office staff handled the phone duties, billing, and scheduling. Andrew oversaw everything, predominantly client services and design work, but today, he was noticeably absent, and I stepped in to fill the void.

"Andrew?" I gently rapped on his office door. "Everything okay?" No response.

I ran out to pick up lunch for the office, and when I returned, Andrew was polishing forks before placing them on the table.

"Are you okay?" I asked.

"I'm fine, Skylar. Just not feeling a hundred percent today."

Sandy sent a scowl my way. I brushed it off and went to help Andrew. We always ate a civilized lunch in the office. It surprised me at first, but I think it was just a further extension of his keen eye for design and beauty. Placemats, stainless silverware, and glasses were placed on the large glass table. I, too, appreciated the pause during the day.

"My dear," Andrew had preached, "paper products and eating at one's desk is uncivilized. We are not animals here."

Everyone took their seat, and again, Sandy gave me the look of a sixteen-year-old clutching the most phenomenal gossip.

"What?" I finally asked. "What's going on?"

"You have been requested," she said.

I looked at her quizzically. I peered at Andrew, who appeared rejuvenated after the morning's falter. "What is she talking about?" Everyone was giddy by this point.

"Well," he mused, "it seems a Mr. Matthew Cherning called and requested a meeting with you specifically."

"Matthew who?" I tried pretending I hadn't been thinking about Matthew Cherning and his dimpled chin for the past week. Surely, I was just caught up in the excitement of the evening and my curiosity about Matthew would quickly fade. "That's weird."

My palms began sweating in my pockets, and my heart picked up speed at the thought of another engaging conversation with Matthew, but then guilt emerged. I should not take this meeting. I should stay away from any man that captivated me. I loved Neil. Neil was my husband. Husband, I repeated in my head. I heard the important words ring in my ear—vows, wedding, white dress. No good can come of a business relationship with a man who piqued my interest. But I wanted to learn more about Matthew's life, his friends, and what made him tick. It was all I could think about. Matthew's genuine interest was refreshing compared to Neil's tolerance of my creative career. I wondered what my life would have been like if I hadn't married at such a young age. While Neil had filled all my voids when I walked down the aisle, would he still as I grew, changed, and developed?

"Weird or not, you are going to that meeting," Andrew declared. He reached for a bottle of red wine and gave himself a generous pour.

I glared at him, hoping he would understand my disapproval of wine at lunch, not to mention the alcohol on his breath every morning, his four o'clock scotch, five o'clock vodka, and beyond.

"Going to the meeting with you. Right?" I was more telling him than asking.

"I don't think so, honey. The gentleman asked specifically for you."

"I can't take this meeting. I'm an assistant."

"This is true."

"You're the designer. This is your company," I confirmed.

My thoughts twisted around one another, evoking an intense fear I had never felt. I didn't feel ready to take on a job by myself. Andrew was my safety net, guiding me along, and with him at the helm, he avoided any beginner mistakes I might make. Without him, I could ruin everything.

"True as well," said Andrew.

"I'm not ready."

"You are ready, my dear."

I absorbed Andrew's words and let them settle in my brain. If he thought I was ready, maybe I was. Maybe I could find a way, but for the moment, fear overtook any rational thoughts.

"I'm not."

"You are," he said.

"I can't."

"You can. And you will."

"It's a mistake. He made a mistake," I implored.

Finding a way out of Matthew's job was necessary. Somewhere deep in my gut, I knew. I knew Matthew was a beautiful storm descending on my life. But it also awakened a desire for emotional connection that I had never imagined I wanted.

"Skylar, the man called and asked for you. It's no mistake. Get over it!"

Truthfully, it felt rewarding to be wanted, but he didn't even know my abilities beyond Christine and Ivan's apartment. Now, the training wheels Andrew had provided would be removed and shelved for the next assistant somewhere down the line.

"Did you set up a meeting?" I asked.

"Yes, Thursday at 5:30 p.m. He wants to meet after work."

"Okay," I sighed, "I guess I'm having a meeting with Matthew Cherning on Thursday."

Thursday arrived faster than any Thursday in history. I perused my pint-sized Manhattan closet for twenty minutes that morning, fashioning an appropriate outfit. My stomach searched for calm amongst a tsunami that had built all week. I wanted to look professional but not stuffy, and cute but not trying too hard. Pants flew off hangers, and sweaters draped over piles of rejected choices as I wreaked havoc on the shelves once assembled like soldiers as Neil preferred.

"Sky, what happened in here?" Neil asked, glancing at the mess.

"Just deciding what to wear to my first client meeting," I said, distracted by the piles of clothes.

"I don't think it really matters, Sky. Why are you stressing about it? Just wear your normal get-up. Which tie do you like with this shirt?"

"Neil, it's my first client meeting on my own, and you always say looking professional is important. If I look businesslike, the client will take me seriously. It's important."

I wouldn't tell Neil my findings on Matthew after doing some research. My new client was listed as one of the most eligible bachelors in Manhattan, and I fantasized about hours of conversation with him. He seemed like a man who attracted overachievers and beauty queens who laughed at precisely the right moment, making her man feel witty and smooth. I quietly envied those women and their power, their ease in landing a guy like Matthew Cherning.

Maybe Christine had encouraged him. I was sure it did not reach further than that. Or maybe it did. Our conversation had meandered naturally without a lull, and I replayed our words over and over in my head. If I felt it, didn't he? I saw something in his eyes as our chat unfolded, a look confirming maybe he felt it, too.

December was sweater weather, helping guide my decision. The winners were trendy black pants, a wool mock turtleneck, and a pair of low black leather boots. The boots had lost their shine, but they would have to do. And the sweater color . . . hmm. Round two. A stack of sweaters confused me with a kaleidoscope of colors represented. Cream? Heather gray? Cranberry? Cream. Crisp and clean, it would give me an angelic appearance. I could have sprouted wings. Matthew seemed cool compared to me. I feared appearing unsophisticated and tried averting judgment from a poorly planned outfit.

At 4:45 p.m., I dragged myself to the luxurious Clarence House ladies room. Luscious silks cascading from eight feet up displayed colors so rich my pupils readjusted when taking in the inordinately dense colors typically only found in nature. Like frogs in the rainforest, or Caribbean oceans on the clearest of days.

This showroom catered to budget-less projects. Price did not require justification, and the beauty and detail was unrivaled. Prior to my meeting with Matthew, my makeup and hair would need some TLC after a workday rivaling a marathon. All seventeen floors had seen my leather boots, hauling my extra-large LL Bean canvas tote with navy trim filled with fabric samples, wood chips, and furniture information sheets. Several other bags adorned with various showrooms' logos had joined my collection. Andrew could barely keep up with all the new clients, ranging from an entire house in Palm Beach to several bathroom renovations throughout the city.

Thankfully, rare were the days that my body sat like an office clerk. Every day was different, and I enjoyed being in constant motion. I loved the pace, the various stages of projects, and, of course, the creativity. There was no doubt in my mind that someday I would have my own design firm and appreciate pursuing my passion every day.

My makeup was mostly preserved, needing only a bit of touch-up, but my hair looked like I'd had an argument with a low-flying bird searching for a nest. I brushed and tussled my hair until it looked like hair, not hay.

I pulled up the email with Matthew's address. West 11th Street. Stepping out on the curb in front of the D&D building, I debated taking a taxi, but the waves of yellow cabs surging up Third Avenue all whizzed north with dark lights atop their wet roofs, indicating they were occupied. December's chill cut through my down parka. The subway was close by, and I would only switch trains once. I hated the subway in the winter months. I froze above ground yet sweltered beneath the crowded city streets. Living uptown provided the ease of strolling to the D&D building, but even with that convenience, I still preferred downtown.

Downtown evoked a sense of being in a different city. Although many friends lived within blocks of my apartment, I found comfort downtown. My nerves mounted as the train headed south, and I fought to balance my emotions and control my perspiration under my heavy coat. As I emerged from the depths of the subway, snow spiraled from the clouds like a magnificent mobile above me.

Beautiful, yes, but it was not helping my sad hair situation. I questioned why I worried about how I looked for this meeting, but admitting the truth would confirm feelings I denied.

Walking toward 11th Street, I mentally reviewed the agenda for the meeting. Assessing the space and the client's objectives were my goals for the evening. At the red brick building, the doorman performed his duties and welcomed me.

"Good afternoon, I'm going to . . ." I fumbled for the address, but my gloves were cumbersome.

"Mr. Cherning?" he asked.

"Yes, how did you know?" I was surprised, but he just laughed.

"Go ahead up, sweetheart. It's Penthouse 5. Elevator is down the hall and to your left."

chapter fourteen

Peering into the mirrored walls of the elevator, I assessed my snow-damaged hair and smudged mascara, compliments of the flurries. I'd hoped to look more professional, and I shook my head upside down as I reprimanded myself for caring too much about my appearance. The elevator doors drew apart from their center, revealing a large, open loft. I pursed my lips and glanced side to side to gain some bearing on the space. I gulped, unsure if my nerves were in anticipation of seeing Matthew or being the lead designer on a project. My inside voice boomed, *You can do this. Get your act together, Skylar.*

Matthew swiftly approached, taking long strides, anxious to greet me. "Skylar, hi. Thanks for coming."

"Hi, Matthew. I'm excited to see your apartment. The building is really cool, old-world New York."

He paced a little, and we stood in the uncomfortable silence.

He finally said, "I like your jacket. I, uh, it's so nice to see you again. I mean, so I can show you the apartment. You know, for work and stuff."

I almost didn't recognize him without his neatly pressed designer suit and starched white shirt. His attire of baggy black track pants with white racing stripes down the sides, red Jordan high tops, a wrinkled and mismatched T-shirt, and a black baseball cap averted my attention from the agenda I planned.

Seeing Matthew casual and comfortable was somehow

more appealing than the suit and tie version. He seemed more real.

"Heading to play some basketball later, I hope you don't mind . . ." He gestured toward his clothing. I panicked that perhaps he'd recognized my silent once-over as my eyes examined him from head to toe.

"Oh, no, of course not. Not a problem."

"Here, let me take your coat. It's getting nasty out there, huh?" I assumed my disheveled hair triggered his comment, and I tucked some loose strands behind my ear out of desperation.

Matthew assisted me with my coat, but somehow, my arm became trapped in the sleeve. I shook my arm a few times, loosening Matthew's grip, and watched the coat float to the floor.

"I'm sorry. I guess I'm a little nervous. Maybe you make me a little jittery," he joked.

I felt a tingle in my belly yet decided that ignoring his comment was the only way through the situation. But I heard him loud and clear.

"It's okay. The weather isn't too bad." I took a step back, as if the distance would break the pull of attraction drawing me in.

"Can I get you a drink?"

"No thanks, I'm good." The last thing I needed around Matthew was a drink.

His awkward, uneven smile tugged at me. I felt a comfort and ease in his presence despite my nerves, yet I didn't understand why. He'd let his beard grow in a bit. It covered his jutting jaw, and I tried convincing myself it would be awful kissing his scruffy face, but it wasn't working. Unfortunately, I found the scruff kind of sexy.

He leaned against the island in the kitchen, crossing his arms against his chest.

"So, how's your day going? Andrew treating you well?" he joked.

"He is. We've been so busy lately. Design is actually fun for me."

"That's great. Seems like you truly enjoy it. That's one of the reasons I wanted you on the project. You just seemed so passionate when we spoke at the party. I admire passion in every aspect of life. Don't you?"

I paused and tilted my head, contemplating his question. Passion. I had never thought of myself as passionate, but he was correct.

"Yes. I guess I never looked at it that way. I love the idea of creating spaces within a client's home where their most intimate moments play out. Creating a backdrop where people experience real life that no one else sees makes me think carefully about my designs. I imagine someone sitting on the sofa crying from a loss, or the announcement of a pregnancy, the excitement of new life before anyone else knows, in the confines of a room I created. That's the stuff I think about when I'm designing." My honesty surprised me.

Neil never noticed my passion. Perhaps there was only room for his technology obsessions in our marriage. Not only did Matthew recognize I was a passionate woman, but he appreciated it, which made me feel seen in a new way. Neil viewed my passions as insignificant and inconvenient, and I wondered why I never recognized his disinterest until I heard Matthew's observations about me.

As Matthew led me on a detailed tour of the vast but empty penthouse, we passed a large canvas oil painting leaning against a blank wall. The figure of a man in the distance, waving at a train leaving the station, caught my attention. My eyes lingered on the canvas, slowing me down as I tried to keep up with Matthew.

"I really like this painting. Are you into buying art? I know some great galleries," I said.

"I like it too. My fiancée, I mean my former fiancée, was a painter. No matter how I tried, I couldn't leave that piece behind. Part of me wants to, wants to leave it all behind, erase the memories and reminders, but that's just not me."

"I understand that struggle. If you're interested, we can go to some galleries and pick out some new pieces for the apartment. Start fresh."

"I love that idea. Shopping for art sounds like a lot of fun. I'd enjoy that."

My mind zoomed, imagining a day meandering through galleries with Matthew. A day observing him in real life, out of his apartment.

"So, there are two bedrooms, three bathrooms—two full and one half—an office, a living room, and a dining room area that kind of includes the kitchen," he explained.

A small staircase revealed an unbelievable outdoor terrace. My teeth chattered as we stepped outside, and I watched Matthew trip over the top step in slow motion, bracing his fall with open palms. He glanced up at me, beet red from embarrassment while laughing, and I watched his dimples dig deep in his cheeks.

"Whoops. That was embarrassing. But I can't hide my clumsiness for too long. C'mon, let's go back inside," he said.

I followed him down the stairs and approached the bar stools at the prominent kitchen island. He had a small wood dining table with four metal folding chairs and a worn leather sofa. That was it.

"So, whatcha think?" He was trying to be cute, but it was just awkward.

"I think it's great. The flow is amazing, and the views are spectacular. Do you have any design ideas or requests?" I felt a giddiness rising within me and fought to stuff it away. Matthew hung on my every word, blatantly charming me. Most guys played it cool, hiding their interest, but Matthew's goofy delight was unabashed.

"Don't know. I want it to be comfortable and cool, even though I'm not so cool. Maybe we can fake it. And, of course, I want you to design it." The edges of his lips turned up toward a smile as he pointed at me, accentuating the "you."

A wave of excitement whipped around me. When I realized I'd officially gotten the job, my chest expanded with pride. He wanted me to design this huge apartment. ME! I imagined jumping up and hugging him, but that would have certainly crossed the line I was holding between us. How would I handle daily contact with Matthew? The mix of the bad and good intoxicated me, and the rush left me lightheaded.

"I would love to work on this project with you," I gushed. As the words left my mouth, I berated myself. Oh, my God, Skylar, try to sound professional. I worried the connection I felt toward Matthew wouldn't go away. But with this apartment, I could prove my skills and take one giant step closer to opening my own business. I wouldn't pass up this opportunity.

"Great! When can we start?"

We reviewed the generous budget and various details about the apartment and furniture selections as I twisted my wedding ring around and around my finger.

"Here you go." He dropped the key in my palm. "And I'll let the superintendent know you may have full access."

We ambled toward the elevator. As he reached for my parka from the closet, three coats dropped to the floor, and just as he fumbled to re-hang them, a pile of hangers toppled to the floor in disarray. I giggled, finding his clumsy nature charming.

"I'm just a design assistant, you know. Why not Andrew?" I blurted out.

He leaned forward on his palms, rising from the mess, leaning uncomfortably close to me. His whispering tone would be inaudible if it were not for his proximity. "When I spoke to Johnny, he couldn't stop raving about you. Let's just say Johnny was not happy with your departure. I don't know. I guess when we met the other night, I just felt a connection, like you would get me."

He'd called Johnny about me? Our eyes clicked together for a moment, confirming the undeniable. Matthew grabbed a navy blue ski jacket from the closet and called the elevator.

"I'm heading to basketball now . . . Does your husband—it is husband, right?"

I stiffened from his words and nodded as best I could.

"Does he play hoops?"

"No, he's a science geek. Not a sports guy." I shook my head, envisioning Neil clumsily running the length of a basketball court.

"Got it. I'll walk out with you. When can we meet again?" he asked.

"I'm hoping I'll complete the presentation before Christmas," I said.

"I have to wait that long?" He looked disappointed.

"Well," I continued, "it takes time to assemble."

"Maybe we should schedule another meeting before then. You know, a check-in."

His smile emerged again. I smiled back and felt a wave of heat come over me. His energy and vibe diverted my attention from all other topics.

"I can't believe you worked for Johnny. Such a small world. He would love to see you."

"Pretty crazy. I see him a few times a year, but it's not enough. We had a lot of fun together. Were you at his launch party?"

"You mean that disgusting basement with no air conditioning in the East Village in the middle of July? I literally thought I was going to have heat stroke."

My laugh erupted at a high pitch, and I quickly covered my mouth. I nudged Matthew as we tried reining in our laughter.

"Seriously, though, why did you guys pick that place?" Matthew nudged me this time.

"I don't know," I said between fits of laughter. "I think

some guy who worked with us knew someone at the company that managed the building. I think Johnny negotiated to get the space for free if that guy could invite his friends or something like that."

"I have to remind Johnny about that. Man, that was a fun night, though."

I wished we had met back then and wondered why we hadn't. "I know. We were so excited. I felt so alive that night. We thought we had really made it. Little did we know how much hard work would come after that night."

"I like hard work. Don't you? I mean, I love how it feels to work hard, achieve something, and then look back on it. The process is the most fun for me."

My brow furrowed. "Hmmm. I never really thought about it that way, but yeah, I think you're right. Those days with Johnny were the best, and the most difficult. We even had the electricity turned off one time because we couldn't pay the bill. It was electricity or five hundred yards of fabric for the new line."

Matthew's words stayed with me as I understood why working for Johnny impacted me. I recalled the hard work and recognized opening my own firm would require a diligence I enjoyed.

I loved how my conversations with Matthew flowed with ease. My skin sensed his proximity, and talking for hours with him would have been the easiest way to spend the night. In a strange way, it was as if I had known Matthew before that day, and I imagined how wonderful it would have been if we had met at Johnny's party. He was awkward but adorable, and I reprimanded my mind for fantasizing how it would have felt to go on a date with Matthew. I had felt lucky to have met Neil so young, relieving me of endless dating like my friends endured, but conversations between Neil and I never had this incredible flow. Neil was either uncomfortably quiet or talking about himself. Communicating with Matthew was fluid, and his goofy nature made him approachable and provided me comfort in sharing my truest self. That's the part that gave me pause. Matthew exuded a comfort within himself that transferred to others. That comfort washed over me.

Matthew gave the doorman a friendly fist bump. The cold air hit my face, and I shuddered just a little.

"You okay?" he asked, looking over at me. I nodded, surprised he even noticed, and watched his long strides gain some distance in front of me. Matthew approached a black luxury car parked outside the red brick building. Opening the rear door, he motioned for me to get in. I rubbed the nape of my neck.

"Oh, no, no. That's too much; I'll grab a cab."

"Skylar, I insist. It's freezing out, and you live all the way uptown. Please?" He looked at me with pleading eyes. All the way uptown . . . don't remind me.

"Okay, but honestly, this is really unnecessary." Clients routinely offered me a glass of water or a cup of coffee but never private transportation.

"It's no big deal."

He leaned over me and spoke to the driver.

"Lukas, can you please take Skylar home? She will give you the address."

"I'll talk to you soon?"

"Yes. I'll touch base in a week or so," he said.

Matthew pushed the car door shut and gave a slight wave. I sat in the low leather seats, peering up at him. Pinpricks danced up my back, and my smile couldn't be contained.

Lukas maneuvered through the dark, wet streets. Streetlamps adorned with evergreen and red satin ribbons trimmed in gold caused the light to dance on the damp asphalt. Sidewalks teemed with shoppers scurrying while completing their Christmas lists as we headed uptown. My eyes rested before arriving back in the other city known as uptown, all while dreaming of a downtown life where hours of conversation with a goofy, charming guy would fill my days and nights.

chapter
fifteen

Sarah Waldbaum sauntered into her torn-up apartment, gingerly stepping over bent metal nails and deflated cardboard boxes caked with gritty dust particles. "Andrew? Andrew!"

Her flat, Midwestern, sing-song voice echoed through the empty, light-starved foyer. I marveled at her intensity as she daintily held her handbag, removed a large plastic bag from within, and then placed her leather bag into the plastic bag like evidence from a crime scene, protecting it from the swirling dust.

The scale of the windows suited the space, but the dreadful northern exposure and unfortunate view of a brick wall provided negligible light. Sarah brushed her hands together, making a slight clapping noise and removing any dirt from her manicured hands. A hint of neutral brown lipstick stained her thin lips, neither drawing attention to them nor making them disappear. Her wide waist was perpetually wrapped with a narrow lizard skin belt fastened with a polished gold buckle, and a strand of large pearls circled her neck. I wondered if she ever allowed warm kisses from the sun. It seemed Sarah's robotic personality concealed her true feelings and thoughts, and befriending her had become a goal. If I could soften her just a bit, make her comfortable, I'd find the real Sarah. I thought about whom I revealed the true Skylar to and who saw the people-pleasing, sugar-coated version.

By acquiring an apartment on Park Avenue, Sarah had achieved her goal of prestige and bragging rights by living on one of the most exclusive avenues in New York. The modest eight-hundred-square-foot apartment needed a comprehensive renovation. "Park Avenue," she boasted when anyone inquired, or didn't inquire, for that matter.

It was a humble apartment compared to most of our projects, yet it lingered due to her obsessive nature. Several times a week, Sarah demanded the general contractor report on-site for extensive reviews.

"George," she said as she glanced at the contractor in his soot-covered navy blue chinos and jacket, "if we were to move this cabinet over three inches, would you have space to build a small additional cabinet, matching the wood, of course, that could pull out like so, with bars to hang dish towels? It would be wonderful to get those dirty dish towels off my countertop." George sneered at me as Sarah continued, "I realize you would need to remove all the installed cabinets and, of course, rebuild this one to accommodate the new dish towel cabinet."

Sarah finally lifted her head from the two-toned zebrawood cabinet in question, staring at George for answers, and in return, George stared at me. My eyes ping-ponged back and forth between them.

Andrew excused himself and stepped into the hall. George's eyes pleaded with me as the meeting entered hour two.

"Well, Sarah, yes, that's a wonderful idea you have. It most certainly would be helpful to have a cabinet devoted to hanging dish towels."

When Andrew didn't return, the stress of handling Sarah weighed on me.

"I think we should review the shop drawings and evaluate the possibilities, you know, from a space perspective. Of course, there would be some added cost, so we need to assess that as well."

My diplomacy was not up to Mrs. Waldbaum's standards, but it seemed to satisfy her momentarily. I scanned the entrance for Andrew. "George, what do you think? Is this something we might be able to accommodate?"

His beady brown eyes burrowed through me. "Yes, of course. Anything is possible." His Polish accent was thick, but after fifteen years in New York, it had mellowed. "But you know it will be a trade-off. The other cabinet will now be narrower. We need to see if that will affect the interior dimensions of the cabinets. Do you know what you're putting in the other cabinets?"

Sarah kneeled over, her bag within a bag near the window, maneuvering the bric-a-brac scattered throughout the apartment.

Unhurried and cautious, Sarah removed a green leatherbound notebook from her handbag.

"Ah. Here it is." She turned toward us with her head still glued to the tiny notebook. "Lower kitchen cabinet number one. Limoges platter, pink and green floral. Fifteen inches. Limoges serving bowl, blue scrolls. Fourteen inches. Lower kitchen cabinet number two. Bernardaud teapot. Birds and feather pattern. Eight inches."

I looked over at George as his eyelids slowly sank like tiny pebbles plopping into a clear lake. I noticed his struggle in keeping them open and entertaining Sarah's detailed list of cabinetry contents.

Andrew strode in, and as he spoke, I caught a whiff of scotch the moment he opened his mouth. "Sorry about that. How's it going?"

George's lids rolled up when Sarah returned to the meeting area we had created.

"Andrew, come with me into the kitchen. I think I have a brilliant idea," she said. George and I didn't follow.

"Is she kidding me?" he asked in a whispered scream. "We will need to remake all the lower cabinets in the kitchen!"

"I know. Calm down. Let's just let her flesh out the idea, and we can dissuade her later. Just bear with me. I bet she'll find some reason why it won't work between then and now anyway, not to mention she will never pay for the change order. Trust me, it will work out."

"Okay, but wow, Skylar, what a waste of time this is. I have five other renovations going on, and this is by far the smallest project!" George's hands flailed through the air. "If this wasn't Andrew's project, I would have put a time limit on these meetings. It's killing my day! I've ignored at least six calls already."

Our previous meeting had lasted more than three hours as Sarah contemplated a glass shower enclosure. "Let me see; if it swings this way, how will I step in and out of the tub?" Sarah walked through the motions, stepping in and out of the non-existent tub, then repeated this exercise, imagining the glass pivoting in the opposite direction.

The meetings took a toll on everyone's schedule, and I wished Andrew would manage his client better. When I had my own firm, I'd remember the importance of setting limits on challenging clients. I zoned out as the meeting dragged on through discussing tile patterns.

I watched as Sarah cocked her head like Scooby-Doo on a mission.

"Well, let's see, what if we turned this around and had the inserts run this way?" Sarah bent over, straight-legged with her rear high in the air, and shifted the tiles. She grimaced as her fingers touched the dust-encrusted tile. I snapped out of the brain fog when my phone vibrated in my hand with Neil's number on the screen. I knew Sarah only cared about Andrew and happily ducked out of the meeting.

"Hey. What's up?" I whispered.

We rarely spoke during the day, given my meeting schedule and the lack of privacy in both of our offices.

"I need to go to San Fran on Thursday. You want to come?"

"I don't think I can pull that off. I've been picking up the slack around here now that Andrew's not himself lately."

"Well, can't you just call in sick or something? I thought we could spend the weekend out there. You know you don't have to be a martyr, Sky."

"I know. It would have been nice, but there's just too much going on at work, and I'm not going to lie about being sick, Neil. Plus, I told Charlie we would hang out on Saturday."

I anticipated Neil's possessiveness. Charlie, my best friend, had moved to my hometown when we were twelve, just after my sister was diagnosed. The belly laughs and silly cooking experiments had transported me miles from the realities of my home life.

"Really? You didn't tell me that. Well, I'm glad I'll be away then. Seems you've already booked up your weekend."

"I didn't realize I needed your permission before making plans with a friend."

"No, it's fine. I can handle being ditched by my wife."

"No one is ditching you, Neil. I just made plans with a friend, and now you're leaving, so it doesn't even matter. Can we talk about this tonight? I'm in the middle of a meeting."

"Whatever, Sky. You're always in the middle of a meeting. I'll see you tonight unless you have plans with your friends."

"Why are you being so dramatic? I really don't appreciate the attitude."

Neil hung up in the middle of my sentence. The gnawing guilt started in my gut and crept up my belly toward my throat. I wished he could be happy that I had a career and friends, instead of him compounding my anxiety. I agonized about going to my uptown home, given his judgments.

chapter
sixteen

In Sarah's pursuit of perfection, it was necessary that she touch, feel, and experience every item. Her expectations resulted in a full-day appointment for plumbing selections. Prim and proper, Sarah inspected faucets and shower valves, grasping each one like Goldilocks testing chairs.

"Too clunky; too slim." She contemplated the assets and drawbacks of each piece. It took hours to finalize merely one decision.

Next, Sarah strode down the long aisle flanked by display toilets. "This is a lovely commode, but it seems a bit low," she commented, continuing her stroll toward the far end of the twenty-five-commode lineup.

Circling the first toilet in line, Sarah analyzed it from every angle as if she were a judge in a world-class toilet competition. After looking at it for long minutes, she approached, lifted the lid, and sat.

"This one is nice. I feel comfortable on it." She wriggled her bottom on the seat.

I couldn't believe my eyes. My giggle slipped out, and I quickly excused myself to the opposite side of the showroom to gain some composure.

The sales representative heard my laughter and caught my attention. Her high brown leather riding boots kissed the hem of her prairie skirt, and tortoise shell framed glasses slipped down her nose as she peered over them, observing the comedic scene playing out before us. She looked over, hiding her laughter as Sarah stood up and walked to the next toilet, where the ritual was repeated. Plop down, wriggle rear, and comment aloud.

"This one dips a little in the middle. It's nice, but it feels a little elongated for my shape."

I struggled to contain my giggles as Sarah sampled every commode in the showroom, straight-faced and contemplating the pros and cons of each. Somehow, Andrew kept it together.

At one point, a boisterous laugh escaped my lungs, and I choked on trying to contain it. My eyes watered, and finally, a silent, uncontrollable hysteria took over. Andrew looked over with a glare at first, but my laughter instantly infected him. Sarah looked up.

"What?" she sneered. "Is it unusual to try out one's commode prior to purchase?"

I could not speak. I was too far gone. Tears flew from my eyes as I escaped to the ladies' room. Once my breathing steadied, I applied lip gloss and then returned to the showroom. One sight of Sarah back on the toilet, and I collapsed into hysteria. Maybe Neil was right. Maybe I wasn't ready to fly on my own if I couldn't keep my composure during a simple task like shopping for toilets.

chapter
seventeen

I trudged through the unpredicted rain to a client's apartment. Andrew had instructed me to supervise the delivery and installation of the bedroom and living room carpet. I hadn't met this client, but I agreed to fill in for Andrew while he claimed to be overseeing another job. Lately, he was about as dependable as the weather forecast.

The installers lugged two rolls of custom-ordered carpet into the apartment, preparing for installation over the newly laid wood floors. This client had enjoyed Andrew's undivided attention, which excluded me from design decisions, including the carpet selections. As the carpets unfurled, I realized Andrew had never advised me on the carpet placement, so I immediately called the office. He usually provided me with a sketch of each room, specifying the carpet style number and name as well as the direction of the pattern. It was clear I could no longer depend on Andrew for the details.

"Hey, Sandy. Can you check the file and tell me the location of the carpets that were delivered today?"

"Sure. Let me grab the file." Sandy placed me on hold while I held off the installers.

"I see the paperwork, but it's not labeled."

"Hmm. Are you sure? That's weird. Andrew always—"

"Oh, Skylar, you know he's been a little, well, off lately. You can't depend on him like you used to."

Andrew's tardiness and absences had become glaring. I'd

created a list of plausible excuses I used when he skipped client meetings. So far, I had been successful, and clients had accepted my stories, but it couldn't continue much longer. It was like treading water in the middle of the Atlantic. I now assumed he would not participate in office meetings, and everyone's commitment despite the loss of our captain impressed me.

My call to the showroom was worthless, and as much as I hesitated to interrupt Andrew in his client meeting, I was left with no alternative. I visualized the nightmare that would ensue if the carpets were not in the proper room.

One ring and straight to voicemail. He must have turned his phone off for his meeting—if he was actually in a meeting. I continued trying him numerous times, but after forty-five minutes, the installers grew impatient. We used deductive reasoning, attempting an educated guess, and the blades emerged, slicing the carpet as precisely as finger sandwiches served at high tea.

The following morning, my phone ignited with Andrew's number flashing across the screen. "Morning, Skylar. We have a problem."

My heart sank.

"The carpets at the Rankins' are flip-flopped."

"Oh no. I didn't have a floorplan or style numbers, so I just took a guess based on the sizes of the rooms and the—"

"The bedroom carpet is where the living room carpet should be. We have a big problem."

"I'm so sorry. I'll call the carpet showroom. Maybe the installers can come tomorrow."

"This is huge. You have caused hours of additional work, and I hope you realize if the carpet cannot be reused in the correct room, we'll need to reorder. Then we are talking about tens of thousands of dollars in materials and labor, some of which will come out of your salary. Not to mention the ten to twelve weeks they will wait for the new carpet." Andrew's brusque tone pierced my self-confidence.

"I'm sorry, Andrew. Really, I am, but I tried—"

"I'm not interested in the 'but,' Skylar. Just fix it. Now."

My face flushed, and sweat formed behind my neck. As I dialed the numbers for the carpet showroom, my fingers quivered.

The customer service associate placed me on hold and reported back with good news that the installers could return the following day and attempt to switch the carpets. My stomach gnawed at me for the duration of the day, and my brain could hardly focus on mundane office tasks. Andrew's reminders of the cost we could incur from this mistake haunted me. I wished for the sun to set and rise again so we could begin rectifying my gargantuan mistake.

Desperate for an after-work cocktail, I called Neil, but his phone rang in my ear. Once, twice, three times. That's odd. He always answered my calls on the first ring.

My friends agreed to meet up, and at five thirty, Charlie called with the name and address of the bar. The unfamiliar name didn't faze me. All I needed was a drink to unwind and my closest friends' support.

chapter
eighteen

I must have passed the nondescript entrance to the bar four times.

"Charlie? Where the heck is this place? I've walked up and down the block three times, and I'm freezing."

Charlie laughed through her words. "You're too funny. I'm coming out to find you. You see the bodega with the red neon lotto sign in the window? I'll meet you there in a minute."

Charlie emerged from the bodega in a fashionable black suit and black patent leather pumps. Her long, wavy blond hair bounced on her shoulders as she met me on the sidewalk.

"Hi, honey! You survived the day, huh?" Charlie wrapped her arms around me, and an elixir of her sweet hairspray and perfume tickled my nose.

"I did. But I think the worst is yet to come. Let's go inside. I'm freezing!"

Charlie looped her arm through mine and led me to the rear of the bodega, where we descended the concrete steps.

"Here, this way." She pushed open a flat white door with a tarnished brass knob, exposing the crowded bar.

"Here we are." She smiled. "The girls are on the left. See them at that back corner table?"

I gave a wave in their direction. The exposed brick walls, devoid of windows, wrapped the long rectangular room. Blaring music muffled the creaks from the aged oak planks beneath my feet. Patrons stacked two deep camouflaged a massive mahogany bar. I spied a drink on the table waiting for me.

Charlie's energy was a warm, golden light that could improve your mood immediately. The first time I had seen her from across the large auditorium at freshman orientation, I had assumed she would be snooty and self-involved. It's rare to be grounded with beauty like hers. Long, silky hair cascaded down her shoulders, and I had yet to see a blemish appear on her well-proportioned face. In business, she was a shark, deadly to unsuspecting victims. Charlie had planned on enrolling in law school but postponed it when a friend of her mother's suggested she try her hand at New York City residential real estate.

I looked Charlie over, picking up some fashion tips.

"What happened with the carpet?" she asked.

I hung my head, then lifted it as I replied. "I can't talk about it anymore. It's all I've thought about for the past forty-eight hours, but thanks for asking." I wriggled my body around the bar stools.

"How is Andrew?" Charlie asked.

"Not so great. His drinking is interfering with work, and it's worrying me. He completely screwed me over. This carpet was his mistake. He just disappears these days. I try taking a whiff of his breath in the morning because it usually predicts how the day will go. He's killing me over this mistake, but it's completely his fault." I rolled my eyes in frustration and took a deep breath, calming my nerves.

Pools of professionals gathered, sipping their drinks and mingling. I lifted the generic highball glass, and the vodka slid down my throat, soothing my stress from the day's events.

As we finished our first round of drinks, a waitress arrived bearing a bottle of champagne in a large silver ice bucket.

"Excuse me." The waitress leaned between us. "Compliments of the gentleman at the bar for you ladies."

We giggled in unison, and everyone at the table perked up, searching the bar for the mystery man.

"Which gentleman exactly?" Charlie inquired.

The waitress ignored Charlie while aggressively pulling the bottle from beneath the ice and briskly unwinding the wire securing the cork. Just as the foam grazed the lip of the flute, I felt the warmth of a sturdy hand on my back.

"Andrew let you out for some fun?"

My brow furrowed, and my stomach dropped, shocked at the sight of Matthew.

"What are—you're—I didn't see you," I stammered.

"Just meeting up with some friends. How are you doing?"

My tongue fumbled. "Yeah." That's all I could come up with. The most idiotic word in the world. My embarrassment swelled as I fidgeted with the cuff on my sweater.

I paused, slowly lifted my eyes from the champagne, and found Matthew's eyes mirroring mine. *This is silly*, I told myself. *He's a client, and I am happily married. I mean, I think I have a nice marriage.* My thoughts twisted, hoping I could wring out Neil's flaws flashing through my head. Comparing Matthew and Neil wasn't fair. I categorized my feelings as a ridiculous, childish crush and shoved them far away.

"Aren't you going to introduce us?" Charlie interrupted the awkward silence.

"This is Matthew Cherning. I'm working on the design for his apartment."

"She should be working on it! Instead, she's here playing with you ladies!" he teased.

"Thanks for the champagne. Really, so sweet of you. Join us for a glass?" I asked.

"Nah, you enjoy your friends." Matthew gave a half wave, revealing a tattoo on his right inner wrist. The black ink surprised me. With the Park Avenue parties and the suit and tie career, I had missed his edge. He swaggered toward his friends, and my intrigue about Matthew Cherning ballooned.

"Skylar!" Charlie raised her palms to the sky. "When were you going to tell us you have a hot new client?"

I pushed my connection with Matthew into a compartment I hoped to lock and seal.

"What does he do?"

"Where does he live?"

"Is he single?"

"Guys! Calm down." I needed to remind myself to breathe. I rubbed my clammy palms on my thighs. I didn't want them looking at Matthew. I didn't want them asking about him. Strangely, the thought of Matthew inquiring about any of my friends made me jealous. I soaked up his attention, his interest in me. I shook my head in disbelief. Why did I feel this unexpected connection with him? I wondered if there was something missing in my marriage that Matthew filled.

"I have no idea. He just hired us a week ago, and I barely know him. He works in some sort of real estate business, and I know where he lives, obviously. That's about it."

"He seems to want to get to know you," said Charlie.

The table erupted in laughter. I forced a laugh, playing along, and prayed our racket was not drawing Matthew's attention.

"No, it's not like that," I attempted to whisper. "It's strictly business. There's nothing there." But as the words left my mouth, reality pummeled me. What if he noticed Charlie's good looks or her sense of humor? When my conversations with Matthew flowed and his interest grew with each leading question, it energized me. Neil and I had never had that connection, and it scared me. Discussions with Matthew felt like a heated game of ping pong, a fast-paced exchange of ideas without a pause.

My cheeks ached from holding a flexed smile most of the evening.

Charlie buried her lips against my ear and whispered, "Matthew is into you. Neil better watch out." She pulled away, and our eyes met.

Eventually, my other friends left, but Charlie and I lingered, watching the after-work crowd thin out.

"I'm close to closing this deal, which would put me in the top ten producers in my office. Can you believe it? I'm super excited. I've truly earned this one," Charlie said.

I had loads of respect for Charlie's work ethic. She always went after what she wanted and inspired me to fill my dreams with goals others might dismiss. Charlie pushed me toward my passions and wondered why Neil didn't. Neil couldn't understand why I looked up to Charlie and admired her.

In the past, when Charlie had pointed out how Neil was less than supportive, I had thought she was being dramatic. Maybe she was right. I knew she had my back through it all, and I trusted her opinion even if hearing her views about Neil wasn't easy. Matthew demonstrated things Neil lacked, and the pit in my stomach deepened, realizing what Charlie had been talking about.

"Skylar." It was him again. "I'd like you to meet Frank and Stephen. Boys, behave," Matthew joked.

"Oh. Hi. This is my friend Charlie. We went to college together."

"Nice to meet you, Skylar . . . and Charlie. MC, we need to bounce. Big meeting in the morning," Frank said.

The guys slapped hands, grabbing hold and leaning in for a quick chest bump and pat on the lats.

Matthew pulled out the bar stool next to mine, making himself comfortable. "So, how was the champagne?" he asked.

I laughed as Charlie responded, "Delicious."

She gathered her coat and kissed me goodbye.

"You're going? Why? Stay," I said.

"Good night! Love you. I'm wiped. Hope tomorrow's a better day."

"But Char . . . we . . ."

"No, you stay and enjoy."

I looked at Matthew sitting close to me, and the champagne jostled in my belly. Was this cheating? Why did it feel like cheating? Why did I have to look at Matthew this way? When the flicker of a spark ignited, why couldn't I extinguish it? The match dragged across the rough surface, and I sat help-less, watching the orange embers between us.

"So . . . Skylar Pearce." Matthew seemed a bit buzzed, and the thought of lost inhibitions worried me. "Tell me about your tough day." There was compassion in his voice.

I struggled to recall the last time Neil had asked about my day and cared about my answer.

"I may need another drink to delve into that. How did you know I had a tough day?" I asked.

"Your friend just said, 'hope tomorrow is better.' That was my clue."

"Nothing, really. Just a little . . . or maybe a big mistake. Not my mistake. But I'm taking the blame. But I'll work it out." The sips of champagne swirled in my head, fogging my thoughts. "Well, I should be getting home. My husband will be home soon."

I hoped referencing Neil would squelch what I began feeling for Matthew. A mantra played in my head. *He's a client. I'm married.*

"Wait, I want to hear more about your work. One more drink. A business drink," he said.

"Is there such a thing as a business drink?" I joked.

"Of course there is. We are discussing business over a cocktail."

"I don't think I have ever mixed business and drinks. Not an interior design thing."

"Great! This will be a first. I love new territory."

I couldn't help but laugh and agree. Matthew worked to hail a waitress.

"So," I said in an effort to fill the space.

"So," Matthew said, "what's all this bad day talk?"

I had never felt a gaze so intense and attentive. He actually cared about my stupid work issue.

"Just a little error that I'm hoping can be fixed tomorrow."

"Want to be a little more specific?"

"It's nothing. I just didn't have some information I needed, and some carpets were installed in the wrong rooms. It's a little stressful, but don't worry, that won't happen in your apartment. It's so rare."

"Skylar, mistakes happen every day in every profession. It's a miracle when things go smoothly. You're human." He laughed. "How'd you get to be such a perfectionist?"

"That's easy. My mother. Definitely my mother."

"What's your mom like?" he asked.

I sipped my drink slowly. "She's an amazing woman. But tough. She expected a lot from us. There were two of us, so I guess it was her way of staying in control."

"I'm an only child, so that seems like a houseful and a lot of fun compared to my quiet childhood."

"I'd like to know more about you. I don't even really know what you do."

"Our company buys all kinds of commercial properties. We renovate or sell them off, or sometimes we keep them. Then, we manage the properties. Hotels, apartment buildings, timeshares. I guess we'll see how it goes. I get bored after a while, so I keep adding to our business plan. I like to keep things new. It's my personality. I prefer to be in motion." He laughed.

Fascinated by his career, I held back from asking every racing question in my head. "What part is the most fun for you?"

As he scratched his head, I caught another glimpse of his tattoo.

"I used to love the travel, but I'm over it now. I think I prefer the small details, the nuances of structuring a deal and deciding what we'll do with the property. There's a hopeful quality in repurposing huge structures."

"Can I ask you a question?"

"Sure," he said.

"Is that a tattoo on your wrist?"

Matthew chuckled. "Laser eyes you have over there." Matthew rolled up his right sleeve, exposing the lion figure in black ink.

"It's cool." I resisted the temptation to run my fingers across the ink. I wondered what the lion signified, but he didn't offer an explanation, and I felt awkward asking. Asking seemed too personal, like crossing a line I shouldn't be near. He rolled his sleeve down, tucking the lion away beneath the crisp white cuff.

We sipped our drinks, and the conversation drifted. I forgot Matthew was a client. I forgot the time. Our words were effortless and endless. I became wrapped in a world, an exchange of ideas and beliefs that exceeded any normal definition of a conversation.

I was surprised Neil hadn't called to check in on me. He worried when I stayed out late, yet tonight, he was silent. Maybe he was caught up in his technology babble. I slipped the phone into my bag, avoiding an interruption, knowing fully an interruption was exactly what I needed.

"Now, can I ask you a question?" he asked.

I nodded.

"Why interior design? I mean, why did you leave Johnny? Johnny says he still doesn't completely understand why you left."

My stomach twisted, thinking about the day I left the best job I'd ever had. It had been difficult leaving Johnny. I'd squelched my memories of Johnny, which made walking away from a job that never felt like work tolerable.

"Well, it's hard to say, exactly. I was engaged at the time, and the fashion industry was demanding."

"So, it wasn't enjoyable anymore because of the hours?"

Memories of arguments with Neil resurfaced. His silent treatment after canceled dinner plans or if I had worked on a Saturday. Neil had recoiled into programming magazines, pushing me from his world. His new job at Giotto Technologies had kept typical hours, while mine had been irregular and plentiful.

Neil had suggested I pivot from fashion design to interior design, where my life would be "normal," as he had said. I hadn't wanted to leave Johnny, yet I had understood Neil's perspective and had grown weary of our arguments. I had loved the creativity of fashion and how clothing could influence how someone sees themselves. I had watched our designs put smiles on faces and make someone stand a little taller when they entered a room, feeling confident from their look. After thinking about it, I had realized as an interior designer, I could be even more impactful in designing a home, the personal spaces where one's life unfolds. Impacting how someone felt when they opened their eyes in the morning and returned home after a long day had brought me back to the memories of my sister and the impact our silly paintings made during even the darkest days. Neil had researched interior design schools for me and inquired about scholarships, but when he had kept referring to interior design as a "nice hobby," I had realized my vision was a career that would fulfill me, while Neil had viewed my endeavor as an activity busying my life while he pursued his lofty goals.

"No, it was fun. I don't think I've ever enjoyed anything as much as working with Johnny. I would get to work by seven thirty in the morning, and the next time I looked at the clock, it would be six at night. We would brainstorm and strategize. It was electric. I never felt so alive."

"So, why leave?"

I paused, taking a deep breath and a sip of water. "I guess, I think it just kind of got to be a lot. I was engaged. And it was hard to do it all. Hard to please everyone."

"Huh. Interesting."

"Interesting? Look, we all have our struggles, right? I had to do what was best for me and Neil at the time. I did the best I could do. I prefer it when everyone is happy."

"Yeah, interesting that being engaged had so much to do with you leaving. I just, well, I'm sure you did what you thought was best."

The doubts that screamed at me the day I left Johnny had remained in my head. I wasn't sure I'd done what was best for me. But I knew it had been best for my marriage.

I checked the time on my watch.

"Well, it's getting late. I should be getting home."

"Let me walk you out."

Making our way to the street, he placed his hand on the small of my back, guiding me toward a black luxury car parked in front of the bodega. The hand felt natural, comforting, yet electric.

"C'mon, hop in," he motioned.

"Matthew, you live around the corner from here. This is silly. I can grab a taxi," I pleaded.

"It's no big deal, and you'll freeze out here waiting for a cab. I've seen your teeth chatter. Let's try avoiding that again." He chuckled.

I slipped into the back seat as Matthew closed the door, jogged around the car, and hopped in beside me.

"So, what are your plans for the holidays?" he asked.

"Nothing, really. Some family stuff. Neil needs to work, so I guess I'll be doing the same. It's a good time to catch up on things in the office since clients are usually out of town."

The holidays stung me, like watching the bee circle my skin, knowing what was coming yet never being prepared for the pain. Thoughts of our last Christmas as a complete family scorched my memory. I couldn't help but think of my sister during the holidays. It hurt remembering, and it hurt forgetting. I wished I could fast forward through all the family gatherings, faking happiness and realizing that life just went on without her. It challenged me year after year, and no one truly understood. Neil told me I had to let go and move on, and my parents had buried all conversations on the topic when they had buried their daughter. Working through the holidays became the less painful choice.

"What about you?"

"Same. Family stuff, but I'll be around too." He looked at me and smiled. "Maybe we can get some work done for my apartment, I mean, since we will both be in town."

I could only muster a nod.

Lukas slid the sedan tight against the curb. Matthew stepped out first, and I slithered across the black leather seats. He reached for my hand and grasped my work bag.

"So, thanks for the ride . . . and the champagne."

"You are most welcome, Skylar. I really enjoy talking with you. It's just, it's so comfortable. It's nice."

Our eyes connected. Repeat mantra . . . *You are not feeling anything. He is a client. You are married. Happily married.*

I noticed I had two missed calls from Neil as I undressed for bed. The weight of returning his call fell on me, and I had to force my fingers, pressing each digit deliberately, hoping he wouldn't answer.

"I'm so busy, Sky. I only have a minute. Been a crazy day here. How about you?"

"I'm a little stressed with this carpet error."

Neil laughed. "Oh, Skylar, I definitely don't have time for your decorating drama right now."

"It was upsetting, Neil. And I'm being blamed for something that wasn't my fault."

"Wow. Sounds serious. Can't you just change the carpet and move on, Sky? I mean, I'm sure it wasn't crazy glued down."

"You know what, forget it. You don't get it."

"It's a carpet, Sky, not much to get."

My eyes stung as tears rolled slowly down my cheeks. Neil's interest in my work challenges was extremely limited. I visualized him shaking his head and rolling his eyes, mocking my stress.

chapter
nineteen

The carpet was salvageable.

My shoulders dropped, my jaw unclenched, and I exhaled the air that I had been holding for the past day.

Two installers carefully untacked the carpet in each room and used the remnants from the first installation, piecing together the rugs, maneuvering and manipulating the shape and location.

"I hate that the carpet pattern will run in the opposite direction from what we planned. Now, the stripes will run this way, not horizontally, when you walk in. I'm not sure I love this new plan," the client argued.

Disaster avoided? Please! Please! I fought back tears.

"She's right. It really should be the other way." Andrew turned on me. "Skylar, I don't know how you managed this mix-up. This will hold up the entire project. I can't move the furnishings in until the carpet is laid, and the lead time is five weeks for new material. It's not a great situation."

I secretly prayed Andrew and the client would somehow think the new carpet pattern looked even better, but they would need some convincing.

"Actually, I like the way they installed it. I think it may even be better this way. See how now the stripes give the illusion of the foyer being much larger than it is? Take a look from this angle."

I positioned them at the threshold of the front door. The client squinted, then bent down to look from another angle.

"Huh. I don't really like the carpet this way because it's not how we intended, but it does draw the eye back, I must admit. Andrew, come take a look."

It would be another hour of debating before they finally relented, but it was worth every effort. Andrew created messes, and I got us both out of them while he sipped his all-day cocktails, unfazed by the complications. I seethed from the frustrating situations he triggered.

Andrew insisted we grab lunch, but not at our favorite midtown deli. We usually split a tuna salad sandwich and discussed work, taking time to gossip about the clients.

"Can you believe she . . . What was that outfit . . . He's an absolute . . ."

But today, he chose a dark saloon. He ordered a scotch, a double, the moment we sat down. I wriggled in my chair, waiting to be chastised.

"I'm sorry about the whole carpet thing, but you didn't give me or anyone in the office any information about the installation. It wasn't my fault."

"Oh, Skylar, I cannot possibly deal with this again. I've had enough of that damn carpet. You know you could have avoided the whole thing, but I can't get into it now."

My eyes grew wide in disbelief that Andrew blamed me. Disbelief in his refusing any accountability. His behavior highlighted his drinking problem, and the price I paid increased each day. The quiet voices in my head grew louder, berating me for allowing the carpet installation without confirmation. But then a louder voice replied in defense. This was Andrew's mistake and clearly not mine.

"I should really fire you after that, but I'm going to do you a favor," he said.

"But, Andrew, I thought we went through this. You gave us no information. I'm sorry, but this is on you."

The alcohol was loosening his lips, and I watched him revert to child-like mannerisms. He chewed his food with exaggerated motion like a toddler cutting a hunk of food with its teeth. I wondered if he knew how foolish he looked and how obnoxious he sounded. The businessmen at the table next to us stared.

"We are not through with this. I need to be published, and if I am known as the designer who can't even install carpet in the correct room, it could erase any possibility of that. I won't stand for it."

My ego buckled from the drilling. I clenched my hands under the table and tried to focus on how pathetic he looked. This was the alcohol speaking. My brain understood this, but it burned to hear harsh words from the man who had built me up. If I didn't intervene, the alcohol could steal my job as well as my confidence.

chapter twenty

Andrew suggested we meet for furniture shopping for Matthew's apartment at the D&D building, but he never showed up. It was just as well. Each day now, I wondered if the angry drunk or the sober, level-headed Andrew who hired me would arrive at the office. His absence at the D&D building was a relief.

I headed to my favorite showroom because I knew Matthew would love the California style mixed with an urban edge, and his budget could withstand their prices. Earlier in my career, the exorbitant budgets sent my mind wondering how people acquired such incredible wealth, but now large budgets were routine, and eventually, I grew numb to the numbers and focused on the design. It felt like monopoly money, brightly colored and inconsequential, unlike my reality of true green bills and carefully monitored bank statements.

I walked through the long entry hall clad with black marble floors leading to an elevator bank. Large display windows flanked the hallway, each featuring luxurious fabrics, intricate wallpapers, and specialty furnishings. I pressed the elevator call button, stepped inside, and stood back as a few stragglers bolted in before the doors slid closed.

"Hi," Candice called out as we entered the showroom. "How are you?"

Candice respected my design choices despite my title of assistant designer. After working on several projects together, we'd formed a friendship.

"What can I help you with today?" she asked.

"We have a new project, and I was thinking about that leather upholstered bed you have. In a king. And that walnut dining table, you know, the one I love. What finishes is that available in?"

Candice led me to the sample boards, then pulled tear sheets of the items that listed the available colors and finishes. I whipped through furniture catalogs without hesitation, choosing items with confidence. Candice showed me a fantastic pair of metal sconces for the bedroom, a sofa for the living room, and a pair of club chairs with squared arms and chrome bases. Finding unique furniture for Matthew fired up my creativity.

On the seventeenth floor, I located handsome fabrics and wallpaper well suited for Matthew's personality and space—casual, urban, and comfortable. I envisioned the design as young and masculine but with a hint of softness.

My design process felt effortless, flowing through me easily. As I gained experience, my instincts became stronger, and my designs flowed with less thought. I let my subconscious and natural instincts take over.

My final destinations were a few lighting showrooms for lamps, chandeliers, and more sconces. The bags of fabrics, trims, tear sheets, and carpet samples weighed me down, so I headed back to the office, where I rummaged through the bags of samples, fanning the pieces on the table and categorizing them by room. My design was taking shape. The fabrics displayed across the conference table remained for a few days, allowing the design to marinate in my head.

Meanwhile, designs of built-ins and custom drapery were drafted and sketched. In a week, the presentation would be complete. I looked forward to showing Matthew what I'd created for him, despite my impetuous nerves.

I wished Andrew could join me for the presentation. Even if he was unreliable, his presence gave me security. The pressure of remembering every detail of the design and hoping

I got it right weighed on me. My mind drifted to a fictitious client meeting where a client despised everything about my design as I struggled to convince them. I reviewed my lists, making sure I didn't miss any details, and contemplated fabric and furniture selections.

That night, I had a nightmare where I was a guest on Matthew's new sofa. We were laughing as he fiddled with my fingers. My eyes flew open at the thought of such an intimate moment with him. Nervous jitters fought with my determination to remain professional, and I promised myself to stay focused. I valued professionalism and my marriage, and these dreams could damage both my career and my relationship with Neil.

This project could prove to Andrew, and to me, that handling the pressures of a senior designer was well within my capabilities. I knew I could handle it, but it's one thing to think it and another to achieve it.

The holidays approached, and I hoped to squeeze in Matthew's presentation before the end of the year. I felt proud of the design, yet I hesitated to call him. I dropped the pen I had been fiddling with and went to the bathroom, where I splashed water on my face and stared at my reflection in the mirror.

"You can do this, Skylar," I said out loud. "*You* can do this. You *can* do this." I annunciated each syllable. "Okay, now I'm talking to myself in the mirror. Go make the call already." I walked deliberately to my desk.

"Matthew, hi, it's Skylar Pearce. I've completed your presentation, and I'd like to set up a time to meet." I used my most serious and professional tone.

"Great. I'm—" There was a loud boom followed by a rustling of papers.

"Hello?"

"Uh, I'm looking forward to it. When is a convenient time for you?"

RENOVATION

"Everything okay? There was a bang."

"I just kind of, I guess you could say I fell off my chair. And now I am completely embarrassed," he said.

"Oh, well, don't be. I do that all the time. I mean, maybe not all the time, but it's happened to me. But anyway, I was hoping we could meet at the end of this week."

"That works for me. Is Thursday at five okay? Is that too late? It's just easier for me after work."

"Let me just double check . . . yup, yes, that works. Okay, so I guess I'll see you then."

"Yup. See you Thursday."

I hung up the receiver, and the office phone rang before I could start on some nursery sketches. "Andrew Thorne Interiors, this is Skylar."

"You know, I meant to ask you—"

I recognized Matthew's voice despite the omission of the expected greeting,

"I just thought maybe I could order some dinner for our meeting. I mean, if you're up for it, no pressure, of course. I'll just be getting home, and you'll be coming straight from work, so I thought . . . you know . . . maybe . . . I mean, I hope it's not too forward. It's just a thought. But we don't have to." Matthew tripped over his words endearingly.

I stammered at the unexpected question. My brain twisted, struggling for a quick answer. I had handled the previous phone call so well. I'd remained professional, but now I crumbled. I was embarrassed to admit that most nights, I ate cold cereal at home alone because of Neil's travel schedule. The thought of a proper meal midweek sounded inviting.

"Skylar, you there?"

"Umm, yes." I chuckled nervously. He chuckled, too. "Uh, I don't know, um . . ."

My mind could only see his smile and green eyes. No thought of food. Mantra; *He is a client. I am married. I am happily married.*

"Okay. Tell you what. Give me a call before our meeting and let me know. Sound good?"

Andrew was back in the office, and he looked over at me with squinted eyes. He smirked the minute I put down the phone. "What was that about?"

"I have no idea." I preoccupied myself with the nursery drawings, but my heart raced with excitement. Dropping my eyelids down for just a moment, I forced oxygen into my lungs, hoping it would tame the zooming beats in my chest.

"Are you okay over there?" he asked.

"Yeah, fine, just working on this nursery sketch." I kept my eyes on the page.

How could a simple phone conversation shift my temperature? My emotions held me hostage. Neil's voice and perpetual balance would set me straight. I wanted Neil's attention; I wanted him to focus on me, but he often fell short of comforting my insecurities. I called him anyway.

"Hi! How's your day?" Cheer dripped off my forced words.

"Hey. Uh, yeah, it's, wait, hang on," he said. I heard the static of the muffled phone and Neil's distant voice.

"Hey, sorry, we're just trying to get this evaluation out today. Yeah, yeah, that looks good. Just, uh, move this to page four." Neil juggled two conversations. "What's doing at home?"

"Not much. Finishing up a big presentation for next—"

"Babe, hang on a sec." Neil muffled the phone again.

Annoyance seeped through my ears as I listened while Neil conducted work and left me waiting. But then I reconsidered, empathizing with the pressure he endured at work.

"Sorry, Sky. So, what's up?

"I have that big presentation on Thursday. Alone."

"Hold on one sec, Sky."

The phone was muffled again, and I could only hear sound but no words. I watched the clock tick as I waited. And waited. And waited.

"Oh, you'll be fine. Or can't you just have Andrew join you?"

"Neil, if you can't talk, that's fine, but I can't sit on hold like that for so long."

"You're kidding, right, Skylar? I'm not matching fabrics for rich trust fund families here. I'm actually creating something. It's not all fun and games here. It's actual work with my brain."

"Are you kidding with that? Are you saying I don't work? That my work isn't important?"

"Listen, let's not get off-topic. You're reading into what I said. You're so sensitive. The meeting will be fine. Andrew helped with the designs and stuff, right? I mean, it's not on you at the end of the day. You'll be fine, Sky. Now stop biting your lip."

My anger began melting away as I laughed at Neil's knowledge of my nervous habit from thousands of miles away.

chapter
twenty-one

Stepping out of the shower Thursday morning, I overthought what I should wear to my meeting with Matthew that evening. After considerable deliberation, I pulled out my favorite pair of black boot-cut pants and slid on my low black leather boots before rushing to the D&D for a full day of shopping with Andrew before my five o'clock presentation at Matthew's apartment. Other clients needed our attention, and I paced the marble entry for forty-five minutes before calling his cell.

"Hey. We are still meeting uptown today, right?" I asked.

"Oh. Yeah, I don't think I can make it," Andrew said in a weary voice.

"Did I wake you? Are you still in bed?" I asked, annoyed.

My tone was harsher than anticipated. I think I struggled with Andrew's drinking more than he did. It had slowly crept into his professional life like a snake methodically suffocating its victim. There had been no inciting incident or dramatic circumstance, just a steady demise.

"Yeah, I mean no. I'm getting up now. Just a late night. You go ahead and shop the list. Whatever you get will be great. You're a lifesaver, Sky," Andrew said.

"So, you're not coming?"

"You can do it, Sky. Truth is, you don't really need me."

"Andrew, listen, I don't want to step over the line, but you know we need you. Your business can't succeed without you. You have got to make some changes," I implored.

"Okay. I'll see you back at the office."

"Andrew? Do you hear what I'm saying?" I asked.

"It's fine. I'm fine. Business is fine. And I have you. My secret weapon. Stop worrying."

"I am worried. I don't know half as much as you do. I'm still learning."

"Oh, Skylar, don't be silly. You know everything. You're ready to fly. Why do you think I let you take on the Cherning project alone? Just take a deep breath; it will all be okay."

I pressed my fingers at the bridge of my nose, just between my eyes, and squinted as tight as I possibly could, pulling a deep breath of air into my lungs.

I focused on smaller items for existing clients, spending the morning scouring showrooms for navy blue textured leather and art deco sconces. My search required focus. Some days, things fell into place smoothly, like a tongue and groove, and others taunted my patience. Browsing through multiple showrooms and examining hundreds of fabrics, scouring for the perfect piece, was my strength as a designer.

Numerous designers made a name for themselves through the repetition of a signature design, but I knew this technique could never fulfill my creativity. Visions of new designs filled my head. I relished the newness of each project and enjoyed the challenges of parameters set by the client's desires and space.

At the end of the day, bags in hand, I hailed a taxi. I slid across the navy pleather seat patched with silver electrical tape.

"Nortrom and Hudson, please," I called out to the driver.

He sneered and tapped the meter. My neck snapped back as he placed a heavy foot on the accelerator. The inside of the cab was silent. I tried to decompress from my day in the D&D, staring out the window and watching the holiday bustle of New York flash through the glass. We whizzed past red and gold ribbons dangling from light posts and evergreen garlands draping doorways. Pedestrians wrapped in scarves and knit hats scurried to find warmth.

I was not ready for the holidays. Neil adored the season, and I ignored my own painful memories for him. My smile and forced laughter made my stomach wince in sadness, but indulging in grief would never bring my sister back.

Back at the office, details of my upcoming meeting circled in my head while my stomach churned. I skipped lunch and focused on the presentation, pushing Matthew's dinner proposal far from my thoughts. Maybe if I ignored my feelings, they would disappear. It only made me think about him more. Why couldn't I be satisfied with what I already had? But my desire for a fulfilling personal life matched my quest for a satisfying career. And both seemed to be stumbling.

"Sandy!" I called back to the dining room. "Where's Matthew Cherning's number?"

"Cell, home, or office?" she bellowed back.

"I don't know . . . something!"

I launched into a panic that my return call was long overdue.

Back at the office, Matthew Cherning's profile appeared on Sandy's vivid computer screen.

Mantra; *I am happily married. He is a client.*

"It's from the article in Forbes last year," Sandy said, noticing my unnatural gawking at the photograph on the computer screen.

"Forbes?" My head jerked from the screen to Sandy.

"Apparently, he's one of the thirty under thirty in New York. You didn't know?" she commented.

I didn't know. In fact, I wanted to know more about Matthew Cherning.

I lifted the landline phone receiver and pressed the ten digits displayed on the computer screen in the "cellular" row.

"Hey, Matthew. It's Skylar." My voice was sheepishly hushed.

"Hi. We still good for tonight?"

"Yes. Absolutely. I'm sorry I didn't get back to you sooner. Work just . . ." I searched for an appropriate excuse other than "I've been forcing myself not to think about you, which only made me think about you even more."

"I'm glad you called. Do you ski? I'm thinking of renting a house in Utah."

"Ski? Well, not really. I did a few times as a kid, but not since then. I'm so sorry I didn't call you back about dinner."

"Have you ever been to Utah?"

My stress waned as Matthew focused on his Utah getaway, completely unphased by my failure to call him back.

"I thought about calling a few times but somehow got distracted. Utah?"

"Sky, you gotta let it go. So not a big deal. You're really hard on yourself, huh?"

My neck relaxed, and I appreciated Matthew's understanding nature. "I guess. I just didn't want you to think I was ignoring you."

"It's okay. Really. None of us are perfect."

"Well, I've had to live up to some high expectations over the years. Kind of just get used to it." I knew my parents couldn't help but place their hopes and dreams in me after the loss of a child, but the burden of overachieving for them was weighty.

"Lukas will be there at six thirty with the car."

"Lukas? No. Matthew, it's not necessary."

"Lukas is bored. He needs something to keep him busy. Just ask him for yourself. I'll see you later."

At 4:30 p.m., I gathered the design boards. Lukas stood outside the office waiting for me. "Good afternoon, Skylar. How are you today?"

"Thanks, Lukas. I'm fine. How are you doing?"

"I am well, thank you," he replied with a smile.

Lukas removed the case from my hands and placed it in the trunk.

"Thanks." I ignored the swirls of anxiety agitating my stomach.

I got this. Breathe. I am prepared; I know what I'm doing; I can handle this. Breathe. Throughout the weeks of preparation, I'd felt a connection with Matthew and gotten a clear vision of the peaceful oasis I was creating with him in mind, but as I stepped toward the presentation, apprehension and jitters stole my conviction. The ease of choosing fabrics and paint colors for Matthew wasn't lost on me. The familiarity I found with him gave me freedom and confidence when assembling details for his apartment. I understood this man and what he needed: a space that could give him comfort, tranquility, and respite. Although I didn't know the details of his loss, I recognized loss, danced with it, smelled it, and wrangled with it. I knew Matthew's anguish and how I could transform his apartment into a home.

"You're looking very professional this evening, Mrs. Pearce," Lukas said.

"I'm trying. Got to look the part," I joked.

He laughed. "I know how that goes. I'm sure Mr. Cherning will be happy with everything. He's a good guy. Best boss I've ever had."

"That must make work a little easier to wake up for each day, huh?" I asked.

"You got that right. And after all Mr. Cherning has been through, I'm just happy I can make his life a little easier."

I devised a follow-up question as the car swerved to the curb in front of Matthew's building. What had Matthew been through? His life seemed perfect and easy from the outside, but I understood the exterior never tells the full story. Asking for details about his life was tempting but seemed unprofessional. I preferred asking Matthew such personal questions rather than snooping.

"Good evening," the doorman said. "Mr. Cherning is expecting you."

I wondered if it would be annoying having people like the doorman and Lukas around all the time. I remembered when my sister's at-home nursing had increased, filling our house with women in white uniforms scurrying around her bedside. Although they had relieved me from the daily chores my mom had expected of me, their presence had felt like an invasion. Like the thick velvet rope separating those invited and those waiting for a chance to enter. I wondered if Matthew welcomed extra hands around, as opposed to being alone.

"Good evening, Mr. Cherning." I smiled broadly, indicating my intentional humor in my greeting, telling myself I was a talented, intelligent woman who could be professional and ignore the sexy smile that lit up when I entered his apartment. Matthew graciously took my coat without any mishaps, hanging it carefully in the closet. I fiddled with my watch and felt my body temperature rise. I silently panicked that I'd left a few samples at the office, although I'd triple-checked every item. Matthew's eyes found mine, and as he smiled, a wave of comfort dulled my anxiety, and my doubts vanished.

"Where would you like me to set up?" I asked.

"Not too many choices are there?" he chuckled.

His laugh sent hot pinpricks up my spine. A few innocent words and I was transformed into a fourteen-year-old girl swooning over the boy across the lunchroom.

"Let's go to the island in the kitchen," I suggested.

"Sounds good to me."

I placed my handbag on the floor, leaning the large portfolio against the island. Matthew looked anxious to see what was on the presentation boards.

"I can't wait to see. I am so ready for a transformation of this place."

"I think everything came together nicely. It will take a

little time, but it will be worth it, I promise." I rolled my shoulders back, forcing confidence forward. The heat Matthew generated would be iced by my professionalism. I'd worked for weeks on this project, and now, proving my abilities and handling a major presentation on my own was my only goal.

I placed the boards across the island and led Matthew through each design.

"Wow. You have every paint color and all the molding details. This is incredible. Even the grout colors."

I reached across the boards, pointing to a fabric for the primary bedroom. Matthew simultaneously reached out, and our hands collided. The heat I had sworn to extinguish ignited throughout my body like a loose ember falling on newspaper. We both lifted our eyes from the boards and made eye contact as if to say, "Did you feel that?" We fell silent. I pulled my hand back as if scalded and placed it neatly in my pocket.

"You okay?" Matthew asked.

I nodded slowly, clearing my throat and continuing as if there were no sparks. After my presentation, we reviewed each room as Matthew made decisions and I took detailed notes.

"How do you keep track of all these fabrics and numbers?" he joked.

"Organization is all it takes, really."

Matthew picked up one of the boards but lost his grip, and I watched it slam to the floor.

"No. C'mon, Skylar," he said as he gathered the board from the floor. "There's a lot more to it. I could never be this creative. It's a lot. Not just organization."

Even with his clumsy nature, I wished he would stop being so perfect. I need to find a flaw to focus on immediately. He couldn't really be perfect; he just seemed that way to me for some indescribable reason. I shook my head and sobered up from the spell he had cast upon me. His crooked smile didn't quiet my hastened heartbeats.

"I'd love to see the places you shop for all this stuff. How do you make sense of it? So much to choose from. I think I would go crazy," Matthew said.

"Really? I'll take you if you want. It's not really that exciting. Well, I mean, I guess it's kinda cool if you've never been before."

I continued, logging every fabric and piece of furniture. Matthew sat patiently while I collected the information.

"I'm not sure if this would be overstepping the boundaries, but any chance you'd want to join me for a glass of wine before you go?"

"I mean, I'd love to, but I really should be going." I knew getting out of his personal space would smother the heat.

"I have all this wine that my partner keeps giving me, and I don't know the first thing about wine. I just thought maybe . . ."

Matthew's eyes dropped to the floor, and my goals of strength and professionalism dissolved. I wanted to stay. "Maybe one glass would be okay," I said sheepishly.

Matthew jumped toward the cases of wine and pried the box open.

"Cheers," he said as the smooth red wine fell into the cups. "To new beginnings, new friendships, and new design."

We sat awkwardly on the floor, and I formed a mental note about Matthew needing wine glasses.

Matthew's attention rested firmly on me rather than the cabernet. The anxiety of presenting without Andrew had drifted away, but now, a new anxiety replaced it.

Mantra.

"Cheers." I lifted my glass to meet his. "How long have you lived in the apartment?"

"I bought it about eight months ago. I was caught up with some personal stuff, and work is crazy, so I didn't have the time or energy to focus on making it feel like home. But I'm ready now."

"Did you grow up in New York?" I asked.

"No. Just outside of Chicago. My parents are still there. They all went back after college."

"How'd you land in New York?"

"Law school. And business school. And you?"

"Well, I come from a big family. I have one sister and a brother." As the words slipped through my lips, I felt a rock settle in my throat. I paused and took a breath. I sipped the wine and pushed away the swelling tears. I could see my sister's, Chrissie's, face on her last birthday. Candles spilled a yellow glow across her face and kerchief-wrapped head. The passage of time played tricks on me. Sometimes, I felt I had just laughed with her, and some days, I couldn't remember her smile.

"Skylar?" Matthew broke the silence as I watched my memory reel.

"I'm sorry. I don't know why I'm telling you this. I had a sister."

"I'm sorry. Wow. That must have been awful for you. I get it. I get it."

"It was a long time ago, but it's not something you ever get over."

"Death is not something you recover from. Unfortunately, I know that all too well." Matthew paused. "I don't know why I'm telling you this. We're like doom and gloom here tonight, but I was engaged. And, well, she's gone now. Car accident. A little over a year ago. That's why I bought this place. I couldn't stay in that apartment with her smell and scuffs on the floor from her shoes. It was just too much."

"I'm so sorry." It was all I could muster. The ache, the compassion I felt, was bigger than he would ever know. I refused to cry and focused on the flashing lights from the city below, working hard not to let a single tear drop from my eye. I was not letting this wonderful night veer into a pity party for either of us, but it hurt. I knew the pain of loss and the excruciating sorrow.

"I'm sorry for you, too. Really sorry." Matthew leaned over to refill my glass as the buzzer sounded.

"I should get going. Sounds like you have company."

"Nope. That's our dinner. If you're hungry. I just thought it might get late, and we both need to eat, right? I mean, I need to eat; I'm starving. If you need to get going, I understand. Totally up to you."

Matthew walked toward the elevator. This meeting had turned more intimate than a typical work meeting, yet a warm embrace of familiarity and comfort filled the space where guilt should have lived. The juvenile crush I had on Matthew had changed that evening. The vulnerability we shared in revealing our jagged pasts brought a connection and a feeling that he understood me like no one else. Explaining the pain when youth and death converge is almost impossible, but I didn't need to explain anything to Matthew; he just knew. Over the years, I'd tried explaining the ache to Neil and even Charlie, but it was no use. My words inevitably fell short. Words were superfluous with Matthew because our experiences said it all, and I was thankful I had been open and honest about a part of my life that haunted me every day. Perhaps I had felt sharing such ugliness would push him away, not realizing it would only bring our connection one step closer, transcending beyond just a cute guy who made my cheeks blush. The newness could not compete with a long, steady, dependable relationship, but this new connection with Matthew wasn't comfort alone; it was also thrilling.

Garlic wafted from the brown bags in his arms, and my mouth watered. I swallowed. "Matthew, this is not necessary."

"I know. I wanted to. We both need to eat dinner," he paused for a moment, "And it would be nice to get to know you a little better. I mean, we have so much in common."

He looked up at me and smiled. I helped him unpack the bags of food on the kitchen island and accepted his invitation for dinner.

"I didn't know what you liked, so I kind of over-ordered."
He reached for plates.

Matthew must have ordered every dish off the menu from a premier Italian restaurant in Manhattan. "I didn't know they offered takeout at this place."

"Technically, they don't," Matthew said.

Matthew insisted I try every dish until I couldn't take another bite, and we laughed over our determination to taste-test despite our fullness. The conversation meandered through the cities I couldn't wait to travel to, our favorite foods, and the Yankees versus the Mets.

The wine was nearly finished. Matthew poured the last drops into our glasses. We sat at the island, silent for a moment. My eyes dropped, and a surge of tingles ran from my gut down through my toes. It felt good. I couldn't remember the last time I'd felt a rush of passion physically swirl through me. I tried pinpointing the moment when Neil and I fell into a routine that extinguished the passion we had once shared. I couldn't recall ever feeling desire like this with Neil, and it hurt thinking about what my marriage lacked and how I never knew this deep connection was missing.

"I should go." I quietly pushed the words over my lips. I didn't want to go. I just knew I should.

"I'm really enjoying this evening. I'm happy for a change. Please indulge me." Matthew smiled and moved through the awkward moment. I lowered myself back to the floor.

"Tell me about the process for the apartment. What happens next? How does it work?" he asked.

"I'll generate an estimate so you can see how much everything will cost. Following that, if you approve, we place orders for the furniture we discussed this evening. Furniture will be delivered in eight to twelve weeks. We can deliver the items as they arrive, or I can store them in a warehouse and deliver everything over a couple of days. It's really your choice. In the meantime, we can begin the floor refinishing, bathrooms, and paint."

"Let's deliver everything in one shot. I like that idea. I've got to say I'm excited about this."

What was he excited about? Me? The apartment? Of course, the apartment. *What am I thinking? We are in a business meeting. I am married. Neil. Think about Neil.*

He stood up and waited for me to stand as well. We walked to the elevator, and Matthew helped me with my coat. He placed his hands on my shoulders, smoothing the wool of my jacket.

I looked down, embarrassed and flattered at once. I almost admitted that I enjoyed his touch.

We both stepped into the elevator and rode down in silence. Lukas waited outside and opened the car door for me.

"Well, I hope you liked everything. I think it will be spectacular when we are done," I said.

"No doubt. You're amazing, so talented, Skylar. I know it will be incredible," Matthew replied. "Maybe I should grab your cell number? You know, just in case, work stuff. I promise not to harass you." He chuckled.

I rattled off my ten digits. "Should I write it down for you?" I asked. I need to stop this right now.

"No, why?" Matthew looked confused.

"How will you remember it?" I asked.

"I got it, don't worry. Have a good night." Matthew firmly closed the door, turned, and walked back inside. I leaned my head back on the leather seat and gently closed my eyes. What just happened?

What was I feeling? I had been with the same man for the past five years. Yet tonight, I felt something I had never felt with Neil or anyone else. The connection between Matthew and I was undeniable before our meeting, but learning he, too, had suffered a loss made me feel understood. This shared tragedy gave us a special connection. I never realized I could have an easy yet deep conversation without effort. I never knew this existed in relationships. My head whirred. I had another six months of close contact with Matthew ahead.

Repeat Mantra.

"Everything okay, Miss Skylar?" Lukas asked as we pulled into the moving traffic.

"Yes. Thanks."

"You know, I haven't seen Mr. Matthew like this in a long time."

"Like what?" I asked.

"Well, you know, happy. Relaxed. He is always so stressed and focused on work. Seven days a week. It's been hard."

I played along. "I can imagine. Maybe the new apartment will feel like home to him and that will help."

"Yes, he hasn't really made a home for himself since, you know. He's been keeping busy. Very busy. It's been very hard for Mr. Matthew," Lukas said.

"I know, Lukas. I know."

chapter
twenty-two

The next morning, Andrew fidgeted with the key in the lock before the door gave way to a vacant apartment we were assessing for a client who resided in Europe.

Walking into the space, I felt tiny. My fingertips brushed against the slick, polished wood walls, gliding from panel to panel. The soles of my shoes wobbled from the uneven, buckling wood, and the scent of mothballs sat in the air. A hint of dust blew by, tickling my nose. Achoo! Achoo! Achoo! I wondered why I always sneezed in packs of three.

"Wow." Andrew was stupefied. "They weren't lying when they said no one has lived here in many years."

My feet continued forward as my head swiveled. The elegant draperies hung from ceiling to floor, exaggerating the ten-foot ceiling height. Sunlight penetrated through the enormous windows, lighting the tattered silk drapes. The apartment had been ignored since the early eighties. Furniture was wrapped in silk frayed like knees on worn jeans.

The antiseptic kitchen, vacant of food, was larger than many New York apartments, with two islands. The home came complete with a dining area, an endangered species in the Manhattan real estate market. My eyelids dared not fall and cause me to miss a detail. Bedrooms on a grand scale with dollhouse-sized furniture begged for a renovation.

"Can you believe this place? It's a relic from the past." Andrew said before picking up his phone. "Hi, it's Andrew

Thorne. Yes, we are here in your apartment." He paused to listen. "Well, now that I've seen the property, I really think you'll need a much larger budget to make any impact."

He was being kind. The owner resided in London yet kept the apartment in case his children chose to attend university in New York. It was staffed but not updated. Charles's proposed $50,000 budget for "freshening up" the apartment, including our fees, would not allow for much improvement.

Andrew continued, "Due to the scale of the apartment and the current condition of the furniture, fabric, and drapery—" The potential client must have interrupted him. I watched Andrew's face scrunch in confusion. He was silent for some time.

I explored the apartment, observing every detail. I never imagined an apartment this size in Manhattan. I had been in large apartments, but this was, well, a whole other level. It was a minimum of five thousand square feet. I prayed Charles would increase his budget and this would become our next project. Returning to the massive family room, I noticed Andrew had created a temporary office space.

"Okay, yes, I understand."

It sounded like they were finishing up the call. "What's the story?" I asked.

"He needs to get a clue," Andrew quipped. "There ain't no way this apartment can be fixed up for fifty grand." He was joking, but not joking. "He's thinking about it. This is exactly the kind of apartment *Beautiful Homes* would publish. This is a hidden gem in Manhattan. I'll call my contacts at the magazine and keep me on their radar."

Andrew's excitement about the apartment and the publishing opportunity woke him from his typical drunken state. I overheard him speaking to three magazine editors, describing the grand apartment in luxurious detail.

The potential client never contacted Andrew again, and our calls went unreturned. Andrew's devastation was drowned in scotch despite my constant pleading. My fears about him were becoming reality.

"We can't win every client, Andrew. You have to stay focused and think about the next opportunity, not just the magazine spread. The right project is just around the corner," I said. I knew stability took precedence, and I wanted the communication lines open between us. But Andrew didn't see it that way.

"Are you chiding me, Skylar? Do you not think I know what I need to do? I've been around way longer than you, and I certainly don't need your advice. You're just all pumped up now from that Cherning job, which is a joke. I could do that job with my eyes closed. Don't get ahead of yourself, my dear."

My insides caved and twisted from his harsh words. I bit the inside of my cheek, thinking it would stop the tears, but one escaped. I had planned an appointment at an art gallery with Matthew later that day, but I wished I could cancel after Andrew's tirade. I collapsed on the tattered sofa and called Neil.

"Sky? Is this important? I'm in the middle of something," he said before I uttered a word.

"Umm, do you have just a minute for me?"

I heard Neil excuse himself from his colleagues.

"What's up?"

"Do you think I'm good at design? I mean, am I wasting my time?"

"Skylar, this is why you pulled me out of a meeting?"

"Andrew just unleashed on me and basically told me the new job I'm working on is easy, that he could do it with his eyes closed. It just hurt to hear that."

"Look, what you do isn't really work, Skylar. It's creative, fun, up for interpretation. If the client likes it, then it's all good, and it's not really about talent or being good at it; you're just pleasing someone. If you can just do what the client wants, follow their orders, you're good to go."

I closed my eyes and couldn't form any words in response to his painful interpretation. His words scalded me, and the worst part was he didn't even realize it.

"Skylar? You there?"

"I am. Andrew is just so focused on the magazines and notoriety, and I just want to create the perfect space where my clients' lives can unfold. I want to design comfortable homes that suit them. I see my clients as individuals and work from their personalities and vibe. It's not just a paycheck to me."

"Well, there's your issue. Like I said, you are focusing on fun, not success. Listen, I gotta jump, but I have to side with Andrew on this one. Drunk or not, he knows what he has to do to make a living and build a business. It's okay that you don't, but you can't be hurt when he just tells you the truth. I'll call you later."

Sandy passed by and returned with a fist full of tissues, staring at me with empathetic eyes. I forced the beginnings of a smile but broke down in the middle.

I self-talked myself into remaining professional and kept the appointment with Matthew, but Andrew's and Neil's words echoed in my head, causing severe self-doubt. I just had to spend one hour in the art gallery, and then I could go home and cry all night. The self-doubt ballooned, and I couldn't understand why it felt like they were both against me. Maybe I was the unrealistic one. Maybe they were right, and I wasn't seeing things clearly.

"Wow. This place is so cool," Matthew said as he strode through the gallery doors.

Matthew's positive energy comforted me. As we strolled through the gallery, I pointed out several pieces I envisioned in his apartment.

"Are you okay?" he asked.

"Yeah, why?"

"I don't know. You seem a little, I don't know, somber today."

I stared at the floor and pulled a tissue from my pocket. Matthew put his hand on my shoulder and forced eye contact.

"Hey, what's going on?"

He led me to a bench in the back of the gallery, and we sat while I gained my composure.

"I shouldn't be talking to you about this. It's not professional. It's not right."

"I understand that, but I don't feel we have a typical relationship, do you?"

"No."

"Okay, so let's just pretend we're friends for a few minutes. Would that be okay? I hate seeing you so upset. And I'm a really good listener, I promise."

It surprised me how easily I shared my struggles about Andrew and Neil. My words spilled out, lifting the weight of the day. Matthew listened and nodded as I rambled, sometimes stumbling over words.

"And now I just don't know. Maybe I'm the one out of touch. Maybe I'm not seeing things clearly."

Matthew placed his hand on my knee and said, "I assure you this is not about you. You are seeing things the right way. Look, everyone has their own goals and their own individual approach to achieving those goals. You and Andrew do not share the same goals, so of course he's not going to understand you. Skylar, your magic is that you do care about the client. You care about the meaning and purpose above all else, the process and how you can create a space for a client that reflects who they are and their lifestyle. I understood that from our first conversation. I see you, Skylar. I see exactly who you are."

I lifted my head to Matthew. He was right. I didn't want to be like Andrew or Neil. I wanted to do things my own way with my own vision.

"Thank you. I don't know how, but you just clarified things for me." Matthew had a way of delivering a message honestly and without fluff, and it grounded me, dissipating the self-doubt that fogged my brain.

chapter
twenty-three

As the new year settled in, Andrew mourned the loss of a project that could have attracted the magazine editors and had a moment of sobriety when he received an invitation to participate in another show house. We all walked on eggshells, hoping the old Andrew was back, but I knew it was too good to be true. The show house was a grand estate on Long Island's Gold Coast. It met all of Andrew's requirements. They offered him the best room in the house, the primary bedroom, with architectural molding details and soaring twelve-foot-high ceilings.

"I swore I would take a break from these show houses!" Andrew said. "But this one is hard to pass up. The magazines will be all over this." Show houses were great for Andrew's quest for publication. He could curate designs without any client interfering with his agenda. They were fun, but I preferred creating spaces with a client in mind. The challenges clients posed were interesting, and I loved determining what design suited not only the space but the personality of the client.

It was eight fifteen in the morning of the day we previewed the estate. I pulled on my boots and fought the angry gusts of winter wind to the subway. Freezing above ground, sweltering below. I emerged in my preferred city of downtown. Andrew sat in his black sedan, waiting for me. Plopping into the passenger seat, I unwound my tangled scarf.

"Good morning!"

"What's so good about it, my dear? You're mighty bundled up today."

"Well, that wind is brutal. You look a little tired."

"I guess I may have had a little too much to drink at dinner last night," Andrew snarked. I knew the drinks would sneak their way back into Andrew's routine, and the hopes of the old sober Andrew returning were swept away with the morning's wind.

Weaving through the narrow downtown streets, Andrew approached the midtown tunnel. Forty-five minutes later, we swerved through five acres of manicured gardens, then crossed through the estate's iron gate. I heard the gravel grinding beneath the rubber tires. The house displayed black iron window frames containing the original glass. Ivy wove up the stone facade, and the slate roof elegantly displayed details of yesteryear. Andrew pushed open the weighty oak front door.

"Andrew, hello. Welcome. Come in," the curator said.

He was an older gentleman, trim and jolly, with white hair and a lime green bowtie.

"Hello. We made it!" Andrew said. "I'd like you to meet my assistant, Skylar."

"Here, let me take you to the primary bedroom." He waved his hand, indicating the direction.

Our steps echoed on the marble floor. At the crest of the stairs, we entered the bedroom. It was fit for a king.

The proportions of the room were enormous. An ornately carved fireplace, intricate original molding, and expansive leaded glass windows created a dramatic backdrop.

"Look at that fireplace. It needs some repairs but could be spectacular." I caught Andrew's eye, and he smiled broadly.

"Are there plans to have the rooms published?" Andrew asked the curator.

Here we go again. If Andrew's work gained notoriety, would the alcohol slip away? Would the fame be enough to sustain him?

"Well, of course, we hope some magazines will show interest, but as you know, there are never any guarantees," he said.

"That was pretty amazing," I said when we were back in the car.

Andrew's energy was palpable, but he remained quiet. Pondering the possibilities, I guessed, designing the room in his head. I didn't push him. Andrew clicked the phone to speaker and began to dial.

"Hi, it's Andrew Thorne. How are you?" Andrew paused, listening to a response. "Yes, of course! Of course!" he responded. "I'm just leaving a meeting about a fantastic opportunity that just came my way. There is this unbelievable show house planned for the spring in the most incredible estate. What's that? Oh yes. And I was just wondering if you would have any interest in the story. You know, maybe follow me through the process, before and after shots. Could be a nice spread."

Listening to one side of the conversation, I watched as his hands gestured with each word spoken, and I almost reached for the unattended steering wheel. Speaking to editors invigorated Andrew, and I prayed this opportunity could change his ways.

Our first appointment after the show house tour was with a client who owned a glamorous dress shop with fancy country club types springing in and out of the store.

"Hello," Andrew sang as we entered the shop, "we've come bearing gifts."

"Whatayagat for me?" The client's gruff voice sounded like cigarette smoke had eroded her vocal cords. Her New

York accent was thick like mud. Leaving her shop in the middle of the day wasn't an option for her, so our design meetings about her house were always held in the back office of her dress shop.

We trailed her to a back office covered in dresses, sample books, and papers piled high like stacks of pancakes. Her wide rear swished and swayed. We recommended reupholstering the chairs and installing new drapery, freshening up her outdated dining room.

"This is fabulous." She draped the bronze silk Andrew suggested across her arm.

"Isn't that wonderful?" Andrew encouraged. "We could use this for the drapery. It would be incredible!"

She held the fabric up to the light and then examined it closely. "Hmmm. I'm not sure. It seems a little dull, don't you think?"

Andrew held up the fabric in different lights and began convincing her. He excelled in demonstrating exquisite charm and finesse.

The landline phone on her desk whirred, and she transformed into the shop owner. "The fabric must be here by Wednesday . . . No, no, I can't . . . Look, if you want to do business, this is how it's gonna go." She flicked her wrist, indicating her annoyance with the call.

Andrew had to work hard on selling the chair fabric, enduring twenty minutes of deliberations. In the end, she chose a stunning brown-and-cream print that played off the bronze silk.

After she agreed to the fabric, the client dragged us through the stockroom to retrieve a check from the safe. She flaunted her newest dresses, aiming to impress. Andrew and I oohed and ahhed to satisfy her. As wacky as some of our clients were, I hoped I would someday navigate colorful characters and challenging situations as well as Andrew. I learned from his techniques in preparation for the day I would be on my own, with my name on the door.

Next on the schedule was the Slater residence. The wife, an adorable stay-at-home mom with two tenacious boys, wore her sweatpants low on her hips, and her long-sleeved cotton T-shirts looked as if they had been rolled in a ball for a few days. I tried ignoring the brown smears on the leg of her sweatpants and the blue ink on her bum. The edges of her sleeves were tattered and discolored, while her unruly hair begged for a brush. Katherine was searching through the house when we arrived.

"I can't remember where I put my keys," she said.

She ambled through the first floor, lifting toys and removing pillows with no sense of urgency. It seemed unlikely the keys would be found, given the mess throughout the boys' rooms. The boys raced across the kitchen floor on scooters.

"No school today?" I asked.

"Didn't I tell you?" she asked impatiently. "I lost my keys, and Henry leaves for work very early. So, here we are."

Despite the war zone of toys and clothing, the decor was impeccable. High-quality pieces with price tags to match. She never questioned prices, never visited showrooms, and never complained. I thought her numbness might indicate she was medicated, or perhaps over-medicated.

Andrew presented the fabric selections for throw pillows.

"Great. Love them. Let's do it," she agreed, barely glancing at the fabrics. "Let me give you that check I owe you," she said, burrowing through kitchen drawers. Eventually, her checkbook surfaced from the clutter. She scribbled black ink across the green check, leaving a mark nothing like a signature.

"Would you mind taking the boys to school?"

I froze, shocked at the request. I didn't move a muscle and let my eyes glance around the room, searching for Andrew's face. Andrew huffed from aggravation. His eyes made a half roll, and he turned away, concealing his annoyance. There was no way Andrew felt comfortable playing Mr. Mom driving carpool, but I knew declining would be difficult.

"Of course we can. Not a problem," Andrew said. Happiness filled his voice.

We hoped for a quick exit, getting our school bus duties over with immediately, but it morphed into twenty-five minutes of preparing the boys for school. Andrew lifted his wrist more than a dozen times. Tapping his toe and bouncing his knee didn't encourage the boys to move faster.

I opened the car's rear door, and the boys slid across the immaculate sand-colored leather. As Andrew shifted the car in reverse, I heard the click and whoosh of soda cans cracking open.

"You're an asshole!" screamed one of the boys, and before my head could crane back to intervene, I heard a thud.

"OWWWWW! You're the asshole! Why'd you hit me?"

Another thud. Brown foaming liquid flew through the air, splashing the window. It flowed onto the boys' faded jeans and formed a puddle beneath them on the leather seat.

"Boys? What's going on back there?"

Andrew could not see the destruction, but he leaned toward the rearview mirror in investigation. Less than a quarter of a mile from the house and there had been cursing, hitting, and a soda spill. The school was two miles away, yet the drive felt like twenty miles with the continued bickering despite Andrew's plea for peace.

"Boys, we're almost there. How about we just sit quietly?" Andrew suggested.

"How about you sit quietly, asshole!" one of the boys screamed at Andrew.

Andrew's lips pursed, and his face turned red in anger. Well, actually, it may have been more of a purple. I had never seen Andrew this angry, but it was justified. We were professionals, designers not babysitters.

They gave one another a high five and laughed.

"Now, now, boys. I'm sure your mom wouldn't want you using that kind of language. I don't want to have to tell on you."

"You can tell her whatever the fuck you want. She won't believe you," one said, then he clenched his fist and struck his brother's shoulder with force.

"Sucker!" He laughed.

Andrew increased his speed, and relief set in when the boys finally jumped out, continuing their fighting through the school's front door.

"Well, that was a nightmare." Andrew sighed.

"Don't look in your back seat. That's another nightmare."

Andrew cocked his head around for a glimpse. "What the heck was that?" he screamed. "Those little brats! Why the hell did that over-medicated, plumber-seducing mother give them soda? What was she thinking?"

Andrew filled me in about the time she had summoned our plumbing supplier to look at her scratched primary bedroom faucets.

"I don't think I was able to make Mrs. Slater happy," Stan had reported after his visit to her house. "When I arrived, she was wearing nothing but a silk robe, which was draped open."

He'd told Andrew that when he had entered the primary bedroom, Katherine had dropped her robe and stood naked in the doorway. I always wondered if he had jumped at the opportunity, but he had denied any unprofessional behavior.

Neil viewed my clients as prim and proper, but large bank accounts didn't ensure appropriate behavior. It was a side of the business I never anticipated yet found interesting, entertaining in a way. I saw the true messy interior of people who curated a perfect exterior for the outside world.

I tried imagining a client soliciting me, and a half-naked version of Matthew appeared in my head. How my mind conjured such an image made me cringe in embarrassment. I could barely handle a little flirting and daydreaming, forget about naked intimacy. I crammed the image into the corner of my mind, hoping it would never reappear.

chapter
twenty-four

Furniture orders for Matthew Cherning were placed, invoices generated, deposits paid, and delivery dates approached. My cell phone whirred with Matthew's frequent calls regarding his apartment: "Just wanted to confirm you received my check." or "Can you help me with new sheets and towels?"

"Mr. Cherning," I answered his first call that day with a hint of sarcasm.

"Mrs. Pearce." His words bounced against mine. "How is the wonderful world of interior design?"

"It's quite well today. Busy. Always interesting around here."

"Hmm. Is that so? I'd love to hear more about it. How about we grab a drink so you can fill me in."

"Matthew." My tone was apprehensive.

He interrupted my thoughts. "Wednesday. No big deal. One drink, Sky. That's it. Don't overthink it. We can talk business the entire time."

I laughed. Was I overthinking it? I wished the pull would weaken, but our easy conversations had become deeper, more gratifying. I pushed Neil's face beyond the limits of my brain, convincing myself a meeting on a Wednesday was not a date. Wednesday is a weeknight, a perfectly acceptable night for a business meeting. If it were a Thursday, that would be different. Besides, Neil had been gone for weeks, and I was tired of nights alone.

"Okay, one drink. Just one." I insisted. "And just to remind you, our focus will be the details for your apartment."

"Yes. One drink. I'll pick you up at six from the office."

Heat rushed through my chest. Feelings I'd fought over for the past few weeks blazed. Not good. Not good at all.

"Sandy, where's the Danzik file?" I asked. I wanted to drench myself in work.

Thump. The huge binder landed on my desk.

"You're a brave woman, Skylar. Good luck with that one," Sandy said.

The entire office had avoided reorganizing the overgrown file. The Danziks had several homes and kept us on retainer for their incessant needs. I knew Andrew would be thrilled if someone organized the file, and it ensured no one would bother me after the unexpected invitation from Matthew.

"This is duplicate, this is garbage, this is in the wrong section," I mumbled to myself as my mind ruminated.

Around and around and around. A rhythm set in, relaxing my brain until Matthew invaded my thoughts. I muscled them aside, replacing his face with Neil's. What was it about Matthew that had me twisted? I had seen hot guys before and had never felt a twinge of temptation.

Matthew wasn't the obvious hot guy in the room. He was quite handsome, an endearing, approachable handsome that could be lost on some, but not me. I saw it all. I imagined attention from a man with such looks would captivate me, but I realized there was more. Something richer seized my attention. Something about Matthew Cherning changed my direction, like a teenager sorting through laws of attraction. Why him? There was something more powerful than mere chemistry, and sorting through it was challenging.

I glanced at the clock and calculated Pacific Coast time. It would be a good time to catch Neil. "Hey. How's it going?" I asked.

"Good, good. I'm just a bit slammed right now," Neil said.

"Oh, okay. I just wanted to hear your voice." I prayed it

would hit my reset button, reminding me of all we shared. The years of memories.

"That's cute. I'll be home Friday, and I promise no work this weekend if you promise, too."

"Great, I've been dying to see that new Picasso exhibit at the Met. Maybe we can check that out."

"Ummmm, maybe. You know that's not my thing, Sky. I mean, I'll go if you really want to, but I was thinking a movie and some Chinese food would be great."

During our courtship, I'd thought Neil loved museums but later learned he'd only gone to pacify me. I should have known not to even try, but I always held a little hope that maybe he would realize my interests were just as important as his.

"The exhibit is only in New York for a few weeks. I have an idea. Why don't we do both?"

"Really? I'm in California working my ass off all week, and you're dragging me to a museum? Come on, Sky."

"What's the big deal? We never go to museums anymore, and the exhibit will be gone soon. I'll agree to your Chinese food, which you know I hate."

"Whatever. You go do your artsy thing. I'll figure something out. But I can't believe you're choosing that over me after you haven't seen me in weeks. It's just surprising, but whatever. Work, clients, Andrew, and now a museum, all come before me. I'm used to it."

"Used to it? What does that mean? Okay, listen, I'm not doing this. I'm not getting into a big fight right now. Let's talk about it when you get home."

I could forget the museum and give Neil the weekend he envisioned. I hoped the time together would remind me of all the good stuff we shared. I packed up the file and tried recalling the beginning of our relationship, replaying the happy moments.

Andrew interrupted my thoughts. "You finished that whole file today? I cannot believe it."

I appreciated the awe in his voice and noticed the scotch in hand. "Yup. Everything's done. Is it okay if I take off early?" I asked. I needed fresh air, and Andrew's scotch would soon kick in. I wanted to escape before he created a scene or unleashed his temper.

"That's fine. Let's meet at the Renzi apartment at eight thirty tomorrow. The paper hanger is starting, and I don't want him speaking to the client."

A meeting that early wasn't in Andrew's vocabulary anymore. Hangovers stole his mornings, leaving me alone on appointments.

I packed up and walked outside, where the sun pleasantly hit my face. I paused, tilting it to meet the rays. The brisk air persisted, as expected in early March. Winter still hung on, and sunny days were a gift. My feet traveled, and my body went along, but my head had no interest.

Why did I agree to have a drink with Matthew? What good could come of that? Only bad. Only complications. Only someone getting hurt. Why did I agree?

Bam!

Ouch! I looked up, and I had walked directly into a delivery guy maneuvering a metal hand cart on the sidewalk. My forehead seared with pain from the crash.

"Ma'am. Oh no. Ma'am, are you okay?" He scrambled. I hunched over on the sidewalk, holding my pounding forehead in my hands. "Are you okay?" he repeated ten more times.

"Yes, I'm, wow, that hurts. I'm okay."

"I'm sorry. I guess you didn't see me. I'm so sorry," he repeated.

"No, it's okay. It's my fault. I wasn't paying attention." Which was the truth.

"You'd better get some ice on that before it swells up," he advised.

I raised my right arm out into the street while holding my forehead as yellow cabs raced past me. I spotted an open cab and struggled to stand tall and wave my arm, grabbing his attention.

As the vehicle slowed, I staggered toward the rear door. Then, some hipster dude ran in my path and jumped into the cab. I tried to scream, but tears replaced my yelling.

I finally found a cab and let my head rest back on the vinyl seat. With the onset of severe throbbing and my eyes closed, I focused on my breath. Deep breaths. Without warning, my head flew off the seat and bounced a few inches.

Ouch! Freaking pothole! My tote bag flew off the seat, landing sideways on the wet floor of the cab. Seriously? Who had it out for me today?

Lipstick, tampons, pens, receipts, and gloves covered the floor. I hunched over, grasping for items, throwing the wet stuff back into my bag. As I lifted my head from the floor of the cab, BAM, another pothole.

The top of my head hit the plastic divider. "Shoot!" I couldn't keep it in.

"Sorry. Pothole," the driver said.

Thanks for the warning. I should have taken the subway. The ride from hell came to an end. Climbing out of the cab, I was reminded how uptown felt foreign and uncomfortable compared to downtown. In my pain, I ached for comfort, and my uptown neighborhood failed miserably. I remembered my sister's pain and how my mother's tenderness and healing touch soothed her.

The sun still shone, and arriving at my building only exacerbated my malaise. I couldn't go inside. No way. Even with a throbbing head, I could not bring myself to go into my desolate apartment. It wouldn't bring me comfort because nothing about it felt like me. The décor was a compromise that kept Neil happy. Sometimes, my whole life felt that way.

I pivoted and retraced my steps toward Third Avenue. My head pounded over and over.

I strolled north on the avenue, watching people maneuver through their daily lives. Mothers pushed strollers beside seniors walking at a snail's pace. Everyone enjoyed the sunshine.

"Hi!" I said as I entered my favorite boutique.

"What happened to your head?" the owner asked as she approached.

I hadn't looked in a mirror yet. "Is it that bad?"

"Well, it's not so good. What happened?"

"You don't want to know."

I didn't want to get into it. Wait. It dawned on me that I would see Matthew the next day, and excitement was replaced with dread. I'd look like an injured hockey player for our not-a-date appointment.

"Are you looking for anything special today?"

"Yes, actually, I am. I'm going out tomorrow night after work and could use a new outfit. A work thing, but you know, not too business-like."

So now I was buying new clothes for a drink with a client I had the hots for. What was wrong with me? So many things it's hard to know where to start.

"Gotcha. I'll pull some things for you. You're what, a twenty-six in pants, right? And a six in tops?" she asked.

"Yup. that sounds about right." I sat in the closest chair and closed my eyes.

She heaved the heavy velvet drape aside and hung multiple hangers on the chrome bar. "Here you go. Try the black skirt with that gray sweater together. It's awesome."

I turned and struggled with the drape. "Oh, my God!"

"Everything okay?" she called over.

"Not really. Just saw my face. Wow. You were being kind. I look like I lost a fistfight."

She laughed. "Let me know if you need other sizes."

I stripped to my lingerie and hesitated. I turned around, examining my body from all angles, imagining Matthew seeing every curve for the first time. A flash of his hands sliding down my back sent a warm purr through my chest. "Stop.

Stop," I whispered to the familiar stranger in the mirror. "Stop. You are married. Married to an adorable, brilliant man, who is successful and loves you and . . ."

"Everything okay in there?" the saleswoman called.

"I'm fine." *I'm not fine. What am I going to do about my head?* The swelling and bruising were already underway. I slipped into the black skirt and gray sweater as encouraged. Hmmm, not bad. In fact, pretty cute. I stepped out for a second opinion.

"Wow! That's fantastic! Wait, let me grab you the perfect boots." She scurried off.

"I must say, this is pretty close to perfect." The only perfect thing all afternoon. "Do you have anything that's, um, like, a little bit, like, sexy, maybe? But appropriate for work at the same time?" My face flushed.

"Of course. Let's show off that cute body of yours! Be right back." She practically ran.

My inner voice shamed me. What was I doing? Why wasn't I buying cute new outfits for a date night with Neil? I used to do those things, but lately, the disconnect between us had left me feeling empty.

An hour later, I waited at the counter as she handed me the receipt and a large shopping bag. It was a splurge, and I knew I couldn't charge one more thing on my credit card for the remainder of the month.

Maybe Matthew wouldn't notice the purple abstract art adorning my face. Not that I should care. He was a client. I was married. End of story.

"Skylar? Are you okay?" The owner held the bag longer than normal.

"Sorry. I guess I just zoned out for a minute. Thanks."

I left the store, teetering, managing my tote bag and the shopping bag while rubbing my forehead. After walking only a block, my cell phone shook my coat pocket.

I dodged oncoming pedestrians, scurried to the edge of the sidewalk, and dropped the bag at my feet. "Hello?" My breath escaped me.

"Hey!" It was Matthew.

"Uh, hi."

"I see you."

"What do you mean 'see me'?" I somehow laughed through my pain, likely from nerves and confusion.

"I see you," he repeated. "I am looking right at you. A little afternoon shopping, I see."

Oh no! My face! No, no, no! "Wait, where are you?"

Matthew walked toward me from the street. His wide yet shy smile exuded warmth, like the sun. Yes, Matthew was like the sun. I wondered if everyone felt the warmth of his lopsided smile or if it was just me. Lukas stood by the car. I recoiled, turning my head to hide my bruise.

"Skylar, hi. We were driving uptown for a conference, and I looked up, and there you were. What's wrong? Why won't you look at me?"

I slowly turned, finally facing him. His eye met my bump.

"Skylar!" For the first time, I watched Matthew's beautiful smile fade. "Oh, my God. Are you okay? What happened to you?"

Well, I was walking on the street, obsessing about you, and walked directly into a metal hand cart. Are you turned on yet? "Yes, I'm completely fine. I was on my phone and bumped into a delivery guy on the street. No big deal."

I kept my tone light. Matthew picked up my bags and, without a word, guided me to his car. As we slipped across the back seat, he took my face in his hands. With his left index finger, he traced the purple bump on my forehead. Unexpected tears dripped down my face. The stress of the day dripped from my eyes.

"Shhhhh," I heard him whisper to me, "it's okay. It's going to be okay."

I was silent. Just tears appeared, no words.

"Lukas, can you grab some ice, please?"

Matthew took out his phone and dialed.

"Hey, Lorraine. I need you to clear my schedule for the rest of the day. Yes, the luncheon, the conference call, everything. We can deal with rescheduling tomorrow. Okay. Great, thanks."

"Did you just cancel your day for me? Please don't. I'm fine. Really, I can handle it."

"Skylar, this isn't even a decision. I'm not going anywhere. This is where I want to be. Let me take care of you. I want to take care of you."

Matthew used his thumb to wipe the tears from my sweaty face while my nose ran like a child's.

"I don't know." I managed to gain some composure. "I should go home."

Lukas knocked on the window.

"Here, lean your head back." Matthew held the ice on the bruise, gently brushing strands of hair from my face in silence.

"I should go home."

"Okay, let me bring you home and make sure you're okay."

"Ugh, I don't want to go home."

"If you don't want to go home, let's head to my place if that's okay with you. You can relax there, and I'll get you back home whenever you feel ready. Sound good?"

I gently nodded.

The intimate moment in the back of Matthew's car quieted the throbbing of my head. What if I missed this opportunity? What if this feeling floated away? No one had ever cared for me so tenderly before.

When we reached his apartment, Matthew guided me toward the guest bedroom with his hands on my shoulders. "Here, why don't you lie down? Is it okay if I help slip off your shoes?" I nodded.

Matthew draped a blanket over me and exited the bedroom, returning promptly with a bag of ice and some aspirin. "Let me look at that bump again. Definitely needs some more icing. Are you hungry?"

Matthew loosened his tie, flung his jacket on the foot of the bed, and kicked off his shoes before he delicately lay on the bed next to me. The awkwardness of lying next to another man never dawned on me because everything with Matthew came naturally. The comfort scared me. I knew I shouldn't feel relaxed next to a man who wasn't my husband, yet the ease I felt despite the situation spoke volumes.

"How's the pain?"

"Eh. On and off. I'll survive."

Matthew chuckled. "I'm sorry you're hurt, but I'm not sorry you're here. I like being around you, Sky."

Should I admit I felt the same? Should I reply in honesty or appropriately?

I said, "My mind wonders whether I should share my real feelings."

"I know you're married, but I also know how I feel. And hiding it isn't the answer for me. I'm so drawn to you, Skylar. I think about you a lot. I think about how I can spend more time with you, get to know you better, and have more of our conversations. I can't deny how I'm feeling. And yes, I know you're married. I understand all that."

"I feel the same things, but I'm struggling with what to do with all these feelings. I would never cheat on my husband. Never."

My phone chimed, and Neil's name lit up the screen. I looked Matthew deep in his eyes. "I'm not the kind of woman who has affairs. I hope you know that."

"I know. I think you should answer it."

I didn't want to answer Neil's call, but what choice did I have? I cringed from the guilt of lying on a bed next to another man, yet it was the only place I wanted to be.

"Hello. Hi, Neil. Yes, I, it's a funny story. I got knocked in the head on the street today, and a client happened to see me, and I'm just at his apartment getting myself settled a bit. Can you imagine? So embarrassing." I paused, listening to Neil, and watched Matthew leave the room.

"A client? Geez, Skylar, what's wrong with you? You sound fine. I think you need to get home now."

"Yes, I'm leaving right now. It all happened so fast, and I just needed some ice and Tylenol."

"Just go home, Skylar. Your clients aren't your friends."

Matthew returned and sat by my side as I hung up the phone. He lifted the ice and examined the bruise, leaning close enough that I could inhale his breath.

"I have to leave," I whispered.

"I know. But I don't want you to. Can you stay just a little longer?"

I shook my head, gathered my things, and headed toward the elevator.

chapter
twenty-five

A week later, it was time to furnish Matthew's apartment. When I walked through the office door, Andrew immediately handed me a blue folder. "This has the complete list of deliveries. Times, phone numbers of customer service, and an updated floor plan." Then he darted off to his desk.

Our office staff had compiled an extremely efficient file, and I appreciated it.

"You ready to go?"

Andrew sat at his desk with a half-empty bottle of scotch and an empty glass. "You go ahead without me. I'll meet you there in a bit," he said.

His presence would be futile.

I arrived at Matthew's apartment at the stroke of nine, as the building's policy was no deliveries prior to nine-thirty.

I checked my notes. Matthew's flight was due in at 5:50 p.m. the next day.

The bathrooms had been updated. Every wall, ceiling, and trim had received a fresh coat of paint or wallpaper. Televisions and sound systems had been installed. Wood floors had been sanded and refinished.

The backdrop was set.

"Morning, Miss Skylar," the doorman said.

"Good morning, Eddie. Big day ahead. I'm going to need your help."

"For you, anything. Mr. Cherning wouldn't have it any other way." He smiled.

Exhilaration filled me, and I eagerly anticipated the compilation of Matthew's gorgeous apartment. I couldn't recall the last time I'd tingled with such passion.

I plopped my bag on the kitchen island and noticed my name adorning a crisp envelope with a small box.

Gulp.

I continued unpacking the folder and pertinent paperwork, creating a mini office on the island. I moved slowly and meticulously. Deep breath. And again.

My fingers touched the envelope, and I could feel his touch. My stomach dropped. The flap was unsealed. The shiny white card had a large red cross in the center. My face scrunched in thought. What the . . . ? Inside, Matthew had written a few lines:

Sky, no accidents, please. I want you in one piece when I return. Can't wait to see your amazing work. Matthew

I closed my eyes, absorbing the moment and his caring nature. My belly flipped as I lifted the lid off the small box. A piece of paper read "Just in case," and beneath it was a stack of Band-Aids. My cheeks grew red while I smiled. I felt light and airy, knowing Mathew was thinking of me even when we were apart. I liked the feeling, knowing I occupied a special space in his head. The buzzer rang like a shotgun, indicating the interior design marathon had begun.

I unrolled carpets, unpacked chandeliers, whatever needed to be done, all while directing the movers. The apartment began to take shape. Four thirty was our cut-off. No deliveries past four thirty. Manhattan buildings had strict guidelines and union rules. For the next hour, I vacuumed carpets, fluffed sofas, wiped down tables, and inspected deliveries for damages. I closed the apartment for the day and made my way through the lobby and out to the street.

"Miss Skylar! Skylar!" I heard someone call. It was Lukas.

"Hi, Lukas. How are you? What are you doing here? Isn't Matthew out of town?"

"Yes, miss. I'm here to take you home," he said.

For a moment, I hesitated in confusion, but then I wasn't surprised. Matthew enjoyed taking care of people. I imagined flocks of women chased Matthew. After all, he was adorable, smart, and successful. Why was he wasting time on me, on a complicated, unattainable relationship?

"Thanks, Lukas. It has been a long day. A ride sounds a heck of a lot better than the subway right now."

He laughed as he opened the door for me.

A trace of Matthew's cologne tickled my nose. I gazed at the empty seat next to me and imagined him there with me. *Why am I torturing myself like this?*

"How's the apartment coming?" Lukas asked.

"It's getting there. I hope he likes it."

"I think anything you do will make Mr. Matthew happy," he joked.

"I'm pretty sure Matthew doesn't need me to make him happy."

"I don't know about that. He keeps to himself these days. You're the first woman he's had me drive since Stephanie."

My interest was piqued, but I resisted prying.

"Really? Huh. I find that hard to believe," I said.

"What does your husband do, Miss Skylar?" he asked.

"He works in technology. He spends a lot of time in California."

"That must be hard, huh?" asked Lukas.

"Yes and no. I'm so busy during the week that if he were here, he might distract me from my work. He likes my undivided attention when he's home."

"Aw, that's sweet. I've been married thirty-eight years. Best thing that ever happened to me."

"What's the secret?"

"It's an everyday job. Just like my job with Mr. Matthew. Every day, I make sure I show her I love her. Nothing fancy, but every day, I make her laugh or hold her hand, and she does the same for me. Every day. For almost forty years, every day."

I leaned my head on the taut leather. Something about Lukas's analysis of marriage made my heart ache. A longing ache. I thought I worked hard to please Neil, but sometimes I wished he worked as hard as Lukas did with his wife. I felt the absence of that authentic dedication in my marriage.

Lukas deposited me back in my uptown world. I held the key up to the door. Neil was in New York that week, adding to my guilt. I wanted to run the other way. Back downtown. Maybe I was creating something in my mind. It had to be. Chemistry. That's all this was. *Snap out of it now, Skylar, right now.* I pushed open the door and crossed the threshold into my life with Neil.

"How'd it go?" Neil asked.

"Great. I was so nervous; you know, first time on my own."

"Well, it was just really the presentation you did on your own. I mean, I'm sure Andrew did a lot of the work. He oversaw everything."

I wondered if Neil understood how his words pricked at my self-esteem. "I guess. I mean, I did most of the work. Andrew approved everything. Although if you're drunk while approving, does it count?" I joked.

"I just mean you didn't do it all on your own. It wasn't all on you."

"Most of it was. I am the lead designer on this job. The client did ask specifically for me. Can't you see how great this is for me, my career?"

"Whatever, baby. I'm glad it's over for you."

"It sounds like you don't think what I do is actual work, Neil. It hurts when you say those things, insinuating I'm not capable. I'm building a career just like you are. Maybe it's not all mathematics and coding, but it was a lot of work, and Andrew is out of the loop these days. You'd be impressed, Neil. I'm contributing more than you think."

"Oh, I know sweetie. I just meant, you know, no need to be

nervous about something so silly. It's really Andrew's responsibility. You don't need to get so stressed about it. It's just furniture and stuff."

"Neil, I take my job seriously. It's not just stuff, and this was mine. My first project as the sole designer. It is a big deal," I defended.

"Okay, okay. You don't need to get defensive about it, sweetie. I just don't think it's worth you getting all worked up about it. It's a fun, creative job. You're just playing with the client's money; they have the luxury of not shopping for their own furniture." Neil said as he rubbed my back in circular motions.

"Are you kidding me?"

"What? What did I do? Come on, Sky, you must know what this 'career' you've chosen really is." He made air quotes around the word "career."

"Please tell me you're kidding?"

"What?"

"Neil, I have a college degree. I have a graduate degree. I've worked my way through entry-level jobs to get to this point in my career. How can you not see all the serious work and training I've put into my design?"

"Babe, woah, slow down. I didn't say that. You're saying these crazy things I never said. Don't be so sensitive. You took it all wrong."

"Neil, you either take my career seriously and support me in my goals or keep your mouth shut because I do not want to hear that crap you're serving up."

Stunned, I jerked his hand off my back, crossed the room, and slammed the bedroom door. Neil ignored me for the remainder of the evening, refusing to acknowledge me when I offered him a bowl of his favorite ice cream. Sleep escaped me. Questions stabbed at my brain and heart. For a moment, I wondered if my words had been too harsh, but the moment passed immediately. I wouldn't let my goals evaporate in exchange for Neil's approval. We'd never had an angry confrontation like that, and although it scared me to rock the boat, I had no choice. Neil snored for hours, unaware of my turmoil.

At five in the morning, I became antsy and headed to the gym. My breath was heavy and deep, and my mind succumbed to the monotony of running. My shirt clung to my sweat-soaked body as the endorphins did their work, pulling me from my funk.

I carefully placed one foot in front of the other on my walk back to our apartment, and the slow pace calmed me. I passed Neil outside the front door.

"Hey. Got a dinner thing tonight. See you after?" he asked.

I nodded.

"Where'd you go? The gym? I got nervous. I woke up, and you weren't there. It was weird."

"Yeah, couldn't sleep."

"I can't believe you actually went to the gym that early. I was hoping for some morning love before work."

Neil's comment confirmed he had no clue how his words made me feel. How could he think I would want to make love to him after he diminished my career and goals before bed?

"Nervous energy, I guess, and honestly, after your behavior last night, sex is the last thing on my mind."

"Now you're just being dramatic. Making some silly conversation more than it is isn't helping. I told you, you don't need to be nervous, Sky. Maybe Andrew should take it over. You don't need this stress."

I felt a sharp twinge in my chest at the thought of handing Matthew's project over to Andrew.

"No, no, it's fine. I can handle it. It's just Andrew's drinking on top of a normal day is rough. I'm taking on a lot more responsibility. It's an adjustment."

"Skylar, you're the assistant. Andrew will deal with the consequences if he keeps drinking. That's not for you to figure out. We'll talk later. I'll be out late at this meeting tonight. No need to rush home."

I felt a wave of relief come over me, knowing Neil wouldn't be pacing the apartment waiting for me. It would be a long day with an unknown timeframe.

I peeled my bike shorts and tank top from my skin. The shower took its time heating up, and my mind drifted to Matthew. My body languished. The wall held my body as my head teetered against it. I allowed my eyes to close and indulge in a fantasy. I could feel his lips touch mine. His body rubbing against mine. My body tingled standing naked outside the shower. As I stepped in, the hot water drenched every inch of me. I stood still. My body twinged. I saw Matthew's face and felt his touch.

chapter
twenty-six

I sprinted for the last block when I realized I was ten minutes behind schedule. Eddie waved as I blew by him. When I entered Matthew's apartment, I caught a glimpse of Andrew, phone to ear, in mid-conversation. "Lost track of time at the gym," I said in a hushed voice.

Andrew waved as he finished his call. "Jorge, you know I can't do that! Can't you just meet me there?" A lovers' quarrel. I sat silently until Andrew hung up and slammed the phone on the countertop.

"Everything okay?" I was delicate with my words, noticing Andrew's furrowed brow.

Andrew grunted and retreated to the powder room, finally lumbering out after a lengthy duration with the scent of alcohol swimming around him.

"Can you make it through the day? It's a long one."

More grunts with a flick of his wrist shooing me away, his eyes avoiding mine.

The electrical fixtures were due any moment, and the electrician would install iron chandeliers, chrome and glass pendants, and a myriad of sconces at noon. As the box cutter cleanly sliced the brown packing tape, the boxes began piling up, and Styrofoam peanuts fluttered across the floor. My hands burrowed inside, feeling for treasures hiding within the snow-filled containers.

"Shoot!"

Andrew jerked his head, "What?"

"The chandelier is bent. We can't hang it like this."

Andrew turned his gaze away, providing zero empathy. As I dialed the customer service number, I predicted a lengthy hold time with feeble musical entertainment by Sheryl Crow repeating on a loop. Finally, they answered. "Hello."

"Hi, Gina. It's Skylar from Andrew Thorne's office."

"Hi, Skylar."

"I just received the Pembroke chandelier for my client Cherning, and the iron is bent in two spots."

"Okay, dear. You need to take pictures, and I'll issue a pick-up request." Her Queens accent destroyed the Rs.

"How long for a replacement?"

"Twelve weeks, hon."

"Gina, that's ridiculous. I'm not telling my client he's waiting twelve more weeks for your mistake." I thought of Andrew's assertive client who owned the dress store. Mimicking her gumption would get me the result I needed.

"Twelve weeks, hon. Don't know what to tell ya." I wrestled with my frustration.

"Gina, there must be some accommodation you can provide for my client. The chandelier was eighteen thousand dollars. He's not going to be happy. You know that, right?"

"Hon, we gotta make a whole new piece."

I dug deep and refused to allow the peacemaker in me to emerge. Representing my clients and protecting my reputation was worth pushing myself out of my comfort zone. "Well, that's not acceptable, Gina. We give you a ton of business. Please don't make me cancel all my current orders. Andrew just placed a huge order last week. I hope he won't change his mind, given your customer service. It's a big risk for our company, and it makes us look bad." I hoped my terse tone conveyed my urgency.

"You think you're the only one? I got a pile here."

"Are you kidding me? My clients pay top dollar for your products, so I'm sorry, but another twelve weeks is not acceptable. This was your shipping company that damaged the goods."

I was teetering on a yell.

"Alright. I'll make a few calls. Lemme get back to you."

I looked for Andrew but couldn't find him anywhere. I paced the apartment, calling his name with no response. I dialed his cell, but it went to his voicemail. I buzzed the doorman.

"Hi, this is Skylar in Mr. Cherning's—"

"Oh yes, Skylar. Hi."

"Did Andrew leave the building? He's tall, light brown hair, in his forties, and probably smells like gin."

"Yes, yes, in fact, he just did."

The sudden release of tension in my shoulders surprised me. Andrew was out of the way. He thought he hid his secret well, but it was clear he was drunk. I could have used his advice and an extra set of hands, but his drinking made him a liability rather than an asset these days.

Matthew had been on my brain since my morning shower. I tried staying balanced, but it felt more like walking on the Titanic. My body tensed, filled with the pressure of making Matthew's apartment perfect and monitoring Andrew's alcohol intake. The electricians arrived an hour late, compounding my stress. I walked Jimmy and his crew through each room.

"Jimmy, I thought I was your priority?" I quipped.

"You are, Sky, but traffic was a killer today."

"Okay, so, these sconces," I said as I held up a polished chrome sconce wearing a white shade, "are for the primary bedroom. These four pendants over here go over the island."

"Okay. Just lemme know the drop on those pendants."

I maneuvered my tape measure, assessing the length for the pendants and chandeliers while one of the electricians held the wires against the ceiling for me to properly judge.

"Try an inch lower."

We only had four hours to install the electrical, and I knew it wouldn't be enough time. Despite the buzz in the apartment and Jimmy's endless questions, Matthew's face steeped in my thoughts. I dreamed of him holding my hand as I whisked him through his beautiful new apartment that I had designed. I imagined him hanging on every word as I shared my dreams of opening my own design firm, watching his excitement for me accomplishing my goals. It occurred to me that Matthew's genuine interest in my life gave me peace and confidence. A heaviness lifted from my chest, replaced by a deep expansion, allowing joy to fill me.

"Sky, you want me to hang the canopy for the chandelier?" Jimmy pulled me from my daze.

"Yes, great idea."

I noticed the blue light on my phone illuminating, visible from across the room. Third ring. "Hello."

"I landed a bit early. Will I be permitted access?" Matthew spoke seriously.

I giggled despite my stress. "Hey, where are you?" I hid my panic, surveying the unorganized apartment.

"How's it going over there?"

"Good. I mean, great. Where are you?"

"I definitely didn't miss this cold weather, that's for sure. I guess only a few more weeks, right?"

"Yeah, hopefully. Where are you exactly?"

"You have a good weekend?"

"Fine, I think. I mean, I can hardly remember it." I laughed. "I've been very focused on my current project."

"I see. Well, I hope the client appreciates your dedication."

"He's pretty awful."

Matthew's laughter relaxed my muscles, which had been clenched over the past two days.

"So, see you in an hour."

The phone hit the marble counter, and I dashed through the rooms.

"Jimmy! You need to finish, like now. I need to get you out of here. The client will be here in an hour."

I hauled the empty cardboard boxes to the garbage chute,

gathering empty coffee cups, pieces of plastic packaging, and random Styrofoam peanuts along the way. Entering the bedroom first, I flicked the switch near the entry, confirming the sconces worked. Check. Now, the bedside switches, one on the left, check. As I depressed the switch on the opposite side of the bed, the light remained illuminated. I could feel my chest tighten. I tried again, with my finger more forceful this time. Nothing.

"Jimmy!!" Screaming was my only option, given my panic and the size of the apartment.

Jimmy strolled in the bedroom, and I said, "This switch isn't working."

As Jimmy began problem-solving, I dragged a damp towel across the lights, then dashed from room to room, removing dust and dirt from every surface. I circled back to the primary bedroom, allowing my critical eye to survey the bed, pillow arrangements, window treatments, rug, lighting, accessories, and furniture. Perfect.

Continuing through the primary bathroom, I slid my index finger across the white countertop and chrome faucets, confirming my dusting had been effective. The massive mirror exposed my embarrassing reflection. I charged out and grabbed my handbag, fishing for some makeup and a brush. I fixed my disheveled hair and melting face.

Stay calm. Breathe. He's a client. You are married. Get. A. Grip.

I picked off fuzz balls, remnants of statically induced Styrofoam, and slivers of brown boxes from my black skirt and smoothed the front of my gray sweater.

"Jimmy!" I screamed, "Client coming in twenty. Finish up and get out of here!"

"Got it. Just finishing up these switches."

The apartment was quiet for a few minutes before Matthew arrived. I tried telling myself to relax, but it only made me more nervous. I was proud of the design, and despite the hard work, the exhilaration before the big reveal fed my soul.

The elevator doors whooshed open, followed by heavy footsteps and a thump. His duffel being dropped, I guessed.

"Honey, I'm home." He followed up with laughter that echoed through the hallway. His footsteps quickened as he approached, revealing that wide, crooked smile coming toward me.

"No, no, no! Close your eyes! Close them!"

"This apartment is insane!"

"Matthew, close your eyes and forget everything you saw."

"Okay, okay. I'm closing them."

I instinctively clasped Matthew's arm and led him to the main entrance of the apartment so we could begin his tour properly, the way I had rehearsed it in my mind from start to finish. He stumbled as he stepped on the area rug in the entry, and we both laughed.

"You trying to kill me, Sky?"

My knees quivered when I heard my nickname. Matthew's black suit showed no evidence of an airplane flight, with it crisply pressed and sharp-edged like on the night we met.

"Okay. You ready?"

"I'm ready."

"You sure you can handle it?" I teased. I released his arm and covered his eyes with my hand. "Okay, here we go."

I lifted my hand, allowing his eyes to scan the space freely.

"Wow! I can't believe this! What a change in only a few days."

Matthew beamed. He removed his jacket and loosened the knot in his powder-blue tie. I pushed my shoulders back and returned the smile. There came the heat again.

"It really came together," I said as Matthew casually took my hand, fidgeting with my fingers. "Wow. I can't believe you did all this. It's amazing. Show me around! I can barely remember what we chose. It was so long ago!"

What I could barely remember was the last time someone had held my hand so sweetly. Neil held my hand occasionally while crossing the street or entering a party, but never with the intention of closeness or connection. Although he'd asked me to be the tour guide, Matthew pulled ahead of me, skipping from room to room.

"I can't believe this is the same apartment! It's incredible!" he said giddily.

We continued through the guest bedroom, highlighting the custom pillows and antique lighting. Then, I revealed the primary bedroom with a custom Tibetan rug and the artwork we had selected together at a local gallery. I grinned, and the knots in my stomach untied as the pressure of perfection was released.

"I'm just . . . I'm amazed!" Matthew collapsed onto the sofa. "I can't get over the transformation."

I positioned myself on the sofa across from him, adjusting my short skirt as I sat and crossed my legs. The room was quiet except for a car's faint horn honking far below.

"When I met you, I knew I needed to be near you, one way or another." His attention was intense. "I'll be living in your vision, your work, everything you chose for me, and that is pretty cool." His eyes caught mine.

I smiled and dropped my eyes to the floor but could not access words. Not words that would make any sense, that is. As a married woman, I couldn't possibly admit how he made me feel special, seen, and valued more than anyone in the world.

"Let's celebrate. I mean, if that's okay. No pressure. I'm just so excited." Matthew jumped from the chair.

My knee bounced involuntarily, and I nodded while the voice in my brain screamed, *NO. You should get up and go home now.* But the truth was, I wanted to stay. I was exactly where I wanted to be at that moment.

Matthew opened the fridge, revealing a lone bottle of prosecco and a container of ketchup. A yawn escaped his mouth, but he tucked his face in his elbow, concealing it. "I'm happy I'm home. I finally have a place that truly feels like home."

"We had a small problem with the chandelier," I divulged.

"A new one will arrive in a few weeks. I'm sorry about that."

"It's okay. Just glad it wasn't the table and chairs. Been dying for those."

The fizz from the prosecco poured over the edge of the plastic cup. "Oops." Matthew laughed as the puddle oozed over the floor. "No one ever called me the smoothest guy. My fraternity nickname was Burnin' Churnin' because they thought it was only a matter of time till I burned something down."

I heard my phone from the entry closet where I had hidden my bags. I let it shrill.

"I'm excited to sleep in my serene bedroom tonight. I bet I sleep better than ever, huh? Better than that box spring and mattress on the floor."

"I hope so. I know you travel a lot for work, so it's definitely better than hotel rooms. How do you like your work?" I asked.

"I love it. I meet interesting people, and I love to strategize. It's really helped me get through some stuff. I focused on the work I loved and didn't give into a pity party." His eyes settled on the bubbles in his plastic cup as he handed me mine.

"So, tell me about your husband. Neil, is it?" Matthew looked up from the glass.

"Yes, Neil. Um. Well, he works in technology. We started dating just after college. That's pretty much it."

"What's he like?" He leaned toward me with intense curiosity that stirred something new in me.

I thought about what it would feel like to have an affair. Removing the smooth gold band on my finger and placing it in a drawer as if that could preserve the sanctity of marriage while lying with another man. I could never do it. I would never be unfaithful to Neil. He was my family now, and I would never hurt him, never go back on my word, my commitment to him. That's just not who I was, not who I wanted to be.

"He's a good guy. He's responsible. He has high morals and values. Let me see," I could picture Neil's face in my head. A posed picture like the one in his firm's literature. Sitting tall, with a fake, dutiful smile and ever-so-appropriate suit. "He's a good guy."

"Yeah, you mentioned that already. What does that mean, Sky? What's a good guy?"

"I don't know. I don't know how else to describe him. He's, you know, steady and level-headed. You know, the kind of guy who comes to the door to meet your parents when you go on a date. That's a good guy."

It felt like a lawyer's defense. Why did it feel like that?

"How did you guys meet?"

"Mutual friend."

"And? There must be a story there."

"I mean, not really. We were at a party that a mutual friend threw. He asked for my number, and it just went from there. He asked me on a date, I said yes, and I guess it just worked out. He was charming in a sea of twenty-year-old goons. Neil always had a plan. He's a very planned-out kind of guy."

"And what happens if things don't go according to plan?"

I twisted my hair around my finger, remembering the time Neil wanted to go to a Black Crows concert. I wasn't interested but cheerfully suggested he go with his friends instead. I finally succumbed after he moped around the house for days, barely uttering a word to me.

"Yeah, he likes things to go his way, and his determination could be mistaken for stubbornness." I sighed, needing to change the topic. "Let's talk about you. What's all this about a pity party you were talking about earlier?"

I peeked at my watch. Nine thirty. Yikes. Matthew released a sigh and leaned back in his chair, pausing before delving into his personal life. He ran his fingers through his hair and massaged his scalp.

"I hate to talk about it, about her. It's just so depressing." He paused again. "She just, it just wasn't, I mean, it just was tragic in every sense. I'm okay. Just if I think about it too much, you know, it just gets overwhelming. We were already planning the wedding." My heart hurt for Matthew, knowing that pain better than most. While some may have found his vulnerability unnerving, his honesty only pulled me closer to his heart, knowing we shared a grief most people our age couldn't understand. We were members of an exclusive club, but no one wants that membership. Even Charlie, who listened and cried with me, was an outsider when it came to the loss of my sister, but Matthew was an insider. Perhaps this was the unspoken connection we both naturally felt, a kinship we sensed but now uncovered.

"I'm so sorry. How long were you engaged?" I asked.

"About six months. She ordered her dress . . . it just never came to be. I never imagined my life would turn out the way it has. Overnight, in the blink of an eye, as they say."

Matthew's eyes looked vacant, staring into the distance at nothingness.

"I can't imagine what that must have been like for you. Devastating. Just when you think you've figured things out, planned the rest of your life." I'd thought I, too, had my life mapped out, but lately, I felt like I was lost without a map when it came to my marriage.

"It's been awful, but it feels good to be around you, and I haven't felt that in so long. I can't explain it. I don't know why. It just feels . . . familiar, yet new at the same time. I don't know; it's hard to explain." Matthew stroked his jawline as he spoke.

"You've had a long day. I should go and let you enjoy your apartment." I stood, making my way to the kitchen sink with Matthew close behind.

"I'm starving," he said. "Any chance you'd want to grab a quick bite on our way uptown? I'm exhausted and hungry, and if I'm being really honest, I would love your company."

A siren blared in my head. *Stop.* Enjoying the evening too much alarmed me. What if I liked being with Matthew more than Neil? My gut silenced the fear, convincing me I could handle spending time with Matthew. *It's a quick bite. I mean, Neil isn't even home. I did work a long, hard day, and I am starving. It's not a big deal, just grabbing a bite. That's it.*

"Actually, I barely ate today."

"Let's do it," he said, smiling ear to ear.

Lukas greeted us as we entered the car.

"What are you in the mood for?" Matthew asked.

"Not Italian. Other than that, I'm open."

"Sushi okay? There's a great place on our way."

I nodded while my head, heart, and gut continued debating my decision.

"Lukas," Matthew said as he leaned forward between the front seats, "let's go to that sushi place I like on Central Park South."

Matthew's hand brushed against mine in the car. Our pinkies lay side by side, and our eyes acknowledged the contact.

"Oh, sorry. But I can't deny, I like how that feels."

I just looked at him for a moment. "I'm not sure what to say."

Was holding someone's hand really that bad? Wanting to hold his hand was even worse.

The car stopped, and I was stunned when Matthew gently tucked a loose hair behind my ear. I felt my face flush as our eyes clicked together.

"You keep amazing me. I am just always amazed by you, and I'm not sure what I can do about it."

"Matthew. How are you, sir? I have your table ready."

Matthew greeted the tall gentleman with a firm handshake, knocking over a glass as he reached across the bar. We both giggled as he blushed with embarrassment.

"Hi. Nice to see you, Nick; sorry about that. We'll sit at the sushi bar tonight."

I was relieved. It wouldn't feel like a date at the sushi bar.

The two sushi chefs gave shallow bows in our direction. I replied with a tentative wave. Matthew slid a chair out from the bar and gestured for me to have a seat.

"Will you have the usual, Mr. Matthew?"

"Sounds good to me. Skylar, what do you like?"

"I pretty much like it all. But I definitely want salmon. Neil hates salmon, so I can only eat it when I'm not with him." My stomach quivered after I uttered Neil's name, wondering why I compared two men who weren't in a competition.

He draped his arm around the back of my chair and brushed my shoulder with his fingertips. I felt a flutter in my belly.

Was sharing sushi just as bad as holding hands? While the wrongs of my behavior haunted me, our conversation naturally blossomed, easing my mind into forgiving my infractions and relishing our time together. I wished I hated him, enabling me to get up and run home to Neil like a good wife, but I couldn't. Neil had expectations, and fulfilling them became more difficult as my career blossomed. Perhaps my growth made him uncomfortable, but fitting the mold wasn't who I wanted to be anymore. Sacrificing my career, my dreams, while Neil took center stage and thrived wasn't enough for me. In fact, it was insulting. Matthew saw me the way I saw myself, passionate about my clients and my designs. I knew my desires were improper, but I was absolutely where I wished to be at that moment.

"Sure. Salmon it is."

Our conversation about his fiancée wouldn't leave my thoughts. I wanted to know more about Stephanie and his life since the accident, but I hesitated.

"So, do you date a lot?"

Matthew turned to look at me and laughed. "Why do you ask?"

"I don't know. Just curious. Have you had any relationships since . . .?"

"Stephanie? No, nothing major. Just, you know, a few dates here and there. Nothing that felt like, well, natural. Did you date a lot? I bet you had your pick. I bet you had men fawning all over you."

"Not that I know of. But then again, I have no aware-ness of those things. I never had enough confidence to believe someone would be interested in me. I remember one summer at camp when a counselor came to our bunk and said this cute boy wanted the number for the girl in the blue bathing suit. Some other girl jumped up and said, 'It's me; it's me.' Even though I was wearing a blue bathing suit, I sat quietly. I never believed it could be me."

"Really?" Matthew shook his head and ran his fingers through his hair. "That's crazy. How could you not know? That's, wow. Look at you."

"What? I don't know. I think of myself as average, just like everyone else. Nothing special or different."

"Seriously?" Matthew's face collapsed in his hands. "Skylar, are you for real right now?"

My unease from his compliments made me giggle.

"Skylar. God. What isn't extraordinary about you? Here you are, this driven woman. Determined. Every time I turn around, you reveal some new skill or talent. Your strength is so . . . sexy. And on top of all that, you're beautiful and kind and compassionate. I just, I can't believe you don't see it. But I guess that's what's so cool about you. You don't know what you've got. Your modesty is charming and sweet."

I must have blushed several shades of red and rubbed my fingernails back and forth. "That's a lot to hear."

"Why? It's all true, Skylar. You are the real deal. You should know that. Look at me." I lifted my gaze to meet his eyes, which were intense and held truth. "Skylar, you need to know. You need to know how amazing you are. You should know."

I dug through my memories of Neil, wondering if he had ever drenched me in praise. Matthew's words felt like being wrapped in my grandmother's hand-knit blanket. The warmth, the security, was unconditional. I couldn't recall similar words from Neil, but I hoped they were filed away in early memories that had become hushed over time.

I dug a whisper from the back of my throat, "Thank you. And what about you, Mr. Successful? You seem to have it all. You live this extravagant life with travel and drivers and professionally designed apartments."

"Yeah. All that and no one to share it with. No one who gets me. And I would have traded it all to save Stephanie."

"I'm sorry. I didn't mean to open your wounds."

"No, no, it's okay. I'm just being honest. We're being honest here, right? I mean, I work hard, and I love what I do, and with some luck and the right connections, I've been fortunate in achieving success. Success in my career, that is. I meet a lot of people, Sky. You do, too. Every day, we encounter so many different people through work or a party, and, well, how often do you meet someone who you just click with—something just connects?"

He avoided my stare for a bit, then turned toward me. My appetite had diminished. I didn't know how, and I didn't know what the fallout of this encounter would be, but my perspective had changed in a few sentences. A new sensation enveloped my heart and head, a space that was now occupied by Matthew Cherning.

Lukas directed the car east. My phone whirred with Neil's number on the screen.

"You need to get that?"

"It's Neil."

"I'm sorry if I kept you too long. I don't want to cause trouble for you."

"No trouble. I guess he was just worried. It'll be fine."

"I don't want to cause an issue, but I can't say I regret dinner tonight."

"Same, and thanks for the sushi."

"Thanks for the spectacular apartment."

"You hired me to do a job. I take that seriously."

"I know that. That's what I was trying to explain to you earlier. That's why I wanted you to design my apartment. You know that, right?"

I looked away and sucked in extra oxygen. His pull was getting stronger. My heart sank, knowing the job was almost complete, but my brain reminded my heart the end was for the best, but the evening had brought a closeness and honesty between us.

Matthew gently pressed his lips to my forehead. "Sadly, this is goodnight."

As I turned the key in my door, I glanced back at Matthew, fighting the urge to return to his car.

chapter
twenty-seven

Andrew's obsession with fame consumed him. When semi-sober, he spent long days wooing various magazine editors and publishers.

"I'm one magazine spread away from millions, Skylar. That's all it will take to have people buzzing about me."

"Andrew, is that what you really want? You would need to expand your business. You'd have to release some control. Can you do that? Your clients are so dependent upon you," I reminded him.

Andrew poured himself a scotch. I peered at my wrist. Ten forty-five in the morning. Not good.

"Are you doubting me, Skylar? I know I'm better than the designers in those magazines. I just need the perfect project to get the editors' attention."

Andrew's goals and increased drinking were certainly misaligned. Frustration from his lack of fame took its toll. It seemed the alcohol numbed his pain and disappointment. The firm was thriving and financially profitable, but Andrew craved fame, leading him to neglect his usual responsibilities.

While Andrew chased notoriety, I focused on the clients—their needs, wishes, and visions. They entrusted us to make their homes comfortable, and the power of that was never lost on me. Andrew never saw our projects as anything other than a step toward interior design fame. Creating Matthew's apartment had challenged me. Balancing the design and the intricacies of his desires had reminded me of the trust he had placed in me to set the backdrop for his private moments. Andrew never understood my connection with each client.

As my one-year anniversary at Andrew's firm approached, I worked longer hours to make up for Andrew's missed appointments, his errors on important orders, and his impatience with clients. I designed, billed, filed, and ordered. In Andrew's absence, clients began requesting my interior design services, and my confidence grew as I took charge of each task like a pro.

I shouldn't have complained to Neil about my frustration with Andrew. I knew better than to expect empathy from my husband.

"If you bring in the business, you deserve a percentage. That's how business works, Sky."

Neil's face was shrouded by the newspaper.

"I know, Neil, but it's not that simple."

He dropped the paper a few inches to make brief eye contact. "Skylar, you may as well work for free."

"I'm learning, Neil. He taught me how to run an interior design firm. The creative side and the business side."

"Yeah, well, now he's a borderline drunk at risk of losing his whole company. If you weren't there, he'd be screwed."

My internal struggle brewed, erupting into a full boil. I felt loyal to Andrew, and helping him through this rough patch seemed like the right thing to do. But as Neil pointed out, it was unfair for me to carry the load, pushing off my own desires. Neil never understood my emotional attachment to situations beyond him. I knew my feelings dictated too many of my decisions. I needed to find a balance. Andrew had given me opportunities and mentored me, and I was grateful.

"Look, I know Andrew hasn't been a perfect boss, but I've learned valuable skills working for him. I've grown, proven to myself that I'm a good designer. Through all this stress with Andrew, I've realized I'm capable of doing all this myself, on my own, without Andrew." As the words fell from my lips, my belly dropped, nervous Neil would be judgmental and not support my dreams. I knew the risks, but I wanted the reward of owning my own business. And knew I had the skills now.

"What does that even mean, Skylar? Are you suggesting you open your own design firm? Do you know what that takes? The time involved? While you may know how to match paint colors and fancy fabrics, you know nothing about running a business. Assuming you can get any clients, you would be doing it all yourself, working all the time, and where does that leave me? Us? How can you expect us to have a normal family if you don't even have time for your husband?" I stood in disbelief and wondered what he meant by normal. My husband thinking my pursuit of a successful business transformed us into an abnormal family made my heart race.

"Since design school, I've dreamed about opening my own firm. I tolerated Francine and Andrew, waiting for this exact moment, where finally my vision filled spaces."

"I'm not sure what happened to the Skylar I know, the woman who supported her husband. I work my tail off, and all I ask is that my wife support me and be there for me. Instead, you're off on some crusade beautifying million-dollar apartments in Manhattan. I know you want to have something to keep you busy, and design is a great little hobby for you, but I think running your own design firm is just beyond you, Skylar. It's just too much for both of us."

I crinkled my forehead in confusion before the anger swelled. "This is not a hobby. Let me get this straight. You get to go out and pursue your dreams, your goals, a career, and even fly across the country weekly while you build your career, but I should stay small? I should stay in a job that's toxic and unfulfilling? My goals are irrelevant? I can tell you that is not how it's going to be. You can kick and scream all you want, but design is not a hobby, not a joke, and starting my own firm is my dream that I guess you will just have to tolerate if you can't find a way to be supportive."

"Babe, listen, don't blow this out of proportion. I'm just never going to be your cheerleader. That's just not who I am." I hurt from the disconnect, the blatant misunderstanding of why I worked so hard at reaching for my goals. My thoughts settled into the reality of who my husband was, and it burned.

Matthew's project was complete, but his routine check-ins never ceased. When my phone rang, I welcomed the break after hours of paperwork in the office.

"Did you know that Michael is the most popular boys' name in the US?" Matthew said, ignoring an obligatory hello.

"Uh, no."

"Sorry. Just picked up the Daily News, and slightly perturbed that Matthew is third. I prefer first place, if you know what I mean." He chuckled.

"Yeah, I get that. You don't strike me as a happy-with-third-place type of guy," I said.

"So, how are you? What'd you do last night?" he asked.

"I guess you could say it was a crisis management situation."

"Well, now I'm intrigued. You okay?"

"Yeah, I'm fine. Things at work have gotten a bit crazy."

"Maybe now's your time, Sky. You know it's just a matter of time before you are flying on your own."

"You think?" I asked.

Matthew's comment blew me away. He truly understood what I strived for in my life. Thoughts of my own business had been held back by Andrew's alcohol and Neil's preoccupation with his own career goals and what he thought was best for us. Both men sucked the life out of me, but then there was

Matthew. The successful, smart woman inside me was buried beneath two men who needed me so fully there was nothing left for me. Matthew needed nothing from me yet awoke a belief in myself that I had forgotten existed. It had ignited the moment he chose me to design his apartment.

"Of course I do." He laughed. "Call my friend Solomon. He's an attorney and can give you some help. How to establish your own business, get things in order. Just to get you started."

I sighed and inhaled as my gut fluttered and flipped. Was I ready for this? How could I do it all myself? How would Neil feel about it? I didn't want to betray Andrew and leave him alone with a mountain of problems, but would there ever be a perfect time to put myself first? The caretaker within me emerged, urging me to smooth out the bumps and save those who needed help. Growing up with a sick sister and navigating the trauma of her loss, I had become a caretaker focused on smoothing out wrinkles in life and filling my void by rescuing those who needed saving.

My eyelids drifted shut for a moment, and my sister's face appeared. All the accommodations in the world hadn't relieved her suffering. I snapped my eyes open, halting the sadness from invading my thoughts. I wanted to save Andrew, but my experience proved saving anyone from their own reality was impossible.

I understood the fragility of life. As much as I wanted to, I couldn't cure Andrew's addiction, or Matthew's pain, or Neil's self-involvement. I needed to save myself this time.

I sat at my desk sketching new ideas, but my mind wandered, playing out an overdue conversation with Andrew. I was done holding it all in and marched into Andrew's office without a solid script in my head. The nearly empty bottle of vodka on his desk glared at me, but waiting for a sober moment wasn't an option anymore.

"Andrew, do you have a moment to talk?" Andrew's face

appeared ruddy and moist.

"I've been here almost a full year, and my responsibilities are much more than when I started. I feel I've learned the job rather quickly, and I've even brought in a client, not to mention the clients who have specifically requested me on their projects. I was hoping we could discuss a raise. I've worked hard, and I believe I've earned it." The words flowed easily and without doubt in my voice. Andrew sat silent and sipped his vodka.

"I see. Sounds like Neil thinks you deserve a raise, so I should just give you one. Is that what you think? He's so controlling. Does he ever let you think for yourself?"

"Well, no, why would you even say that?"

"Because it's true, Skylar. Do you really think that arrogant husband of yours knows anything about this business? Maybe if he stopped running away from you to California all the time, he would have a clue. That guy doesn't give a damn about your career, only about his. So, let's just put his thoughts where they belong, and that's out with the trash."

My body fought the urge to double over as if a fist struck my gut. Was that how he saw Neil? Did everyone see Neil that way? Had Andrew's alcoholic state revealed the hardcore truth or just a mean alter ego of the Andrew I once adored?

"Andrew, he's my husband; of course he cares about my work. He just thinks I deserve compensation that matches my time and effort, that's all."

Andrew leaned forward and rested his elbows on the desk, inching closer to me. "Skylar," he whispered, "here's a newsflash: Neil isn't the great husband you think he is. He's never shown a shred of interest in your work here until now, until it's about money. I'll consider a small raise, but what I won't consider is listening to a man like Neil. He's lucky a woman like you puts up with him." Andrew lifted his glass and gulped.

"What are you talking about?"

"Geez, Skylar, that guy keeps you locked up in a box, and

you don't even see it. A real winner you picked. I may drink a little too much sometimes, but at least my boyfriend supports me instead of just tolerating me."

Andrew's bombshell had me sorting through numbing disbelief and questioning myself in shame. Andrew's impression of Neil resonated and sharpened my view of problems with my husband. Before, they'd appeared blurry to me, and I'd thought invisible to outsiders.

Neil saw Andrew's flaws as well, but what about me? Both men overlooked my desires in their analysis. Neil and Andrew were driven by their own agendas, neither of which included my personal career goals. A new urgency pushed me to form my own business. Otherwise, my dreams would escape or be stolen.

chapter
twenty-eight

Daydreams of scurrying through my own office cluttered with fabric samples gave me new fervor. I knew I was capable, and Matthew's confidence in me boosted my courage when my self-doubt set in. He believed my own design firm would be a reality.

I spent my free time creating a logo and transforming a narrow corner of the living area into a cozy workspace. Matthew would often stop by my apartment after an uptown dinner while Neil was away. At first, the awkwardness of Matthew walking through my marital home tangled my nerves, but he had a way of instantly melting my anxieties with his laugh. He would toy with the logo designs, discuss marketing ideas, or sit on the floor in his suit and put labels on folders. Matthew pitched in with big and small tasks as if his name were on the door.

Working for Andrew became less enjoyable. At the end of each day, as I packed my bag, I imagined my last day with Andrew. Would I feel sad or celebratory as I walked toward the subway? I trudged through each day, closer to the final one with Andrew, closer to my own new beginning.

A small desk and a low bookcase I found at a flea market made my office feel separate from the remainder of our living room. Just seeing the office each time I entered our apartment made my arms tingle with goosebumps. Except when Neil was home.

"Do you really need all this stuff? I mean, we're losing a

ton of our living space. Is this really necessary?" Neil quipped on one of his rare weeks in New York.

"It's not that much space, Neil, and you're gone most weeks," I defended.

"It's just our apartment is being taken over by all this, this stuff. Things aren't that bad with Andrew. Would it be so bad to just stay there, and we can have our apartment back?"

Neil didn't like to be inconvenienced. He liked things a certain way. I would be lying if I didn't recognize Neil's disdain for my desk and my dreams. He viewed the change as an "invasion of his space" rather than an expansion of his wife's blossoming career.

"You know his drinking isn't going away, Neil. I know I can be successful if I open my own firm, and I've had some great feedback from clients. In fact, one of them is helping me set up my business as a favor."

"Who's helping you? I can help you, Skylar. You don't need anyone else." Neil's tone changed as he enunciated each word clearly.

"The guy whose apartment I just finished, Matthew Cherning. He owns a real estate business, and he thinks starting my own firm is a no-brainer," Uttering Matthew's name in front of Neil made my stomach flip from nerves. Would my words reveal Matthew wasn't an ordinary client? As his name fell out of my mouth into the conversation, I regretted it. Matthew felt safer without Neil knowing about him. I wished I could take it back and keep Matthew to myself, far away from my marriage and Neil's grumbles.

"I don't need another man helping my wife. I can help you just fine."

"Neil, you don't know anything about running a business. You're a computer guy. This man can really help me set myself up for success."

Neil flung his glass in the sink and stomped toward the bedroom. As he walked past me, I whispered, "I just want us to be partners in my career endeavors, not only yours."

He continued past me and the faint words I had struggled to share without him stopping before slamming the bedroom door behind himself. I sank into the sofa, replaying the conversation in my head, wondering where it went wrong. Envisioning my own company up and running hurled me closer to my dream yet further from a comfortable marriage.

The following week was rough for Andrew. His partner confronted him about his excessive drinking, but Andrew only spiraled into more drinking rather than heeding the advice. I waited for a sober moment, giving Andrew one last chance to recognize my value and increase my salary. The moment presented itself on the first warm spring day. We had a client meeting in the Hamptons that required over an hour of driving time. We would be alone in the car.

"Morning. You have the Wellister file?" I asked as he climbed into the car beside me.

"Yup. Right here," Andrew said. He lifted the large canvas tote as evidence.

"Great. All the client meetings have been confirmed for the day. We are on a tight schedule today," I said.

Andrew resembled his pre-binge drinking self, with his shirt neatly pressed and the stubble gone from his chin. As we merged onto the Long Island Expressway, I inhaled and prepared for another confrontation with Andrew. Just thinking about it caused a ripple in my stomach and beads of sweat on my upper lip.

Andrew's attention was on the road, but at least I knew he would be sober for the conversation.

"You know, I want to just circle back about getting a finder's fee or percentage of the clients that I refer to the firm."

Neil's voice boomed in my head: "Speak up for yourself.

He's taking advantage of you. You can't let people walk all over you." His voice had both encouraged me and scared me. Neil had pressured me to come home with a win. I wished his passion included watching me create my own firm instead of viewing it as an interruption to his life, an intrusion he couldn't support.

Andrew's eyes flew at me as my words hit the air.

"Skylar, don't you think that's a lot to ask? I mean, I've had my firm for, what, over twenty years, and you've been working for me for a few months? I hardly think you deserve more than what I'm already paying you."

Ouch. Maybe the absence of alcohol agitated him even more. The realization that he placed no value on my efforts hurt. I inhaled deeply, regrouping while wondering if he remembered our recent conversation on the topic. "Well, I guess what I'm saying is those clients would not have found you if not for me, so . . ."

"Skylar, you don't know that. That's ridiculous. They come for my talent. My reputation, not yours. Stop listening to that greedy husband of yours." Andrew balked.

My back was soaked with sweat. I gripped the seat tightly, hoping it could ground me. I heard Neil in my head: "Fight, Skylar. Fight." My fear of confrontation seized my words, and I reconciled my loss as a survival technique. "Keep the peace" was the mantra that won.

Andrew ignored me, busying himself with superfluous phone calls. The car careened down the expressway, every slight bump in the road jostling my queasy belly. By the time we arrived in the Hamptons, I had decided to resign, and the only questions were how and when I would give my final notice to Andrew.

After a long day of back-to-back meetings, we arrived in Manhattan after dark.

"What a day," Andrew said. "I'll see you tomorrow."

I reminded myself he was a barely functioning drunk. My mind flashed to the time he became unleashed while I was on the phone with a client because I mispronounced the word "damask." Apparently, I accentuated the wrong syllable. I used his recent anger toward me to keep me from procrastinating and telling him I was leaving.

"Actually, Andrew, I think we need to talk about that." I surprised myself with such a bold leap, but I knew I needed my freedom.

The streetlamp gently illuminated his face, and a sadness rolled through me. I didn't want to leave Andrew, but resigning seemed the only path to my destiny.

"I think it's time for me to move on. It's been great working with you, but I just think it's time."

Andrew stood stone-faced, then let out a raucous laugh. "Oh, Skylar. Don't be so dramatic. Please, you can't leave me. I mean, where would you go? What would you do? That's ridiculous. I'll see you tomorrow." He turned away.

Rage surged within me, and my heart quickened, leaving me breathless. Ridiculous? Where would I go? Had he gone insane? I imagined grabbing the lapels of his cashmere coat and shaking him until he grew dizzy.

"Andrew," I said as I grabbed his arm before he went too far. "I've done a lot for you, and I'm a great designer. I actually care about the clients. I've had enough of your disrespect. I'm done. I'm done picking up the pieces while you're off drinking. I am done."

His mouth gaped open in shock.

chapter
twenty-nine

Matthew had once disguised his daily phone calls as work-related, but now he didn't bother with the false appearances. His enthusiasm and genuine interest in my daily tribulations fed me when Neil couldn't be bothered and belittled my efforts. I wondered why Matthew invested his time in my little nothing firm. Why did he care about the computer program I chose or my silly business cards?

I juxtaposed Matthew's supportive advice against Neil's fits of disgust that I didn't work things out with Andrew. Despite having pushed me to ask for a raise, he seemed angry that I'd taken the extra step of quitting. Preoccupied at work, Neil had no interest in or time for the details of my "little project," as he put it.

Neil's drive to obtain a level of financial success that would far outshine his father's meager earnings eclipsed anything blocking his path. After I had met Matthew, I had realized how Neil growing up in a family that lived paycheck to paycheck had affected his behavior. Matthew was more comfortable in his own skin, unconcerned with proving his success.

Perhaps Matthew's life lessons had shaped his perspective. He seemed older and wiser than Neil. He saw the panoramic view of life and had less focus on the tiny parts that make up the sum. His genuine support and philosophy were dangerously attractive.

Matthew and I ticked down a checklist of tasks necessary

to launch my firm, acutely aware of the steamy emotions bubbling beneath the surface. Inevitably, there was a brush of a hand or a swipe of a loose tendril of hair that set fire to my chest. I wondered if he felt the same burn. His hugs were not quick anymore, and his eyes lingered longer than appropriate. My daily routine now incorporated Matthew. A call, a quick lunch, and with Neil's increasing absence, I had plenty of time for setting up my new company.

Matthew's words calmed the overwhelming self-doubt Neil had planted in my head. I easily imagined a life with Matthew, and the daydreams scared me. I knew the truth, the reality of our lives, yet saying goodbye each day pained me. He brushed my cheek with his knuckle, and our eyes often locked before I dropped my head, disengaging from the connection that emerged naturally between us, afraid of what would follow.

I cherished his drawn-out goodbye hugs, squeezing me so tightly that I thought he would never let go, and I knew letting go wasn't easy for him, but he had to. Matthew added light into my life when I had never even realized it was dark.

Four days passed without a call or text from Matthew. Had I done something? Said something to offend him? Was he busy with work? Had he met another woman? Ugh. Listen to me. "Met another woman?" As if I was his woman? I felt like I was back in the dating scene, struggling with the games that were previously absent between Matthew and me.

I missed talking to him, telling him about my day, hearing about his. I missed his company and his support. I sent him a short text, and a week plodded by, but still no word. On the eighth day, my cell rang on my way to work.

"Hi there." Matthew's voice was upbeat.

My heart swelled from the sound of his voice. "Hi there," I replied.

"How've you been?" he asked.

"I'm good. And you? Where have you been all week? You've been MIA." I melted into the phone.

"Busy. Trying to get it all done. Travel, deadlines, you know."

"I hear you." I heard the crisp edge to my voice. I recoiled from this new stilted dynamic between us. I was hurt and a bit annoyed. In the past, he'd pushed deadlines and meetings aside, making time for me. The choppy conversation felt like words being lassoed, chased, and wrangled.

"So, can we, uh, grab a drink this week?" he gingerly inquired.

"Sure."

"Thursday?" he asked.

"Thursday," I confirmed.

"Okay, I've got to run," said Matthew.

"See you then."

As I placed the phone on my desk, my gut told me my relationship with Matthew had changed.

He was not my boyfriend. I was married, and our friendship was certainly unconventional. I had no right to have any expectations. Maybe he was just busy. I forced optimism and refused to contemplate the fact that Matthew might be moving past me. I knew there had been a shift, but I buried my unease, focusing on my goal, which I would reach with or without Matthew in my life.

I appreciated how Matthew had enriched my days with smiles, rushes of heat, and deep conversations where I felt safe sharing thoughts about life I never said out loud. The flirty phone calls and daydreams and meetings where we struggled to restrain ourselves were on the brink of disappearing.

Matthew's interest in my daily routine only highlighted Neil's self-involvement. He was completely caught up in his project on the West Coast, which he reminded me was far more important than my "little business venture." My confidence waned with his words. I played a dangerous game comparing the two men.

I hadn't seen Matthew in days, and an uneasiness caused clammy palms. I clasped my cell phone from the moment I woke, anticipating Matthew's call. Scurrying through the D&D building, I continually checked if I had missed any calls. Finally, the phone rang around two, and my jitters erupted.

"Hey, Sky. How's it going?" Matthew asked.

"Pretty good. Super busy shopping for clients today. How's your day?"

"Actually, it's been crazy. Unfortunately, I need to cancel."

My hopes fell like a rock off a cliff. I paused, swallowing my tears, hiding them away as a married woman should. "Totally fine. I get it." I was stoic.

"Yeah, just a lot going on here. Maybe next week?" he asked.

"No worries. Maybe next week," I said.

As I clicked the end button on the phone, I collapsed onto a silk sofa on the eleventh floor of the D&D. My phone buzzed again, and I reluctantly answered.

"Sky?" It was Matthew. "I hated that conversation. I want to be honest with you. The truth is, staying away from you is my only option here. I want more, and I think about it all the time. I know it's not fair. I know you're married. I know it all. My feelings are growing . . . I feel myself falling, Skylar, and I can't. You can't," he said.

My stomach fluttered at hearing that he felt the same weakness. I knew it was wrong, feeling this disappointed, but I also knew my emotions told the truth. It amazed me how, without a single passionate kiss or a romantic evening, my feelings for Matthew ran deep. His drifting from my life had pained me in a way I had never experienced. I tilted my head back, trapping the pools of tears in my eyes as long as possible.

"I know," I whispered. "You're right."

The following week, I officially launched Skylar Pearce Designs. As I assembled binders and arranged catalogs in alphabetical order, I thought about Matthew and yearned to share my news. He was my go-to person for my daily accomplishments and struggles, and I missed him.

I chuckled to myself, imagining Matthew attempting any organization. He was a piles-of-clothes-on-the-floor, dirty-dishes-in-the-sink kind of guy, the opposite of my life with Neil. The disorder was refreshing and so very human, relaxing compared to the upkeep of perfection.

I missed him interrupting my daily life, and I could have used his positivity as my nerves amplified my self-doubt. My emotions toward Matthew vacillated between sadness and anger—anger because I wanted something I couldn't have, sadness because of how deeply I missed it. I felt like a fool, feeling deep emotions for another man while married.

Could I be falling for him, too? My mind raced with questions about love and falling in love, and the only person I wanted to share my thoughts with was Matthew. I'd intertwined my life and possibly my heart with a man that wasn't my husband. My eyes shut in dismay. I ridiculed myself better than Neil ever could.

Neil was in San Francisco again for the "final push" of their new product launch. I had been hearing "final push" for six months, like he was delivering a baby. I conjured an image of Neil in stirrups on the labor and delivery floor, sending that stupid project flying out of his ass. It wasn't that I didn't understand the magnitude of Neil's work, but his intensity could be comical.

Andrew was in my rearview mirror, getting smaller as the days passed. I hadn't realized how much negative energy he'd generated. His spiral downward had been fast and steep, but I was thankful for the experience I'd gained, and for him bringing Matthew into my life, even if it was temporary.

In my soul, I knew Matthew had entered my life for a reason. He'd opened my eyes to possibilities I would never have had the courage to entertain. In a short time, Matthew Cherning had helped me realize the full potential within me. He unearthed my best qualities. I understood myself in new ways through our honest and vulnerable conversations. Although he'd retreated, likely to protect us both, I would not regret that brief time of connection with him. I was thankful for having known him, thankful he helped me see the best version of myself, even if he was gone forever.

chapter
thirty

SP Interior Design's first client had cashed out of an entre-preneurial venture that left him with a few million dollars. Dean was in his late twenties and purchased his bachelor pad on Manhattan's Upper West Side for just under two million dollars.

The pre-war building displayed ornate architecture with an intricately carved white marble lobby providing as much warmth as a courthouse. The archaic elevator was confining and rocked like a boat as I stepped inside.

Exiting on the eleventh floor, I detected the smooth scent of marijuana wafting around me, intensifying as I approached Apartment D. I extended my finger toward the small, worn buzzer and pushed. Nothing. I tried again. Nothing. I lifted my fist, but before I could knock, it opened. A cloud of smoke puffed into my face.

"Heeeeeyyyyyy!" Dean drew out the phonetics, display-ing his tooth-filled grin. Curly blond surfer-like locks bounced against his shoulders as he moved. "C'mon innnnn!"

My uniform of black boot-cut pants with a matching blazer seemed formal amongst the mattress lying on the floor and mismatched bean bag chairs. My eyes scrutinized the space, promptly noticing a red bong on a small chrome bar flanked by black leather stools that had possibly been stolen from a seedy bar. Dean plopped himself into the bean bag chair.

Massive canvases coated in vivid graffiti art covered the

walls. Dean leisurely turned around, joining me in contemplating the paintings.

"Wow. These paintings, they're incredible! Where did you find them?" I asked.

"Aren't they awesome? I bought them in LA. The artist is incredible, right? Zander Jones Lanspo. He's the man."

Curled up in another bean bag chair was an attractive brunette dressed in a stunning designer pantsuit. She had kicked her heels off, exposing her cherry red toenails. Dean's baggy jeans and a white T-shirt complimented his bare feet perfectly.

"Sooooooo," Dean drew out the one-syllable word like pulling taffy. "What's up?"

"So, for a start, are we keeping any of this furniture?" I gestured toward the generic wood table.

"Just the art." He began to laugh with this comment. He looked at the girl, and they both laughed for a bit as the weed kicked in.

"Babe," she moaned between her laughs, "what's so funny?"

"I'm going to take some measurements. Can I start in the bedroom?" I asked.

"That's cool."

I measured the room and could hear Dean saying goodbye to the woman. A few minutes later, he joined me in the bedroom.

"That's my girlfriend for, like, almost a year, I think, but I, I don't know. I may need to break up with her." Dean chuckled a bit. I remained focused on my work and continued into the living room for more measurements. Dean followed close behind. "I mean, she's a lawyer and smart and everything, but, I mean, she's hot. She's definitely hot."

I listened and nodded, focusing on my pencil flying across the graph paper in my arms, wondering why his love life had anything to do with me.

"I mean, the sex is great; we have a lot of fun. I just don't know. What do you think?"

I looked up from my pad. "Me? Are you asking me?" I had seen clients cross boundaries with Andrew, but this was a first for me. Dean's eyes were now merely slits. "Are you in love with her?"

He bowed his head and closed his eyes. "I'm not sure. What is love really?" Dean lifted his head. "How can you ever really know?" He had a point.

"It's funny," I said. "I've asked myself the same question. Is love born out of the history you share with someone? Is love loyalty from knowing someone for a long time, or is it a comfort that allows us to be the best version of ourselves? I don't really know the answer."

Dean's questions brought Matthew to mind. While Neil grumbled at the thought of my new firm, Matthew had pushed me toward my dream. Two of his friends had already called to set up meetings.

I thought I loved Neil, and maybe I was unfairly comparing a long-term relationship to the excitement of something new. But weeks after I'd last seen him, my feelings for Matthew still ran far deeper than a crush or lust. Perhaps this was an emotional affair. It would wane in time because Neil was my family. He was the steady voice of reason when my head floated away, as he liked to say.

I pulled my thoughts back to the apartment. "Let's talk about some details about the design," I said to Dean.

"You're married, right?"

"Yes, I am."

"I mean, this chick is pressuring me to take it to the next level, and I don't know, man; I don't think I'm ready for that."

"I think love is a gut feeling. Does she feel like a true partner? Do you support each other through your hopes and dreams? I think that's important, don't you?"

"I think we do. I mean, I don't really know. We don't really talk about that stuff. We have a lot of fun together, but goals and dreams? It's just not like that, but you're right, it really should be." Dean slumped into a beanbag chair. "The artwork, it's got to stay."

"I think so too. How else can a relationship last after all the newness fades? I visualize the art as the most important part of the apartment. Clean, allowing the primary colors of the art to take center stage," I said, refocusing on my role as designer.

"Skylar, come over here. C'mon," Dean patted the blue bean bag next to him as if he were beckoning a dog. I obliged and fell into the soft "chair," almost rolling onto the parquet floor. Dean reached for the bong next to him and filled the metal bowl with marijuana.

"Okay, Skylar. It's your turn," Dean held an orange lighter in one hand and the bong with an outstretched arm toward me in the other.

"Oh, I'm good. But thank you. I'm really fine."

"Skylar," his sing-song tone taunted me. "C'mon. It will be fun. We'll hang out. And talk. Get to know each other. It'll be fun."

"No, no, thank you," I insisted.

My first client, and he was pressuring me to get high with him? This was not in the job description I'd imagined. Matthew and I would have had quite a conversation about this if he were still in my life.

"Just take a small hit. It's mild," he said.

I thought about my reputation, how others would perceive me if it ever were revealed that I'd smoked marijuana with a client. I scrolled through the pros and cons. Pros: it would please the client; this is my first real client, so I need to make him happy; securing my relationship with Dean could lead to lots of referrals. Cons: it could hurt my reputation and cause potential embarrassment; it was unprofessional for sure.

Dean lit the weed in the bowl, and I again refused, saying, "Well, the art is enormous and in primary colors, so I don't see how it couldn't steal the show!"

Dean laughed loudly. "I'm glad we are on the same page," he said.

I pitched my vision of keeping the all-white walls in the apartment and creating interest through layered textures and variations of white. Dean bought into the plan, and I envisioned the design in my head.

"Yeah. It'll be super cool. So, what am I doing about Melissa?"

I stared blankly back at him. "Melissa?"

"Yeah. Melissa."

"Who is Melissa?"

"Melissa!" Dean yelled while laughing. "The girl. You know, who was here before?"

"Oh! Melissa! Yes, okay. Sorry. What about her? If you don't feel like she's your partner and you guys don't talk about goals and dreams, I think taking it to the next level would be challenging."

Dean shuffled his feet as we walked toward the door. "Yeah, you're right, Sky. Hopes and dreams, that's the important stuff. I agree."

I stumbled into our pitch-black apartment around midnight.

"Where were you? I tried calling you." Neil's voice was hoarse from sleeping.

"Sorry," I whispered.

A crash followed a bang as I knocked over a floor lamp in the darkness.

"What time is it?"

"I think around eleven."

"Skylar, you're being so loud. Is this how your new business is going to be? Coming home late? I have real responsibilities. Unlike you, I don't just pick pretty paint colors. I'll be writing code all day tomorrow. You know, thinking and stuff."

"Is that what you think I do all day? Eat bonbons and point to colors?" I asked.

Neil forcefully rolled over, turning his back to me, and huffed a few times for effect.

I lay in bed, struggling, searching for sleep through my anger. Squeezing my eyes shut, counting to ten, then twenty, then fifty, trying to slow my mind.

My blood whooshed as the pace of my heartbeats increased. Is that what Neil thought of my career? Maybe he was just irritable from the constant travel and time change. Maybe he didn't really mean it. But maybe he did. It wasn't the first time he'd insinuated my career was a luxurious hobby that required no effort or ability.

I tried rationalizing his snarky remark, but underneath the layers of denial, I could feel the truth. I could sense his dismissal of what I took seriously. He never appreciated how much I enjoyed helping my clients, building relationships with them, and creating a unique space that I dreamed up.

He focused on the frivolity of interior design, not the power I had in my role as a designer. Neil equated compensation with value. Did he not value the work I was doing because of the salary? I knew the money would come if I was happy in my career, and I believed in my talent and training. There was no question in my mind about my ability.

I drifted off despite being furious, and my dreams were vivid. I pictured myself sitting in the middle of an empty room with two windows positioned on opposite walls. Peering in one window was Matthew, and in the other was Neil. Neil wore the suit he wore on our wedding day, and Matthew was in his basketball clothes. Their mouths were moving, and Neil made grand gestures with his hands toward Matthew, but I couldn't hear the words. Everything was silent despite the moving lips and arms. Matthew's demeanor remained controlled as Neil's gestures grew larger and more dramatic when the floor beneath me turned to sand, and I sank steadily until my nose and mouth were covered. I felt the lack of breath in my sleep but remained paralyzed and unable to wake from the dream. Finally, my eyes fought their way open, and I gasped for the air I'd been deprived of. I wheezed and squealed as panic overcame me.

"Could you keep it down? It would be nice if you had some consideration for me. It's not often I'm home during the week, so when I am, it would be nice if I could actually get a good night's sleep. You already kept me up late," Neil barked from the far side of the bed.

I rolled my eyes in the dark and slipped out of bed, tiptoeing across the apartment toward the kitchen. I glanced at the Tiffany clock, a wedding gift from Neil's aunt Millie. Two forty-five. I replayed bits of my dream, searching for some inner meaning. My coughing had begun when my voice and breath had been taken away, and I knew I couldn't let that happen in real life. If Matthew were there, he would be worried about me, not annoyed that my coughing disturbed his sleep. Matthew agreed interior design wasn't a hobby or a game; it was my career. A career worth fighting for even if I was up against my own husband.

chapter
thirty-one

I would never turn away business, especially a referral, so when William Parri contacted me with his formal business attitude on display, I worked to soothe him.

A television executive, William boasted an ego larger than those of the on-air talent. It pained him to fraternize with hired staff such as myself. The apartment he'd purchased was anything but low-key, likely an attempt to equally impress friends and women. Manhattan's newest, most buzzed-about building was nearly complete with two soaring towers, a luxury hotel, high-end retail space, luxury apartments, and the headquarters of a major television network. Apartments sold rapidly due to the fantastic location.

"We'll meet in the new apartment," he demanded. "Construction is ongoing, but it's far enough along to see the space."

The opportunity to preview the building triggered my creativity and imagination. The buzz had been going strong for months, an accomplishment in Manhattan's fast-paced real estate market. I gushed to Neil about the opportunity to design an apartment in such a building. Without my daily calls with Matthew, I had turned to Neil, engaging in conversations that were missing in my life. I had hoped he would show me we could develop meaningful connections around the excitement of my new business.

"It's a little ostentatious, don't you think, Sky? I mean, this guy is only buying this apartment to say he lives in that expensive building and impress people. You sure you want to be a part of that scene? Personally, I think it makes you seem kind of, I don't know, shallow, don't you think?"

I inhaled a deep breath, calming my anger and frustration, closed my eyes, and exhaled before I spoke. I was really trying with Neil, but his negativity deterred me. It was almost like he was trying to push me away with his constant badgering.

"Shallow? Are you judging me based on who hires me? That's kind of shallow if you ask me." I doubted if he would ever understand or respect my career. I appreciated the opportunities this ostentatious building could provide my budding firm. I would prove Neil wrong, push myself to succeed. Maybe this would be the apartment featured in a magazine. Everyone was dying to get a peek inside, including me.

When I arrived at the building, the sun shone bright, and rays bounced off the towers, illuminating the roundabout far below. Only a few pedestrians surrounded the towers since the retail portion of the project was far from completion. Door men and security guards stood at attention in the modern lobby.

Despite the fanfare of the building, its exclusiveness matched William's persona. Like choosing the perfect car or wardrobe, clients' apartment buildings reflected their personalities. Big egos meant high-profile addresses and high-profile buildings. Unconcerned about impressing others, most single guys I knew didn't live in flashy buildings. William wasn't most guys.

I watched him parade through the large glass doors of the building's entry from my seat in an uncomfortable modern chair in the sun-soaked lobby.

"William?" I called as he approached.

His head jerked my way, and his eyes compressed to slivers for a moment. "Skylar, I presume?" he countered in a most serious tone.

William's black ensemble screamed New York City the

way a Stetson hat screams Texas. From the black leather jacket to the black Converse All Stars, William was head-to-toe darkness. He shaved his salt-and-pepper hair in the back, keeping it long in the front, a style typical of a much younger man.

"Let's head upstairs," he said curtly.

No smile. No smirk. No pleasantries.

"I have a lot to review with you," he snapped.

His demeanor jittered my nerves, which I hid well. As the elevator doors parted on the twenty-third floor, I assumed a spectacular view would be included in his multi-million-dollar acquisition. William led the way as I trailed his black silhouette.

"You must be pleased the construction is almost complete," I chirped. Positivity poured from my mouth, only to be met with silence.

My palms sweated from his less-than-welcoming demeanor, but I kept telling myself I could handle it. This was just part of the job sometimes.

William dug in his front pocket for the key, and my cell phone whirred in the depths of my handbag. William snapped his head around, rolling his eyes. I ignored the ringing.

"The apartment is great. Lots of sunlight."

"You've only seen the foyer, Skylar. I think it's too soon to comment," he retorted, not bothering to face me.

I switched to recovery mode. We ambled around the corner.

"This is the powder room. I want all new tile, wallpaper, lighting, mirror, and faucets." Despite the high-end finishes, he demanded they all be replaced with customized pieces. "Living room needs lighting, wallpaper, sound system, television, furniture, pillows, and area rug." Men like William knocked me off balance, reminding me of how Neil left me wobbly at times with his judgments. It was just a symptom of perfectionism. It was never personal—hurting someone was never their intent—they just liked things a certain way.

William's sharp voice brought me back to his apartment.

"My bedroom. Bed, lighting, bedding, night tables, wallpaper or upholstered walls . . ."

"Guest bedroom. Bed, lighting, paint, night table, bedding."

My pen was flying across the page, taking notes like a presidential secretary.

"Primary bathroom, towels, new mirrors, new faucets—these are disgusting—and lighting."

I remained silent, demonstrating my focus.

The apartment's high ceilings and wide hallways were gracious and contemporary. Brazilian walnut floors with dark staining were laid in a stunning herringbone pattern. White marble, accented with black veining, was slathered across every surface in the bathrooms. The floor-to-ceiling windows welcomed ample sunlight and invited Manhattan's cityscape inside. My career provided access to Manhattan's premier apartments, and I was rarely impressed, but the hype about this apartment seemed justified. I remained professional, never letting on that his apartment was anything but ordinary or run-of-the-mill for a designer like me.

"We can accomplish all the goals you have. Do you have thoughts on style or color story?"

"I'm glad you asked. Gray, black, and white. Here are some pictures for your files."

He reached for his black leather bag and removed some magazine clippings. The top one was a black leather bed.

"I will get to work on a presentation and give you a call when we're ready," I said.

I packed up my suitcase-sized bag and swaggered through the foyer. Shoulders back, head high, calling up my confidence. "Thank you, William. It was a pleasure to meet you. I look forward to working with you."

William looked through me and nearly closed the door in my face. I checked my phone as I walked toward Fifth Avenue. Even after all these weeks, I hoped to see Matthew's number, but instead, there was only a missed call from Neil. I resisted dialing Matthew despite my fingers grazing across the first digits of his cell. Sharing tales of the incredible building and laughing about William the jerk would have been wonderful. Maybe Neil would soften soon, and then I could look forward to calling him about interesting new projects. I wasn't giving up hope.

I had already planned William's entire apartment in my head when he called a few days after our meeting. I knew I could design a space where he would feel comfortable while addressing all his parameters. But the call did not go as planned. William abruptly explained that he decided to "go in a different direction with a more seasoned designer." I rubbed my arms, and he delivered his opinions of me from a tall soapbox. "I need a designer with a reputation, a following. I'm sure you understand; this is not a job for an amateur like yourself. You're just too, how can I say it, green for this job." I worried he might hear my heavy breathing on the other end of the phone, and my voice shook as I spoke.

"I understand," was all I could utter.

I held my face in my palms and gasped from the shock of his decision. I hoped Neil would come through and help me navigate my first business disappointment.

"What's up? I'm in the middle of a meeting," he said.

"I didn't get the job. I can't believe I didn't get it. I wanted it, I deserved it, but he said I was too green and inexperienced. I feel so stupid."

"I can't really talk, but he has a point. You don't have much experience, especially in those fancy buildings. I told you running a business is more than just matching colors and stuff. I can't get into this now, but just do me a favor and really think about what you're doing. Maybe Andrew will take you back, and we can resume a normal life. I'll call you later if I have time." I held the phone pressed against my ear long after Neil hung up. The room spun, and I closed my eyes in search of peace. Matthew's face appeared, but I shoved the image aside and replaced him with the only other supportive man I could think of: Johnny.

I opened my eyes and frantically dialed his number. After the fourth ring, I gave up hope and flung the phone on my desk. I just needed one ally, one person who understood my goals and believed in them. There was only one person left on the list, and I knew the risks of calling him, but Matthew truly listened, and after all our transparent conversations, I counted on him understanding me. He answered on the very first ring.

"Hi, wait, hang on; I'm in a meeting, and I'm just walking out of the room." Matthew's schedule paused whenever I called. "How are you?"

"Not so good." Tears flowed as his voice gave me the safety I needed. Sharing emotions came easily with Matthew. "I had this meeting with a new client, and I thought it was fine, but he called and said I didn't have enough experience, and I'm not good enough for his fancy, expensive apartment. I'm such a fool for ever thinking I could do this. What was I thinking? I know dumping all this on you isn't fair, but I'm just so used to having you around, and you always help me make sense of things. I'm sorry, but I miss you in my life."

"You can call me anytime. You know that, and you and I both know you can do this. You are talented and capable. Don't let this one client, one jerk, push you off course. Remember all the chats we had about disappointments and how we learn so much more in life from failure and challenges? No one knows that more than us. You've got to get up, get tough, and get back at it. You can do this, and one day, I can say I knew her when she started her empire."

I giggled, thinking about me running an empire. I didn't need an empire, just some clients who realized how much I cared and a husband who felt the same.

"Skylar, there is no place I would rather be than by your side through your journey." His voice crackled with emotion. "But you know I can't. It's just not right, getting so close, developing feelings. I wish our circumstances were different."

My tears gushed, and I couldn't form a single word because he was right, proving again why this man had a hold on me.

"Please understand, this is not a choice I like or one I want, but what can I do?" he said.

I understood. I nursed my aching heart as I denied falling in love with Matthew.

chapter
thirty-two

My new client, Galina, began her first project with me obsessing about her second. It amazed me how many referrals came my way, boosting my ego even on the days I doubted my abilities. Some referrals were through clients I'd met while working for Andrew, and others came from showroom managers or even an electrician. I thrived on meeting new clients and watching how the relationship and design evolved.

"And after we complete the apartment, we'll head to Miami and house shop. I'm thinking on the water, four bedrooms. Skylar, you'll help me find the perfect house, right?" Galina asked.

"Of course," I assured her. "Let's focus on the apartment for now. Once we place all the orders, we can focus on Miami."

"Oh no, no," she said. Galina shook her finger at me, accentuating her thick Polish accent. "You are coming with me to Miami. At least two days, most likely three. I can't do this alone, Skylar. I need you to make sure the layout is perfect."

Galina's twenty-five-year marriage had recently succumbed to a slow, painful death, as she liked to say. I'd hid my disbelief as Galina had shared all the messy details of her divorce. She had grown weary of being controlled and let me know she began living for herself and her own passions. I didn't know the inner workings of her relationship with her husband, but Galina's strength amazed me.

A referral from a showroom manager had led her to me, and she wasted no time in starting a new life and creating new surroundings as a single woman.

"Honey, he demanded approval before any simple decision, and I couldn't live like that anymore," she said.

Redesigning the entire apartment consumed her, as it hadn't been touched in ten years. Hosting lavish parties and charity events motivated her, and she once again complained about her ex-husband holding her back. "Erase any memory of him," she insisted.

Galina explained how she'd started her fragrance business and how her obsession with scents developed into a small empire. Her tale of success wasn't without hurdles, mainly her ex-husband. As she rambled on, images of what my business might be one day filled my head. I knew it would take time, but if Galina Trebmal had accomplished her fragrance dreams, then my design dreams were certainly within reach. As I looked closer, I discovered Galina and I had much in common, and I could learn from her life experiences.

"We need to review Miami dates for a preliminary trip, you know, just to get some ideas," she said.

"Have you thought about the dining room presentation? Maybe we can place those orders this week before we focus on Miami," I urged.

"I looked into flights already. Where did I put that paper with the flight information?"

At first, the thought of leaving my clients for a few days set my heart racing with anxiety, but then I thought maybe a few days away wouldn't be the worst idea. I couldn't remember the last time I left New York, and a busy schedule kept my mind off Matthew. I agreed that two nights in Florida would be a worthwhile and adventurous business trip, and Galina joyfully clapped her hands when I shared the news.

Neil thrashed and pouted when I delivered the details, but I knew Galina's project would advance my career and my portfolio. A new project in Miami sent tingles up my back in excitement, but Neil didn't share in my enthusiasm. Engaging in his negativity would only bring me down, so I listened while silently telling myself I'd made the right decision. He grumbled some more, but I ignored his discontent.

Galina rattled off the itinerary as the taxi jerked along in the stop-and-go New York traffic to the airport.

"We land at five thirty, then dinner at eight with Oliver, who I met at a convention years ago. You'll just love him. Tomorrow, we'll meet for breakfast at eight thirty sharp and have our first appointment with the relator at nine thirty."

I rubbed my knees, wondering when I would squeeze in necessary calls to Neil and other clients.

The sun blazed the following day, and Galina's excitement grew with each house tour. Each home was larger than the last, as were the asking prices. I preferred the quaint cottage on a quiet side street with a charming backyard, but Galina gasped at the water views and grand entry of the largest house we viewed that day. The project would challenge me but also enhance my portfolio of work, leading to clients with larger budgets.

On our last day, Galina and I scoured the design district buildings.

"Ask for the manager." Galina urged at each showroom, which only highlighted how much I missed the familiarity of the showroom managers and receptionists in New York.

We bounced around the city from tile stores to marble quarries to carpet showrooms.

"This traffic is unreal," I commented.

"With sunshine and palm trees every day, who cares about the traffic, Skylar?"

I vehemently disagreed in silence. Despite the warm climate, I couldn't imagine living in Miami.

"I could never imagine you living anywhere else," she said, "You're a true New Yorker, Skylar."

Her comment warmed me as I stared out the window at the palm trees whizzing by but dreaming of Manhattan with a gleam in my eye.

The design took shape, and I found creative solutions for the large, impersonal rooms with soaring ceilings. She loved the ideas of layering textured fabrics, replacing cold stone floors, and adding heavy drapes and heavily patterned wallpapers. Two days in Florida's design showrooms was all I needed to know that my design career belonged in New York.

chapter
thirty-three

I returned to New York with an inbox full of voicemails and two full days of catch-up work. My phone chirped as I settled in at my desk. Dean was my first call, as he had said it was urgent.

"Sky! Hey. Meet me at New York Digs offices on Thursday. I'm thinking of upgrading to a new apartment. I need your help. We can meet the realtor at 12:30 Thursday," Dean said.

"Let me take a look at my—"

"Sky, I need you. You know I can't decide without you."

His timing could not have been worse. Dean needed a wife to relieve me of the responsibilities he imposed on me, but I knew that would not be happening anytime soon. Although I had completed his apartment, he called weekly. "How do I dim the light on the lamp?" or "I need new towels" or extending an invitation to a restaurant opening or some exclusive party. Dean's New York connections placed him in the center of the city's happening events. He devoured life in Manhattan, making him a great connection for future clients.

Dean's real estate agent had forged a name for himself through edgy marketing. Unlike the old-school players in town, he catered to the young and very rich, successfully tapping into an unclaimed demographic. I arrived early, probing the realtor about his business and the itinerary for the afternoon. I hoped connecting with him would lead to interior design referrals.

We walked toward the long corridor behind the lobby, and

he said, "So, Dean tells me you're the best designer in the city."

I puffed with pride, thinking of Dean bragging about his apartment. If my clients felt proud of their homes, I had achieved my goal. "Well, that may be up for debate. But I love working with Dean. His apartment looks great. Big change from when we started."

"I know; I was up there last week. He wanted me to see his current place and discuss what he's looking to move into. He says you're the boss. In fact, he doesn't have any idea what he wants," he said.

He walked me through the lineup for the day: two lofts in Tribeca, each around twenty-five hundred square feet; three Upper West Side pre-war beauties that begged for renovations; and three possibilities in the West Village—one small townhouse and two expansive apartments.

"These look great," I said.

"Well, when I'm involved, you get the good stuff."

"I bet." I laughed.

He looked about five years older than his actual age, mostly due to his thinning hair. He was a smaller guy but compensated with a healthy ego, which he demonstrated when he cited his earnings and bragged about his "huge" apartment and "waterfront" beach house.

"The townhouse and the ones on the Upper West Side will need renovations. I have fantastic contractors, and personally, I would love that kind of a project, but some clients aren't prepared for that kind of work, as you know," I said, gently reminding him of my capabilities and hoping he could be a source of new referrals.

Noting the time, he grabbed his jacket while dialing Dean on his cell. "Dude, you almost here?"

"Just pulling up in front," I heard Dean say through the phone.

The powerful black SUV swerved against the curb, landing directly in front of the agent's office. We darted from the office toward the car, dodging the marble-sized rain drops pelting from the gray haze above. Hip-hop rap pounded from the sound system with inflated bass. How perfect.

I hadn't expected such a crowd. The driver sat next to an empty passenger seat, while Dean, his financial advisor, the relator, and I sat in the ample rear of the truck, which felt more like an airplane. Apparently, Dean's apartment search demanded a squad of advisors.

The wipers squeaked back and forth as the chatter grew boisterous. Casual comments incorporating "a million bucks" or "buy out" circulated through the cabin. As the truck careened past the Chelsea Market, the chatter subsided as they prioritized their phones and buried their eyes into the small screens. The agent gave us the particulars on the first apartment.

"Twenty-three hundred square feet, two bedrooms, two full and one half-bathroom, a fireplace, and a chef's kitchen, and it's a full-service doorman building."

I wondered if Matthew's company worked with residential buildings. My thoughts veered from the apartment description to Matthew, who often gripped my attention at inopportune moments. I analyzed what allured me. Yes, he was witty and intelligent, but Neil was bright and cute as well. But conversations with Matthew unfolded with ease and ambled through topics that began as heated debates and ended in fits of laughter. The comfort that filled me when we were together captured my attention time and time again. Neil and I never shared a meandering chatter, and over the years, I had found myself avoiding topics and thinking before speaking due to his judgments. Feeling caution in choosing my words was exhausting.

"Skylar?"

Dean's voice extracted me from my battle within. "So, what do you think?" he asked.

"Um, yeah, it sounds interesting," I barely hid my flummox.

After a long day of apartment tours, Dean insisted we discuss his options back at his apartment.

"Wait, pull over, buddy," Dean called to the front of the truck. "C'mon," he said.

"But, where . . .?" I stammered.

"Leave your stuff in the car," he said.

Dean grabbed my hand like a toddler pulling his mother. I could barely keep up with his spacious strides.

"Gregg! What up?" Dean called across the bar and gave him a high five.

"Sky, this is Gregg. Gregg, Skylar is the best damn interior designer in the city."

"Ah, I see. Would you like two of my special martinis?" Gregg asked.

"Best drink in Manhattan, Sky. Just to get the evening started," Dean said.

Evening started? What was he talking about? I needed to go home for work, sleep, and, hopefully, a meal. I was so backed up from my trip with Galina that there was no time for cocktails, even with a client. I watched my phone light up with Neil's number. I hesitated and almost answered, but I wasn't in the mood for Neil's judgments. I could handle Dean.

"Okay. Let's get down to it," he said before my phone hit the bottom of my bag.

"Okay," I said.

"So, what did you think?" he asked.

"Well, I think a lot will be determined by location. Where do you really want to live?" I asked.

"Where do you think I should live?" Dean asked.

"Dean, I can't tell you where to live."

"What do you prefer? I mean, if it was you?" he asked.

"Seriously? I mean, I prefer downtown any day," I said.

"Don't you live uptown? Why are you uptown?" he asked.

"Well, my husband likes it there."

"You should move. I'll call my realtor right now." Dean

pulled his cell phone from his back pocket.

"No, no. Dean, stop. Please. I can't," I begged.

"What do you mean you can't?" he asked.

"Neil, my husband? He likes where we live. He's happy," I said.

"Are you happy there? I mean, you just said you would move downtown."

"You know, I never really thought about it. Neil preferred uptown when we looked for apartments, and when he found our apartment, I just kind of agreed."

"Isn't he in Cali all the time? You should move. I mean, he's never around anyway. You're not moving to Cali, are you, Sky?" Dean asked.

I swatted my hand his way, demonstrating how ridiculous both ideas were. But a move downtown was tempting. I was alone most of the time. Neil would never be open to the idea. I could hear Neil's voice of reason telling me a move would be silly.

I tried to recall the conversation in which Neil and I decided to live uptown, but the memory wasn't available. I remembered darting around town in and out of apartments available for rent and analyzing the pros and cons, and Neil placed uptown as a clear pro and downtown as a huge con.

"Well, maybe you should," Dean said.

"Maybe you're right."

"I am right, Sky. You need to live downtown near me."

I laughed. "Okay, so back to your apartment options, please."

"Yes, back to the apartments," Dean said.

"I kind of love the three-bedroom on West 10th Street. Flooded with natural light, great block," I said.

"You like that better than the brownstone?"

"Well, the brownstone is in a completely different price point, plus the renovations would be hundreds of thousands of dollars on top of the purchase. And you're looking at six to twelve months of construction." The idea of a full renovation of that scale was tempting, but giving Dean my honest opinion was more important than advancing my business. I'd watched Andrew play games in search of advancing his business, and they disgusted me.

"Yeah, I get it. Okay, well, let's sleep on it and talk tomorrow. We may need to see more before pulling the trigger. Cheers to new apartments for both of us," Dean said as he raised his glass and threw back a massive gulp as I left my glass untouched.

A muffled chime caused Dean to grip his back pocket. He unapologetically read through his emails. I watched him lift his hand, covering his mouth as his eyes grew.

"Everything okay?" I inquired.

"Uh, I don't know, give me a minute, Sky?"

With that, Dean swiftly traipsed out of the bar into the street with the phone pressed to his ear. It had been hours since I had the opportunity to check my emails or voicemails, so I made the most of Dean's absence. Three missed calls from Neil and one voicemail.

"Hey Sky, it's me . . . Called you a few times. Where are you? Alright, I guess, call me when you're free. Just like I predicted, you're just too busy for me these days. Hope this business of yours is worth all the sacrifice."

My stomach dropped, and the guilt crept in. Dean returned and ordered another drink and a shot.

"Skylar, you have to help me figure this out," he said.

He lifted the shot glass and swung his head back, devouring the vodka.

"I'm screwed," said Dean. He elaborated on the drama unfolding as his professional and personal life crashed together. Dean was purchasing several trendy burger franchises, but an electric affair with the attorney overseeing the deal had placed him in a precarious position. Clients like Dean failed to see the invisible line that separated business relationships from social ones. Matthew's face flashed in my head.

"She's hot, but she's also married," Dean confided, a minor detail Dean had omitted from the original story. It had been a two-month affair that he had grown weary of as his moral conscience awoke. Dean's situation only confirmed what Matthew and I already knew. Distance wouldn't erase our feelings, but it would remove the danger of hurting someone.

"Dean, I see her point. You went from warp speed to a screeching halt. Couldn't you have played it cool? Not made all those promises. Wooed her a bit less?" I asked.

"I know. I know. I mean, I felt those things. I really felt a connection with her. She's so hot, Sky. I mean, really hot."

"Dean! She's married. And she's your attorney. You cannot sleep with her anymore. Make nice to get this deal done."

"Look, I could fire the law firm and hire a new one. It would cost me a lot to get out of it, but maybe it's worth it. I have moments where I can't stop thinking about her, and then I think I can't do this. But I mean, if she's cheating, there's something wrong with that marriage. Right?"

"Dean, listen to me closely. You can't get back with her. Just smooth this over and close the deal."

"What do I tell her? How do I make it right?"

"Relationships are a big deal. Marriage is a big deal. Make sure you choose carefully. Sometimes I wish I had taken more time, been more mindful of my choices." My words echoed in my ears, reminding me how marriage binds. Marriage locked us together, merged us into one, and I wondered if I could find an exit route even if I wanted to.

Dean bowed his head to the table and held his head in his hands. I realized what a mess I could have made of my life if I had given in to my feelings for Matthew. I would never want this kind of drama. Neil had his flaws, and our marriage struggled at times, but I had invested in our relationship for many years, and thoughts of an affair burning it up prompted a sadness in me. Matthew was right; our closeness had become dangerous.

chapter
thirty-four

Buzzzzzzzz, Buzzzzzz.

"Delivery."

A delivery boy arrived at my door with an oversized navy blue garment bag with wide red stripes. In an instant, I knew it was from Johnny. He hoped I would someday work for him again at his fashion empire, so he invited me to his fashion show every year. I peeled open the attached note.

"Skylar, maybe this year you'll be impressed and come back. A man can dream . . . Give me a call . . . Let's plan dinner, me, you, and Matthew Cherning. See you at the show. Johnny."

Merely seeing Matthew's name on the page sent my breath chasing my heart. I folded the notecard, cramming it into my pocket. Matthew helped Johnny with his real estate acquisitions for office and retail space throughout the world. A fiery surge swept through me at imagining a dinner with Matthew across the table. I understood reality, but the fantasies never ceased.

Johnny's passion for his work reminded me of my own. I pictured Johnny on the day he interviewed me in his meager offices. His navy chinos and navy blue cotton blazer were punctuated with a red candy-cane-striped tie. The hem of his chinos had been rolled, exposing his birdlike ankles. Johnny's strides were impressive, given his delicate, short legs. Tortoise shell glasses completed his ensemble. Johnny was new to the fashion industry and hungry for success. His goal was to build a strong brand identity like Ralph Lauren had achieved. A

magic combination of a strong brand identity, celebrity col-
laborations, and high-profile financial partners catapulted
Johnny into stardom as the golden Oscar does for starlets.

"Who's here?" Neil called from the bedroom.

"Just a delivery . . . from Johnny."

I unzipped the garment bag with anticipation. Neil hadn't
budged from his old, worn-out reclining chair, which I had
relegated to the bedroom. I had to close one eye whenever I
entered the room, banishing its rips and holes from my sight-
line.

I removed the icy white dress adorned with a wide navy
band encrusted with gentle beading that matched the bag.
Johnny magically balanced sexy and elegant. I peeled my jeans
to my ankles and shimmied off my socks. The cut and color
accentuated curves I seldom flaunted. I wished I had the courage to own my sex appeal, but Neil always discouraged it, saying it looked cheap. The white cotton hem, taut against my
thighs, drew attention to my toned legs, and the deep V neckline spotlighted my long neck and defined clavicle. Tucked
inside the garment bag was the crisp invitation to Johnny's
fashion show and after-party.

"That looks . . . well, you know my feeling on those kinds
of dresses," Neil said. "From Johnny?"

"Yup. Fashion week."

"That sounds fun, as long as I don't need to go. They're
all so fake. I mean, they all act so important, and all they do is
make clothes, for God's sake. No one is saving lives or changing the world."

"And you're saving lives in San Francisco?"

"Whoa. What's with your attitude? And actually, we are
changing the world, the landscape of programming. It's over
your head, but our company impacts the world. We're certainly not playing dress-up all day like your friend."

Neil breezed past me into the kitchen, ducking his head
into the refrigerator. His family had lived on a tight budget,

and McDonald's ninety-nine-cent burgers had been a mainstay. I knew his disregard for the money in fashion and design stemmed from this, but now it grew worse with every success I had. I wish he understood how this was part of my world. I'd hoped he might appreciate the technique and talent needed for any design career, but anything in the arts was frivolity at its worst in his eyes.

Johnny was the opposite of Neil. He'd hired me just out of college, and watching his struggle toward success had inspired me. He had filled the long hours with a joyful mix of laughter and severe focus. We had brainstormed over cheap Chinese takeout and refilled coffee cups at one in the morning, but I had been happy and satisfied by our small successes. His meager part-time sales staff had implored the big department stores to place orders back then, while today, they begged Johnny for private label deals.

Johnny had tried to woo me to stay, but in the end, it had been Johnny versus Neil. Neil had hated my long hours, and sometimes he had seemed jealous of the bond between Johnny and me. Neil had pushed me toward interior design back then, yet ironically, it now posed the same issues for my marriage.

Deep in the garment bag sat a shoebox with Johnny's signature logo. I slipped into the navy stiletto sandals and walked to my full-length mirror.

I felt fabulous. My eyes closed, imagining Matthew greeting me at Johnny's show. What if he brought a date? What if he didn't even show up? I wasn't sure which was worse.

"Shoes, too? Johnny's still at it, trying to win you back? Pretty funny if you ask me," Neil said.

"Funny how?" I asked.

"I don't know. He just seems kind of desperate."

"Because he keeps in touch with me? Invites me to his shows and parties? How is that desperate? I find it flattering."

"I guess. He should just move on. I mean, he has hundreds of employees. He clearly doesn't need you. I just don't get it," Neil said.

I wished he would just say nothing rather than these hurtful jabs. I turned my attention back to the mirror, distracting
myself from the insults. As my eyes met my reflection, I stared
and looked deep and found my backbone. I'd had enough, and
I could no longer calculate my words, sparing myself the discomfort of a confrontation with Neil. Just because he was my
husband didn't mean he could take cheap shots at me.

"Actually, Neil, I do get it. I get Johnny completely. Johnny
doesn't need anyone; he's built a huge company by himself,
and I participated in that success. He appreciates me and
understands my value, my abilities, my contributions. I'm
sorry you don't get it or me. Do you even understand how
hurtful your comments are?"

"Oh, come on, Skylar, you're really overreacting. Sheesh,
these days, I have to watch every little thing I say around you.
Your business is really making you stressed out and on edge,
I guess."

I prepared words in my head but thought better of it when
I realized Neil didn't listen to or understand me at all. I packed
the dress and shoes away and grabbed my keys. "I'm going
out." My words had sharp edges.

"Where are you going?" Neil asked, surprised.

"Out." I slammed the door on my way out.

Neil opened the door after me. "Skylar, what's your problem?"

"No problem, Neil. Despite your pessimistic attitude,
I know why Johnny values me. I know why he wants to be
around me. It's really pathetic that I need to explain that to
my husband."

"Skylar, I didn't say you're not valuable. You always twist
my words."

"Whatever, Neil."

I stomped away, disinterested in Neil's response. Nothing
he could say would take the sting out of his cutting statements. Did it make him feel better about himself? Was he

jealous? His focus was always on his work. He didn't keep in touch with many friends from his past and had few friends at work. Neil had no hobbies or passions, so how could he possibly understand mine?

Without thinking about a destination, I headed to the comfort of Southern Manhattan with long, swift strides. Salt burned in the inner corners of my eyes as tears dripped down my nose. I dug my fists deeper into my pockets, clenching tighter as I replayed Neil's demeaning words.

Months of Neil's dissent had created a mountain of hurtful interactions, and today's criticisms landed like a maraschino cherry on top. I walked forty blocks before hunger overpowered my anger. I ducked into an Equinox gym for a quick smoothie and sat at a tiny chrome table more suited for a dollhouse.

My shoulders hunched forwarded. Dejected from my argument with Neil, I slid low, extending my feet far from the legs of the chair, and chewed the straw between sips. My eyes glazed over. A cluster of women poured from the gym, swarming the smoothie bar.

"Skylar!" Charlie waved as she approached. "What are you doing down here on a Saturday morning?"

"Don't ask. What are you doing here?"

"Just took a class; I ate like a pig last night. What's with you?" she asked.

"I just had a blowout with Neil. I ran away from home," I said.

She laughed. "Aren't you a little old to run away from home?"

"He always cuts me down right when I'm fulfilling my goals or talking about someone who supports me. It just happened with Johnny. I can't figure it out. His job is amazing, and he's doing great. I don't know why he can't be happy for me. It's like he can't accept that others appreciate me. I just don't get it. All I know is it hurts. A lot."

"Why don't you come back to my apartment? Maybe clear your head?" she asked.

I wondered why interactions between Neil and me felt different now. Was it my focus on my new business? The attention from Johnny? My feelings for Matthew? Maybe all the time apart from Neil? Had I contributed to this derailment? Maybe this was my fault.

"Sky? Skylar?"

"Huh?"

"I'm trying to talk this through with you, but you're just staring into space. Are you okay?"

Charlie had been spewing advice as my mind generated questions that nagged and begged for answers.

"I don't know. Neil just has no clue how hurtful he can be." I pondered whether I should come clean about my feelings for Matthew. She was my best friend and knew me better than anyone. Charlie never judged like Neil, but the shame I felt about my feelings for another man made sharing the truth difficult.

"Was it always like that between you two?" she asked.

"I don't know." I buried my face in my palms and rubbed my temples. "There's something else. I think I may be comparing Neil to someone else," I admitted.

"What do you mean? Who?" she asked.

"Remember that guy Matthew, my client from the bar?" I said, "Well, we've become close but just friends. Well, we were close. I haven't heard from him in weeks, but we talked every day, and he's amazing. I feel myself around him. We talked for hours about everything in our lives." My face flushed. I couldn't fight a smile despite my sadness.

"Oh, my God! Skylar. Look at you. You're giddy just thinking about him," Charlie said.

"I know but . . ." I felt my grin reverse, and tears formed, quickly raining down. "I haven't heard from him in weeks. And Neil. I'm married. I can't have these feelings."

Charlie wrapped her arms around me, and for the first time, I confronted emotions I had avoided for months. Matthew inspired a part of me that I'd never known existed, discovering repressed parts of myself, and I liked what I found. My sobs bubbled from my gut, riddled with fear and confusion.

"Oh, Sky. This is probably just a phase. Neil's been away so much. You know he loves you. I'm sure he's just stressed out. Let's plan a girl's night out. That's what you need. I'll start putting something together. A little fun with your crazy friends will take you out of this funk."

Neil was packing his bags when I returned home. He glanced up from the suitcase. "I have to go to San Fran tomorrow, remember?"

"Yeah, I remember," I stated quietly.

"You're being ridiculous, Skylar. You're not a child anymore. You don't need to be so dramatic. You left me alone all day, and I'm leaving tomorrow. I thought you would want to spend some time with me," he spat.

"I do. I'm sorry for running out like that. Your words hurt, Neil."

"What about me, Sky? I'm stressed out with this new product launch. What I'm working on is huge. I work my butt off day in and day out, and you don't appreciate how I grind. It's not some little mom-and-pop company. It's a major player in technology, Skylar."

Guilt worked its way into my heart. "I know you have a lot going on, too. I just don't want to fight. Can we grab one last dinner before you go?" I appeased my own discomfort from the dispute. Although I wanted him on the plane as soon as possible, I yearned for a peaceful goodbye for my own sanity. The weight of anger never served me well.

"Not sure. Let me see how my packing goes," he snapped.

chapter
thirty-five

As I dressed for Johnny's show, the reality of seeing Matthew loomed. Johnny had invited everyone he knew to the after-party, and Matthew's name would be on that long list. My palms felt damp and slick at the thought. I dreaded seeing Matthew, the awkward hello, and ignoring feelings that persisted even in his absence. The landline shrilled, pulling me from my uncomfortable thoughts.

"Hey, babe. How's it going? Another boring night without me?" Neil asked.

"Hey. What time is it there?" I asked.

"It's, uh, about two, two thirty. Everything okay at home?" Neil quipped.

I debated mentioning Johnny's show, but after our recent fight, I thought it better not to give Neil any reason to be annoyed. No more bumps.

"Yup. A-okay. Nothing to report," I chirped.

I secretly hoped he would ask about my new business, but I knew it was not his focus. Just a token of interest could have floated me through the week.

"Well, I miss you. Wait, don't you have Johnny's thing tonight?" he asked. I felt anxiety singe my chest and loop through my lungs.

"Yes, it's tonight," I said quickly.

"Are you going?"

Every year, we had this exchange. "Yes, Neil, I am going."

"Really? It just seems so ridiculous. I mean, watching stereotyped humans parading down a stage to display clothing. I mean, I guess if you enjoy it, but it seems so shallow and silly. You haven't worked there in years."

"I know you don't understand, but I do enjoy it. Johnny and I have a special relationship. You know that. I like to be there for him, to support him, and to see old friends. It's fun."

"Okay, well, you go have fun. I'll be thinking of you all pretty while I'm eating pizza at my desk and drinking stale coffee at midnight, stressed out about this deadline." Neil's passive-aggressive comments would not derail my evening.

Dressing for the fashion show, I was relieved of any wardrobe deliberations, thanks to Johnny's gift. I gazed at the full-length mirror, inspecting every inch of my body in the designer dress.

"I look damn good," I said out loud, as if hearing the words would give me added confidence.

My former colleagues greeted me as I stepped into the show. Many had stayed with Johnny, climbing to senior positions in his fashion empire. Seeing them calmed my nerves and distracted me from thoughts of Matthew. I was escorted to a prime second-row seat and busied myself with surrounding guests. My eyes wrestled with my brain as I squelched my desire to scan the crowd for his dreamy, crooked smile.

Focus, Skylar. Focus.

The overhead lights dimmed, and the first model sauntered down the runway to wild applause from the crowd. While observers appreciated Johnny's talent, I knew the incredible hours of work necessary when debuting a new season. Neil made fun of fashion, but Johnny worked much harder than Neil, overseeing a company he had built himself. A packed runway show and after-party proved Johnny's talent and dedication in an industry where most fail. It's not enough to be creative. Johnny possessed business skills that elevated his firm, and I marveled at his achievements. As Johnny waved and bowed, his smile radiated with pride. I closed my eyes, imagining what that must feel like, hoping someday I would feel that pride as well.

A tented roof deck with jaw-dropping views set the scene for an outrageous post-party. Champagne and caviar flowed, intoxicating and impressing guests.

"Skylar! What did you think?" Johnny slung his arm over my shoulder.

"Fabulous. Just incredible. I really loved it. Especially the finale."

"Skylar, I miss you. When are you coming back to work with me? Tomorrow?" he asked.

I laughed. "Actually, I just opened my own firm."

"That's fantastic! Here, I want to introduce you to a few people." Johnny led me across the exhilarating space, crossing through pools of light that created a sexy atmosphere.

"Skylar, this is Seth Middlepunt and his wife, Julia. Seth is working on a cutting-edge technology that will streamline manufacturing like never before. I'm still not giving up on you coming back. Don't worry; you can keep your own firm on the side. Whatever it takes to get you back," Johnny explained.

Seth's name sounded familiar to me. Where had I heard it before? Then it came to me.

"Wait, Seth, are you with Giotto Tech?" I asked.

"Yes, yes he is," his wife chimed in.

"My husband Neil Hessim works at Giotto."

"Yes, Neil works for me. Well, actually, there's one level of management between us. But yes, of course I know him. I didn't realize he was married," Seth said.

"Small world," his wife said.

Didn't know he was married? What does that mean? My

internal sirens blared, but I hid my emotions.

"I just hope we can find a good gym in San Francisco. I'm at the gym Monday, Wednesday, and Friday, and then we all go for coffee at The Grind next door. Tuesday and Thursday, we have lunch at Bergdorf's and get a little shopping in." His wife sighed. "I'm really going to miss it here."

I played along like I knew what they were talking about, but it sounded as if they were moving to California. Seth mentioned he was in a higher position than Neil. Maybe some of the higher-ups were relocating. A twinge of anxiety rolled in my belly. What if one day Neil was asked to move?

"Oh, I'm sure there are ladies who lunch and workout in California just like New York," Seth said.

"But Seth, what about my canasta game?"

Just when I had indulged in enough trivial conversation to forget about him, there he was. His broad shoulders and piercing green eyes entered my space and sent a heat wave rising from my Johnny Tithler shoes and through the designer dress.

"My man! You killed it. Awesome show. When are you delivering my new wardrobe?" Matthew joked.

Johnny and Matthew laughed for a bit, drawing attention from the surrounding crowd. I dropped my eyes to avoid an awkward encounter.

"So, do you know the good restaurants in San Fran? I can give you a fabulous list," Seth's wife asked. My head popped up in confusion.

"No," I stammered.

"Once you get there, call me. We can do lunch and explore the city," she continued.

"I think you must be confused. My husband is based in New York. I mean, he travels to California, but he's not being relocated," I assured her.

"Oh. Really? Hmmm. I thought Seth said the whole department was being relocated. Seth? Honey? Isn't the whole department moving?"

"That's correct," he said. "I think Neil is more excited than any of us. He's had enough of New York."

"I've already connected with some of the other wives, and they're deep into planning their moves. I'd be happy to put you in touch with them."

The beats in my chest first jogged, then multiplied to a sprint. Was I, was Neil, being relocated? As I paused to gain emotional balance, Matthew's face thwarted any hope for poise.

"Skylar." His voice drenched me at the worst possible moment. He leaned in, cupping my neck with his rugged hand and wrapping his other arm around my back. His eyes married with mine for a second, and he parted his lips and took a breath before placing his lips firmly on my cheek. His hand drifted down to rest on my waist. I wilted inside while I arched my back and my shoulders so I wouldn't collapse.

"Feels good to see you," he whispered.

I stepped back from his embrace despite wanting to stay there forever. "Matthew, I'd like you to meet Seth—he's with Giotto Technologies—and his wife." I tripped over my tongue, which had been partially paralyzed by Matthew's greeting.

"Nice to meet you."

"I was just telling Skylar about our big move," Seth's wife said.

"Move?" Johnny's voice pitched higher than normal.

"Giotto is moving out to San Francisco. I think there will be phases of relocations, but eventually, everyone will be making the move," Seth said.

Silence fell over the five-way conversation. The pumping bass and blaring treble took over the hush within our circle. An ache rose from my gut like a swift fist had hammered into my belly. I intentionally widened my eyes to erase the haze that blinded me. I tried to process the information but choked on Seth's words.

"Excuse me, Johnny. Where's the ladies' room?" I pushed

the question through my lips, breaking the silence.

As I speed-walked across the mosaic floors, the deafening music rose in my ears. A burning sensation singed my eyes as I fought to keep the tears from flowing freely. *Just get to the bathroom. At least get to the vestibule by the bathroom.*

Four steps from the hallway to privacy, a familiar strong hand gripped my shoulder, spinning me like a delicate pinwheel.

"Skylar! What is going on?" Matthew's hands gripped my shoulders, his green eyes confused.

"I don't know. Please, please, just let me go. You don't need to bother with this; it's not like we're even friends anymore." My words were barely audible from the expanding balloon in my throat. I tore myself from his grip.

"Skylar. I know, I'm sorry, please, let me explain," Matthew pleaded.

"Whatever, Matthew. I have to go."

I flicked my hand in his direction and ran toward the bathroom to compose myself. Locking myself in the stall, I leaned my back against the metal door, and the tears exploded. I gasped for air between gut-wrenching sobs. My breathing sped as fast as my thoughts. I knew we could never be just friends, but it didn't change the hurt in a moment when I needed him most.

The weight of every aspect of my life crashing down at once overwhelmed me. Matthew was the one who comforted me as I risked creating my own business. Then, I'd watched helplessly as he walked away. My husband, who never shared in my goals, deceived me, and the devastation hovered over me, paralyzing me.

What was happening? Why hadn't Neil mentioned anything? And Matthew. I didn't hear from him for weeks, and he acts like everything is normal? I grappled to make sense of my new reality. A rapping on the door pulled me from my mental tornado.

"Just a sec." I wiped the tears with my knuckles.

"Sky? It's me, Johnny. I kicked everyone out of here. Otis is guarding the door." He spoke gently.

Opening the stall door to Johnny's face was a relief. "I'm sorry. I was just blindsided."

"I caught that. Neil hasn't mentioned anything?" Johnny asked.

"Not a word. I mean, he's been traveling out there every week, but he never mentioned the company's plans. And my business, my new interior design firm, what about that? And Matthew, ugh, It's just all too much, Johnny." My eyes swam in tears.

"Shh, shh. It's gonna be okay. We're going to figure it out, maybe not tonight . . . And if you have to move, I have an office there. You can work for me. My new home collection is launching, and we can get you involved."

"I don't know anyone in San Francisco. I don't even know anyone in California."

"Look, maybe Neil's not sure if he's being relocated. Or maybe he will leave Giotto to stay in New York. And what's the issue with Matthew? He said you did an unbelievable job on his apartment."

"I feel like if I say it out loud, it becomes too real."

"Sounds like it's already real," Johnny said.

"We just have this connection. An undeniable connection. He feels it, too. There's something there. But it's . . . Johnny, you cannot tell Matthew any of this, or anybody for that matter," I implored.

"Of course. Skylar, you sat outside my office for a long time. You are my friend. I would never betray you. I've always believed in you. I beg you to come back every few months because I loved working with you. You're so capable, Sky."

"It's not like Neil is bad or anything; it's just there's something with Matthew that I've never felt. I'm not pursuing it. Nothing has happened, but when we're together, it feels like it's where I belong. He feels like home. Is that crazy?"

"No, Skylar. Not crazy. Not crazy at all," Johnny said. Silently, Johnny enveloped me with his slender arms.

I leaned into Johnny's comforting grasp and allowed my tension to cascade onto him.

"Shhhh. It's gonna be okay. You're gonna be okay, Sky," Johnny repeated over and over.

"I'm sorry, you're missing your party. I'm okay, just go. I know there are a million people looking for you."

"Skylar, c'mon. This is where I want to be. I wouldn't have this big party if it wasn't for you. Remember all those late nights of schlepping clothing samples, begging the buyers to write up an order? You were with me in the very beginning of my business. I will always remember that Skylar. They can wait."

Johnny's words pricked more tears. I had forgotten what it was like when a man had your back. For someone to disregard even his most important night of the year for me. To put me first. Neil never took what I wanted seriously. Johnny valued me more than Neil. I tried comprehending the weird and confusing revelation that my husband never had my back.

Not to mention, he had looked into my eyes and lied to me.

I remembered Matthew's excitement when I overheard him referring me to friends and business associates, bragging about my talent before he drifted out of my world and faded into Manhattan's fissures.

Reemerging into the packed after-party, it seemed the crowd had doubled. Matthew spotted us and pushed his way between the clusters of guests, clasping two champagne flutes between his thumbs and index fingers.

"Are you okay?" Matthew touched my elbow gently.

I wanted to sneer and snarl and scream, but I found words instead. "I'm surprised you're suddenly interested. We haven't spoken in weeks. I don't need you to come to my rescue, Matthew. I'll be fine."

"Can we talk for a minute alone? Outside?" he asked.

"Not now. I'm not leaving Johnny's party." The bubbly champagne popped and crackled down my throat. I breathed deeply and pushed my shoulders back, calling my self-confidence forward. Neil's secrets and Matthew's mixed messages would have to wait.

I mingled and drank, and soon, guests were dancing and feeling the alcohol. I joined my friends, dancing and drinking, numbing the confusion and stinging realities that awaited me. Vodka lost its taste as I lost my inhibition.

Matthew remained sidelined, and I felt his gaze. More vodka would make that go away. I squinted at my watch, pulling it away from my eyes, then drawing it close, struggling to assess the time as the dial spun. I widened my eyes to gain clarity.

Staggering through the charged crowd, I stumbled as Johnny approached, steadying me. I stared into space, racking my brain for answers in this confusing evening. I needed air. Downtown New York air. My body leaned forward, slanted through the doors as I sucked in crisp oxygen and thanked the exterior brick wall for holding my limp muscles.

"Matthew, you got her? I don't want her leaving alone." Johnny came up beside me.

"Yeah, I got her. Okeydokey. Let's get this little lady home," Matthew said.

Johnny lifted my right arm, draping it over his shoulder as Matthew did the same on my left. My tongue failed, and I succumbed to the assistance. My body spilled into the supple leather seat. I tilted my head back, meeting the headrest as my eyelids fell.

"How you doing, kid?" Matthew asked.

"Okay," was the best I could do. "I'm mad at you," I slurred. "You left me."

"Skylar, I didn't leave you. I'm right here."

"You know what I mean. Poof, and you're gone from my

life." I gestured my hands like a magician. I dozed off and woke to Matthew leaning close, stroking messy, loose hair strands from my face. I recognized my uptown block and felt the car stop.

"I can't. I can't go in that apartment. All the things we've collected as a couple, all the years I trusted him, only to realize I've been duped. This isn't a marriage or a partnership. It's been life according to Neil. I just can't walk in that apartment full of lies."

"We can sit in the car for a bit," Matthew suggested.

"Freaking uptown. Ugh. Get me out of here. I can't breathe up here," I slurred.

"But, Skylar, you're home. I know you've had a little too much to drink, but we're outside your apartment. I think you'll feel better when you're in your bed," Matthew said.

"I know exactly where I am. And apparently, this is not going to be my home much longer. Would have been nice if someone told me. You'd think I'd have some say in my life. But noooo, Skylar is a good girl. She makes everyone else happy. I cannot go in that apartment right now with that ugly, torn-up recliner he insisted we keep. I can't look at it, Matthew. I can't be reminded of how often I yielded because I wanted Neil to be happy and my marriage to be blissful. Neil thinks I'm stupid and that I'll go along with anything he says to keep the peace. I can't face all the reminders of my mistakes."

"Are you sure?" Matthew asked.

"If I go in that apartment, I will take a knife to that ugly-ass recliner and gut it beyond recognition. And I am sure when Neil returns, there will be retribution even though he's the one with the big secret. That I know." I garbled my words together.

"Lukas, let's go home," Matthew said.

chapter
thirty-six

Panic set in when I woke the next morning. It took a few seconds to recall the evening's finale. After I shuffled to the toilet, the mirror told the story in full: smeared makeup and tattered hair complemented by bloodshot eyes. Matthew had laid sweatpants, a sweatshirt, and a T-shirt at the foot of the bed when we arrived, and I'd slipped into them before going to bed. My beautiful Johnny Tithler dress lay wrinkled and disheveled. The washcloth's moisture and heat felt heavenly when sliding across my face.

"Morning, sleepyhead," I heard Matthew call from the hallway outside the guest room. I peeked into the hall. The hair on the back of my neck bristled as I laid eyes on Matthew in his torn jeans and blue T-shirt. I smoothed my hair with damp hands and made my way to the main sitting area near the kitchen.

I floundered on the sofa as my eyelids slid closed for a moment.

"I'm embarrassed." My candor surprised me. The comfort I felt with Matthew always allowed me to be myself, to say what was on my mind, and to be heard without judgment. I often buried my own truth, censoring my words while avoiding Neil's disapproval, but with Matthew, I had no secrets. The only secret was the one between us, the clandestine affection that surged within us.

"You don't need to be. You behaved. I would tell you. Coffee?" Matthew's casual tone relieved some of my anxiety.

"Tea would be great. This is a bit awkward." I endured the thick tension. I wondered if he was moving on while I ached to hear his voice. I was mortified thinking about the drunken evening, forcing him to rescue me.

"Nah. I'm glad I was there. Johnny called three times already, checking on you. Oh, here's your phone. Didn't want it to wake you."

I reached for the phone and swallowed hard as our fingers connected during the transfer.

"Fifteen missed calls! I'm an idiot," I said as my palm hit my forehead. "Great way to debut my business. Get bombed and lose a day of work," I lamented as I scrolled through the missed calls and voicemails on the phone. I leaned back and closed my eyes in anguish, fully experiencing the repercussions of my irresponsibility.

"Wow. You're pretty hard on yourself. So, you had a fun night. Big deal," Matthew rationalized. "You'll get it done."

I gripped my tea, trying to make sense of the evening. How could I have possibly ended up in Matthew's apartment for the night? Why was Neil keeping his relocation a secret from me? I began doubting that Neil and I were a team in this world, that we were in it together. I guess that's why he had shown so little interest in my new business. He knew it would be destroyed.

"I'd better be going," I mumbled.

"Let me get some food in you. You need some energy." Matthew's enthusiasm was infectious.

"I don't want to keep you. You've done enough, really."

Inside, my heart said yes, but my brain said a firm no. The thought of my lengthy to-do list overwhelmed me, but being near Matthew quieted the noisy voices in my head. Neil's betrayal had changed me, and it was time I started putting myself first.

Matthew said, "Are you kidding? I would spend all day with you if we could. I walked away from you for the right reasons, Skylar, but if I could make breakfast for you every morning, I would."

I bit the tip of my nail and looked away because the pleasure from the tender image of Matthew scrambling eggs for me before work moved me to tears.

Matthew prepared breakfast while I showered, hoping the warm water would rinse away the guilt and embarrassment of the past twenty-four hours. Instead, the silent bathroom and pulsing water uncovered hidden thoughts. Doubt snaked through my brain. I'd never imagined the possibility of a life without Neil, and now the unthinkable seemed possible. San Francisco? My career roots were firmly planted. I slid the sweats back on and met Matthew in the kitchen. He reached for my hand as I sat at the pristine table. I noted the carved basket weave on the flatware. My mother had a similar set that she used on special occasions, and I remembered the last time I saw it was at my sister's final birthday lunch.

"I'm glad you stayed." Our eyes connected, and he smiled as I bit my lower lip.

The delicious first forkful of pancakes forced a hushed moan.

"So, can we start over? How are you?" he asked gingerly.

"Busy. Stressed. And honestly," I said, then paused, inhaling a deep breath before continuing, "missing you."

"It feels too good, too easy being with you. Then I remind myself you're married."

I dropped my eyes. "I know," I whispered.

"When Stephanie died, I lost hope that I could meet someone I connected with. I don't know what it is about you. I mean, I know exactly what it is. You're smart and kind and driven. I love your passion. I love that you started your own company and care about your clients. You're different than most girls." Matthew's voice reached a crescendo, then backed down to a whisper. "And beautiful." He dragged his thumb across my chin, lingering at the base, driving his eyes into mine.

A lonely tear escaped my eye. "There's a comfort, an honesty we share, and if I wasn't married, I'd spend as much time as possible with you. It's a combination of warmth, security, and a whole flood of emotions I've never felt before," I whispered.

"I'm glad you feel it, too." Matthew rested his elbows on his knees, directing all his attention on me. His cell phone rang, but he ignored it. "I just don't know what to do about it. I tell myself to stay away. I protect myself because I know if this gets started, I—we—won't be able to stop. And I know it's wrong, Skylar. I'm not looking to break up your marriage. It's just that this connection, these feelings are rare."

"I know," I whispered. "But even when you stay away, you're still there in my head."

"You're not alone in that," he said.

chapter
thirty-seven

I spied Charlie's red sweater wrapping around her broad shoulders as I entered the cafe. I looked forward to our weekly lunches. We clucked over healthy salads, gossiping about her neighbors and her friend Gemma's wedding. After the waitress refilled our waters and retreated into the sea of tables, I cleared my throat.

"So, it seems Neil's firm will be relocating to San Francisco. He didn't even tell me; he still hasn't told me. I heard the news at Johnny's after-party the other night. Can you imagine not telling your wife you're relocating, yet everyone else knows? He kept the move a secret, and my anger just keeps growing and growing."

"Wow. That's bad. I can't understand why he wouldn't tell you. I hate asking this, but why are you staying with him? He's just so . . . dismissive of you. It doesn't even seem like he considered you in his grand plans. And honestly, I've seen this for a long time, but I figured you were happy. But if you're not happy anymore and he's turning out to be a real jerk, why stay?" Her words were smooth but felt like sandpaper. "There are better guys out there, Skylar. Of all people, you don't need to settle."

I sipped my water and let her words sink in. Leaving Neil hadn't entered my mind, but Charlie had a point.

"I've never thought about leaving," I admitted. "My family would be so disappointed. They'd never understand. And how do I tell people I'm divorced? It's embarrassing. We took vows; shouldn't we work through these things?" My words came faster and faster as my mind spun from the thought of leaving Neil. The guilt and shame from my relationship with Matthew rattled me. I would never leave Neil for Matthew, but the circumstances Neil had created and the emotions I'd developed for Matthew confused me. My tangled thoughts formed a tight knot in my head.

"Have you spoken to him?" Charlie asked.

"No. He still hasn't told me yet."

"Skylar, you can't live for everyone else. You did that with your sister. Now, you have goals and dreams, and Neil is preventing you from growing and achieving them. I know it's not easy disappointing your family, but you're building your own life. Your parents want you to succeed, to be loved and supported. Not only do you deserve it, but you have the right to have a wonderful partner who believes in you."

As Charlie spoke, all I could think about was the one man who did all the things Charlie outlined.

My body ached, riddled with secrets weighing on me. Confronting Neil about San Francisco burdened me more each day, but I feared the conversation would blow up our marriage. We needed to find the right time, the right place, for such an important decision. He gave no clues about the relocation, and I wondered when he would divulge the truth about my life's future to me. Part of me hoped this was all a terrible misunderstanding, that he needed the right moment. I wanted to give him that chance. I searched for the hope that we could figure this out and get our marriage on track, but he continued back and forth to California, carrying his secret along with his carry-on roller bag, and I plowed through my work, creating a successful business in New York regardless of Neil's impending move to San Francisco. I refused to give up and stop working or accepting new clients while I tried to define my future in the no-man's-land of Neil's deception and Matthew's avoidance.

chapter
thirty-eight

With every new client, I retreated from the turmoil in my personal life, and Pete Jandon's project arrived at the perfect time. He and his wife began the process of building a house four times the size of their current home and hired me at the inception. A job of this scale consumed me, and I welcomed a creative diversion that brought me joy in the midst of the storm around me. In the back of my mind, I hoped accepting such a significant job would cement me in New York, one more reason moving would be impossible.

The couple insisted I attend every meeting with the architect and builder throughout the project. Much like a marriage, I navigated the ups and downs as the job progressed. If my relationship with Neil indicated how I would fare with client relationships, I'd be headed for a tough road ahead.

Pete had a protruding belly and lips so thin they barely existed. His obsession with the stock market seemed more like an addiction, talking incessantly about blue chip this and Dow Jones that. Despite his fortune, Pete haggled over every bill, negotiating as if shopping at a street bazaar in some foreign land.

"Skylar, six thousand dollars? Really? For a chair? How is that possible? I am not paying this," he would rant.

I studied each client, searching for a technique that would diffuse their sticker shock. I easily identified Pete's competitive ego, helping move the process forward.

"Pete, this house is spectacular. We have spent months

perfecting every aspect. The chair is amazing. None of your friends will have ever seen anything like it. My client in Manhattan just bought that other chair you said was too expensive. That will be over nine thousand dollars by the time it's all said and done. I saved you from that one."

I dismantled his agitation with finesse. I handled clients' irritation with ease, and sometimes, I wondered why I couldn't manage Neil's discontent without difficulty. I avoided confrontation with my own husband yet addressed my clients head on, and it made no sense. Why did fear freeze my tongue with Neil? I knew I had the strength and communication skills, yet I dodged disputing with my own husband. I walked on eggshells around Neil, always worrying about his happiness over my own, but I knew crushed eggshells were in my future.

"Skylar!" An excited chirp brought me out of my thoughts and back into the Jandons' living room. Pete's wife, a perky little thing, loved her country club life and filled her days with golf, mah-jongg, and shopping. She considered herself a "natural designer," and managing her had become a necessary skill.

"I need a purple bedroom. You know it's the color of the season. All the girls at the club are talking about it, and you know how design comes easily to me. I know all the trends. The bedroom must be purple." As I crafted the primary bedroom design, I considered throwing a speck of purple somewhere, but I intended to play it off as if I had forgotten about our purple conversation. It's not that I had an aversion to purple, but her version of purple and mine were surely not the same, and I knew, in the end, she'd prefer quality over a fast-fading trend.

During my presentation, I fanned out fabrics for her elaborate bedroom. The room would include gilding, ornately detailed furniture, excessive molding, and layers of pattern. There was nothing serene about this bedroom, and it fit the

Jandons' personalities perfectly. She was all smiles as she pondered the fabrics. Understanding my clients gave me satisfaction, and witnessing their smiles of excitement affirmed my design abilities.

"Wow. These are amazing! I love this one." She pointed to the herringbone. "So, are we not using purple in the bedroom?"

I was prepared. "Well, as I worked on the design, I felt a monochromatic palate would better compliment the furniture selections we made. If you are still thinking you would like purple after we complete the room, we can always add some throw pillows on the bed." She bought into the plan, avoiding a garish purple bedroom.

The young general contractor, John, and I became close allies as the job progressed. We commiserated over the lengthy process and agreed a sense of humor would get us through the job without going insane. His long hair, black like ink, tousled perfectly over his forehead. John likely spoke with me more than his wife. He barely had time for his family with several demanding high-end projects in the works.

Because we worked well together, I jumped when he pulled me into a new project. "I just got this job in East Hampton. They haven't hired a designer yet. I think they'll like you, and it would really help me if we worked together on this project," he said.

I knew exactly why John wanted me on this large job in the exclusive beach town two hours east of Manhattan. Uncooperative interior designers made a contractor's job extraordinarily difficult, creating friction for all parties involved.

As a designer, I wanted a tight relationship with a contractor, providing a lifeline for completing my design visions. When I needed an electrician or a faucet moved, John made it happen. A good relationship with him would be the next step in building my business. When John asked me to join him in East Hampton for a meeting on Friday, I cleared my schedule despite the short notice.

chapter
thirty-nine

Early Friday morning, I drove to East Hampton from Manhattan, meeting John and the new clients at their expansive beach house. The property boasted five acres of grassy, manicured land and a small pond beside an old, abandoned horse barn. The client wanted the interiors completely gutted. New floors, windows, bathrooms, kitchen, railings, molding, paint, and, of course, furniture. It was a sizable project, as the home was 7,500 square feet, plus a guest house adjacent to the pool. The excitement of getting my hands on a project that big pushed my other problems away.

The husband, Brad, seemed smitten with his wife, Lauren, while she, on the other hand, seemed distracted by John. She cocked her head and twirled her blond hair like a high school girl, laughing at all of John's mediocre jokes.

Brad seemed clueless; John was not, leaving his gaze on Lauren just a little longer than he should have. Her white V-neck T-shirt exposed her cleavage, and her hair bounced as she sauntered before John in her snug jeans.

There was something surreal watching the soap opera unfold from afar. I reflected on my life with Neil and the taxing drama in my own reality. Resentment surfaced when thoughts of Neil appeared in my head, only fueling my rage about his company's move.

The meeting went well, and the couple asked for my contract so we could begin the transformation. I dreamed about the possibilities, soaring high from the excitement of yet another new client. As I built my business one client at a time, I was set on proving to Neil that I could run a successful business and fulfill my creative itch. The move to San Francisco loomed around me with two sizable new projects in the works. I seethed thinking about Neil's secret, especially with my business growing, but the glory in digging my career roots deeper into New York helped push California out of my mind.

Back at John's office, his smile lingered from the meeting.

"Lauren's a knockout, huh?"

I changed the subject, focusing on our plans and scheduling for the house. In three weeks, I would make a presentation to Lauren and Brad. Tile, cabinetry, flooring, faucets, appliances, lighting, and countertops all needed quick decisions. Like dominos, the construction process could fall apart if supplies weren't on the job, awaiting installation, so time was of the essence. I took my responsibility seriously for the sake of my clients and John.

I planned a site visit at the beach house, taking measurements and confirming which walls would be knocked out during the upcoming demolition. I left John a voicemail with my schedule and said I would swing by his office and grab the house keys.

I rolled in around noon, and the office seemed rather quiet. Rita, John's secretary, sat at an old Formica desk.

"Hi, Skylar. How can I help you?"

"Just picking up the key for the new East Hampton project."

She paused before breaking the silence by saying, "Um, the client is in with John now."

I looked over to John's office, and the door was closed. "When did they get here?"

"I think she got here about a half hour ago," said Rita.

I approached the door, and I heard moans of passion. I raised my fist to the door, preparing to knock, but hesitated and continued eavesdropping. I waited for silence and then gently knocked. John answered as if he was startled from sleep.

"Yes, uh. We are having a meeting in here. Be done soon."

"John? It's Skylar. Just came to grab the keys."

He opened the door a crack. All I could see was his nose and half of each eye. His body was hidden behind the door. Out popped his hand, and he dangled the key over my open palm. I shot him a look. He pursed his lips together. "Shhhhhhhh."

I silently shook my head, disapproving of John's behavior.

Throughout the ride to East Hampton, my mind stirred with questions for John. He had crossed the line with a client, but had I? Sometimes, someone shows up in your life that you are completely unprepared for, and the connection is irresistible, the feelings pushing you in a direction you know is wrong. I was in no position to judge John. I would never tell Brad, or anyone for that matter, but I thought about the collateral damage from their behavior and knew I could never be so cold. While Neil and I had hit some bumps, I could never intentionally hurt him, and I hoped he felt the same. As much as I was dreading it, I knew it was time to confront Neil.

As the project in East Hampton heated up, so did the affair between John and Lauren. Soon, they didn't even try hiding their flirting from me. We never spoke of it, but they assumed I knew everything. Meetings took on a new flavor filled with batting eyelashes and gentle caresses. They often finished the "meeting" long after our work was done. Brad was blissfully ignorant. Lauren put on a good show and never gave him any reason to question her fidelity, at least not in front of me. I could never tell if it was just chemistry and sex or if there was an actual connection between Lauren and John.

Matthew and I both felt an emotional connection as well as physical desire but never considered acting on our feelings. Perhaps someday, I could look back on my relationship with

Matthew and appreciate that it ended before it became a sordid affair.

I focused on the job and pressured John to focus as well. Lauren kept expanding the project, open to anything I suggested. Ultimately, her satisfaction with John made her a very malleable and decisive client. Maybe we were onto something if John could only keep all the wives this happy.

chapter
forty

Neil rolled in from the West Coast early Friday morning.

"Hey, babe. The redeye's a killer. I'm gonna need a nap." He planted a kiss on my forehead as I applied my makeup for the day. "What's going on in NYC?"

"The usual."

Neil emerged from the bathroom, still drying his hands with the towel as he leaned against the bedroom wall. The air conditioning sent a chill up my forearms.

I asked, "What's doing in San Francisco?"

This was our usual course of questioning and readjusting upon Neil's return. I replayed Julia Middlepunt's words in my head, the words that had silenced the party music and caused the room to spin. While I hoped Neil would come clean, I had given him ample opportunities to tell me his career plans, and each day he remained silent. I was done waiting. I played the conversation in my head like an actor preparing for opening night, wanting my words to impact Neil.

"Busy. Lots of meetings. They pushed back product launch. Always something." Neil yawned.

I leaned back in my chair, inhaled deeply through my nose, and looked up at Neil leaning limply on the wall. The confrontational words pushed at my lips and fell out casually.

"So, I heard Giotto is relocating to San Francisco. Is it true?"

Neil met my stare silently. There were miles between us. The street traffic outside filled the space, and screeching car brakes broke the drawn-out silence.

"Yes, it's true." Neil's hushed tone was barely audible.

All the pleasing and pacifying fell away, and like a quiet smoldering fire leaping to life from a sudden gust of oxygen, my anger blazed.

"Were you going to tell me? Or did it not occur to you? Maybe you don't even care if I go or not. Did you think I would just go along? Give up everything I've worked—"

"Skylar, no, it's not like that." Neil used both hands, running his fingers through his hair.

"Oh really? Really? Then how is it, Neil? How exactly is it? I can't wait to hear how you spin this one. And why didn't you answer your phone the other night? Maybe it's time to tell me everything, Neil. Everything."

"Skylar, what do you want me to do? I have a great job and a great opportunity. I always answer when you call. Now you're acting crazy."

"It's all about you. Well, guess what, Neil, I'm in this too. I have a life here, friends, a career."

"You just started your business. It's not like you've had it forever."

"Are you kidding me? Seriously? You did not just say that. I am so sick and tired of worrying about you, pleasing you, accommodating you. I'm done. Despite what you think of my career, I love what I'm doing, and my business is thriving. Everyone sees that except you." I threw my hands up in disgust and paced toward my tiny desk in the corner of the apartment. "How dare you not tell me, not consider me. Were you going to pack my bags and leave a note on the fridge to meet you in San Francisco?"

"It's not like that. I knew you wouldn't understand how important this opportunity is for us."

"When is this move happening?" I picked up my hairbrush and slammed it on a mosaic tile sample, sending a piece flying through the air. Neil's eyes followed the small blue ceramic shard.

"Skylar, calm down. You need to relax. I've done nothing wrong."

"Don't tell me to relax, Neil. I've been way too calm. It's about time I speak up."

"The company hasn't finalized anything,"

"Neil, that's a full-out lie. I spoke to Middlepunt at Johnny's party. He said Giotto is moving, you are relocating, and he didn't even know you were married. It's time for the truth, Neil."

"We're going to make this work. It's not what you think. I mean, yes, the company is relocating; I just knew you would overreact. And now it seems you are." Neil stepped closer, lifting his arms, attempting to hug my anger away, but I lifted my palms toward him, giving the universal signal for "back off."

"Get away from me. Just go away. I can't even look at you."

"Skylar, c'mon. Don't blow this out of proportion. You're being ridiculous."

"I'm getting out of here. I can't take any more of your lies or your disregard for my life."

"You're joking, right? Disregard? All I do is work my ass off for you and our life. I travel all the way across the country, working long hours so we can have this apartment in New York that you wanted and so you can have your creative little business, which has taken over my apartment, I might add. That's not disregard, Skylar. You are disregarding my life, my career, my sacrifice. How about that?"

"Your apartment? Don't you mean our apartment? And I didn't want this crappy uptown apartment; you did. I'd give anything to be living downtown, and you know that. I told you that, but as usual, you don't really care what I want or how things will affect me. You think you're the only one working hard? I've been out here figuring out how to start my own business, and you couldn't care less. You've never offered to help. All you do is sit up on your high horse, judging me and my career. If you can't be bothered to help your wife build a business, at least keep your mouth shut and stay out of my way." I started to leave, but I had one more thing to say. "You've been lying to me for God knows how long, just assuming sweet, nice, accommodating Skylar will go along with whatever works for you and your life. No way, Neil. I am done with that. I may be your wife, but I'm not a doormat. I'm not invisible."

"Talk about lies; how could you say I don't support you? I'm here. I let you set up shop in our apartment. That's support, Skylar. And this is exactly why I didn't tell you about the relocation. I knew you would freak out and be all dramatic. I have no choice; I have to move. I don't know what else you want me to say. Yes, we have to move Skylar."

"Let's be clear: you have to move, Neil. I can do whatever I choose."

Tears washed my face with each syllable. Neil's words felt like knives in my heart, and I just wanted him to shut up and stop the pain. Although we hadn't spoken since the morning after Johnny's party, I heard Matthew's voice in my head. I needed the support of a friend who understood me merely by looking into my eyes, and this was one of those moments. I rushed through the apartment, gathering my things for the day, exiting with a strong, forceful slam of the door but without a goodbye.

chapter
forty-one

While I sorted through my life's dilemma, I decided I wouldn't let Neil's plans, or our argument, hinder my career. Fortunately, a client's complaints distracted me from my disintegrating marriage. For the moment, I forged forward with my work.

"We are very concerned about the wallpaper. We want to return it. The paper hanger was here today, and he's very concerned that the paper will never look smooth on the wall. We just don't want to risk it."

At this point, steam floated from my ears and head. On top of my problem with Neil, I had a major issue with a client.

The paper hanger had broken the subcontractor's golden rule: Do not discuss any issues with the client. Only the designer. His comments would cause hours of extra work to unravel this mess.

"I understand your concern. I've used this paper many times." It was important to be confident in this moment.

"We just want to return the paper. There are too many issues."

"I am not giving up on this wallpaper. I think it will be completely fine. I can have another paper hanger do the work. I think we are jumping way ahead of ourselves here."

I remained calm but added firmness to my delivery. I hated confrontation, yet I had to manage the paper hanger. I grew skilled at standing up for myself at work and at home as conflicts became more present in my life. I phoned the paper hanger. It was time to stand up for myself again.

"That wallpaper is going to be a huge problem. It's a big mistake to use that paper," he said.

"Your first line of action should be a phone call to me. You cannot speak to the client about these things. Why is this so hard for you to understand? If you can't handle the job, then just say so. If you had called me and had a conversation with me about all this, we could have handled it."

"I like to tell the clients what I think."

"It's clear we aren't on the same page, so it's best if we go our separate ways, and I will find a replacement for the current jobs you have with me."

Severing a relationship felt harsh and uncomfortable, but putting myself and my business first became a priority. Speaking up to Neil had jarred me, but standing up for myself wasn't a choice anymore; it was a necessity.

chapter
forty-two

Later that day, I navigated the streets home after a day full of appointments. I longed for downtown and found my feet choosing an out-of-the-way route past Matthew's street. The temptation to call him was no different than Andrew with his scotch. I dialed the first few digits of Matthew's number, then tossed the phone in my bag.

I wanted to tell him about the paper hanger and my fight with Neil. I knew his opinion would calm me, and he'd support the difficult decisions I made. The phone buzzed, and I prayed it wasn't Neil again. I had ignored his calls all day. I lacked the energy and stamina to dance that dance again.

"Hello?" I answered.

"Hey, you! How's it going? Where are you?" Charlie's voice was light and airy, like summertime clouds.

"Am I glad to hear your voice."

"Is everything okay?" she asked.

"Can you meet me? I'll explain when I see you."

It was an amazing summer evening in New York, and the sun's warmth on my skin was soothing, the way it felt when Matthew was near. I chose a cozy sidewalk table where we could appreciate the downtown vibes. Sipping my rosé, I tried organizing the chaos of thoughts in my head. As much as I avoided it, serious decisions lay ahead.

Would San Francisco be in my future? Not married very long and soon divorced? What a stigma. I'd always categorized Neil as easygoing, but it had become apparent that his mellow personality was contingent on his needs being met, not mine. What did I want? When did my voice matter? Today, I'd shown Neil I would not be ignored. I couldn't always go along with his master plan if I wanted a meaningful life filled with choices I made for myself.

I caught Charlie floating down the block in a breezy floral sundress accessorized with her beautiful smile.

"Did he tell you?" Charlie asked.

"Nope, I just came out and asked him. Straight up."

"Good! You should have said something a long time ago, Sky. You've been living with this secret. It hasn't been good for you, or your marriage."

"It was awful. I couldn't hold back. The brewing erupted this morning. I'm so angry, and it feels like there's a chasm between us."

"Oh, Skylar," Charlie placed her hand over mine on the table, "I know how hard this must be for you. Finding out in the middle of Johnny's party, the whole thing with Matthew, then Neil still not coming clean, it's a lot."

I restrained my tears.

"Did he say when you need to move?" she asked.

"Nope. And I don't know if I'm going, Char. I can't imagine giving up everything I have here in New York. I can't believe he thinks I can toss away everything I've built without a thought. It's like . . . like he's assumed whatever he wanted would just happen without even a discussion."

"Skylar, maybe you're seeing it for the first time, but maybe you chose not to see how Neil treated you," Charlie proposed between bites of arugula salad.

I placed my fork on the corner of my plate and thought about Charlie's theory. I had assumed our disconnect in recent months was related to Neil's constant travel and my meeting Matthew. Had this always been our dynamic? I had thought we were on equal footing. I planted my face in my palms and shook my head vigorously.

"Shhh, Skylar. It's okay. It's gonna be okay." Charlie rubbed my shoulder.

"I can't deal with this. I don't know how to deal with this. I just want to build my business and live happily ever after. Neil screwed all that up for me. And if Matthew Cherning enters my mind one more time, I'm going to scream. I don't know why he still haunts me. We haven't spoken since the morning after I found out about Neil's relocation."

"It's better that you don't speak to him, Sky. You have enough to untangle. Adding Matthew would complicate things even more."

"The damage is done. He's already complicated things for me."

My future weighed on me like heavy snow draped across flimsy tree limbs. Anxiety piled in my chest as I pushed through the door of our apartment.

"Hi," I whispered, fearful Neil wouldn't understand me and start a fight.

"Where've you been?"

"With Charlie. We grabbed a bite downtown after work. I needed some time."

"Would have been nice if you called." Neil's surly tone made me recoil.

"It was a busy day. I had a lot going on, a lot on my mind."

"You could have returned my calls, Sky. It's unacceptable not to return my calls."

I wouldn't dignify his irritation with an angry response. He deflected from his wrongdoing, and his blatant discontent with me couldn't be ignored.

"Can we talk?" he asked when I didn't respond.

I plopped on the sofa, crossed my arms, stared into Neil's eyes, and waited.

"I guess I should have told you when they announced I'd be transferred to California, but I didn't have the details. I was waiting for the specifics. I didn't want to upset you before it was necessary. There's so much planning involved with the move; I didn't want you to stress about it. Can you understand that?" Neil leaned in as if the closer he expelled the words, the clearer they would be.

I hesitated, hoping time would calm my resentment. "I have so many issues with that statement I don't even know where to begin. First of all, you 'guess' you should have told me? No, Neil, you should have told me, no guesswork involved. Second, the fact that you are assuming we are moving is just, well, it's shocking. I have a say in this, Neil. How could you think I wouldn't want to be a part of this decision?"

Thoughts of Matthew appeared in my head. I could hear his words urging me to set higher aspirations for myself, boosting my resolve. I shoved his voice into the corner of my mind so I could concentrate on the argument, but I remained determined.

"Babe, what can I do? It's a huge opportunity. I can't just quit, walk away. Your career has barely started. I figured you'll just start fresh in California."

"Are you hearing yourself? Do you hear what you are saying? It's like I don't matter. Like my world doesn't matter. Have you been paying attention to how hard I've worked at establishing my business? I cannot just 'pick up' in San Francisco, Neil. I don't know anyone. Literally no one. How can I get clients without knowing a soul in that city? I have zero work connections. I don't know the design market. No friends, no family. You don't pay any attention to my business and how things are progressing, but I have two huge new jobs. Jobs seasoned designers would die for." The pace of my speech hastened, and I breathed as if I'd completed a round of sprints.

"It will be an adventure. We'll be in it together. I'll have work friends relocating. Maybe they would hire you. And if your business doesn't get off the ground, you could get pregnant, start the family we know we want."

Dizziness overtook my head while my tongue froze and my mouth gaped open. A screaming baby entered my thoughts, and I shuddered. My career was the only baby I would be nurturing, and Neil's comment only confirmed my feelings.

"What?" Neil lifted his palms in confusion.

"Neil, you just don't get it. Perhaps you never have. I'm at a loss for words, and I can't sit here trying to explain respect and consideration to a grown man. A grown man who took vows to support me, not trivialize me. I don't want a baby, Neil; I want a successful business. Can't you see me working toward my goal? And my business is in New York, the city I love, where my friends and family are, where I built my business relationships."

"I'm speechless. This conversation doesn't seem real. I don't think you know what you're saying, Skylar. I'm going back to California, so you can take some time and get comfortable with the idea of moving. We can revisit this when I get back. You'll come around. I know you will."

My breathing felt rushed, and I felt light-headed from Neil's assumptions. "I'm going to bed before I say something I'll regret."

I didn't feel Neil's side of the bed lower from his weight on the mattress that night, but I did feel the sharp pain of his disrespect.

chapter
forty-three

Lauren and Brad's house was spectacular when the renovation and furnishings were complete. Clean lines and a beachy feel exuded from every room. Stark whites and deep blues covered every inch of the house. Brad loved the design and mentioned thoughts of their future children enjoying the home at every meeting. I cringed. Poor Brad. If he only knew Lauren's loving, doting wife act only happened in his presence.

Lauren and Brad sent silver Plexiglass invitations requesting guests arrive wearing all white for a summer housewarming party. I knew the soiree would be a who's who of Manhattan, considering Brad's high-powered Wall Street job. I arranged to stay at a client's home in South Hampton because, as usual, Neil scoffed at the invitation and refused to attend. John was not as lucky. His wife insisted on attending the elegant party.

I hardly recognized Lauren and Brad's home as I approached. Massive tents and decorative lighting were installed for the gala, and security swarmed the property.

I accessorized my elegant white silk dress that boasted a plunging neckline with long gold chains draped around my neck. I could feel eyes on me as I entered, so I rolled my shoulders back and stood tall. I didn't know many people at the party, yet I didn't hesitate to arrive alone.

"Champagne?" the waiter offered.

I delicately accepted a flute. The tiny bubbles felt crispy in my cheeks. Brad, surrounded by his handsome friends, greeted me as I entered.

"Skylar! So glad you made it," Brad yelled over the DJ's music. "You look . . . well, fantastic."

"Thanks, Brad. Sweet of you to say."

"Guys, this is our very talented interior designer."

Brad introduced me to all twelve men as they complimented my work. When one suggested I speak to his wife about designing their new home, I realized the importance of attending client-hosted events. Brad pointed toward Lauren, urging me to say hello.

The DJ's music grew louder as I approached the pool. I hoped I would make it to the dance floor later in the evening, perhaps after a few drinks. I would never get drunk at a client's party, but a little relaxation never hurt. It was a party, after all.

The painter on the project called out to me. "Heeeeeyyyyy!" He seemed drunk.

"Nice job. The house looks gorgeous," I complimented.

"Wow! Skylar, you're looking great! You should dress like this every day." He began to laugh uncontrollably.

"Funny. Very funny."

I waved and continued moving toward the pool area. The bass pumped, and deftly placed lighting set the mood. I could see Lauren's blond hair in the distance. I caught her eye, and she smiled with delight. We had a great relationship, but maybe she was just happy I'd kept her secret.

Pushing through the crowd, she wrapped her arms around me in a welcoming hug. Her dress was short and skintight. She oozed sexy. Her hair was beachy and flying free in the breeze.

"I am so excited you're here!" Lauren squealed. "Come meet my friends."

Lauren grabbed my hand and led me through the crowd to a group of gorgeous women. Each had a smile glistening white, with teeth like Chiclets gum. Lauren rambled through the names of the women, and I knew I would not retain a single one. I simply smiled and nodded.

"Skylar! Can we discuss this dress? You look incredible. I didn't know you had it in you. You're always so buttoned up for work. I'm glad you loosened up for the party."

I laughed. She was probably right. I could use some loosening up. Her words gave me confidence in a sea of stunning women. Lauren and I approached the bar while her friends trailed behind.

"Cosmos, please," Lauren said.

The bartender quickly got to work. We toasted the new house as Lauren complimented me until I blushed with embarrassment.

"Whoa! These are strong!" I said after a small sip.

Eventually, Lauren and her friends broke away, greeting guests as they arrived. I ordered another cosmopolitan and settled in at the lounge area nestled between the house and the pool.

"Pretty lady, is this seat taken?" A man's voice boomed from behind. As I turned, John's face was above me.

"It has your name on it!"

The cosmopolitans had made their way through me, and I felt my body soften and relax.

"So?" I asked.

"So, I'm trying to make it through this night," he slurred.

"Where's the wife?" I imagined his struggles with Lauren and his wife in the same space.

"I have no clue. She's having the time of her life while I sweat it out."

I had to laugh at the uncomfortable situation, watching John cope with the hornets' nest he'd created. We laughed about the ups and downs of the project, avoiding the details of his affair with Lauren.

"Remember the time the painters sang along with Whitney Houston when she came on the radio? And then broke into full dance mode. Or when I had that explosive argument with the plumber when he refused to follow the bathroom plans?" I recalled.

The evening passed quickly, and my glass was suddenly empty.

John stood up. "Let me freshen you up." Despite John's personal choices, he did great work, and we worked well as a team. I imagined working on future projects with John and how my business would benefit from our collaboration.

"No thanks, John. I've had way past my limit."

I noticed the dance floor suspended over the pool, clear Plexiglass over water. Lights flickered, creating a club-like scene. The music became progressively louder, and the crowd started bouncing. Lauren came bounding toward me, and I nervously scanned the property for John's whereabouts. Thankfully, he hadn't left the bar on the opposite side of the expansive yard.

Lauren screamed my name, grabbed my arm, threw my handbag on a chair, and dragged me to the dance floor. The tightly packed space had everyone shaking to the remixed music. Bodies glistened from the hot summer night and near-aerobic dancing. I released my overworked mind and enjoyed the moment.

From behind, I felt hands on my waist. I laughed, thinking it was John or maybe Brad. I spun around to Matthew Cherning flashing that exquisite imperfect smile. My mouth dropped open in shock, but a smile soon overtook my surprise. What was he doing here? I hadn't seen him in months. He hugged me tight, then danced close without a word.

He took charge and guided my hips to move with his. I could feel guests on the dance floor watching us move together. The alcohol swirled to my head. I put my arms around Matthew's neck. We spun around as one while Matthew kept his eyes locked on mine. I let my gaze drift, checking out his white attire. A wave of heat crested as I looked him over. White jeans torn just a bit near the top of one knee, white Stan Smiths with a navy tab on the heel, and a loose linen shirt unbuttoned just enough to tease. He wore a short, black rope necklace that I had never noticed before. I didn't know how I could resist him looking like that.

Blocking Matthew from my life hadn't cooled the spark between us. The time away had only heightened this moment. The feverish attraction hadn't faded in his absence; it had doubled or tripled. He leaned in close to my ear, held my hand, and said, "C'mon, let's go." I would have gone anywhere with Matthew at that moment. The drinks, the music, and my arguments with Neil all put me in the wrong place at the wrong time with the right man. He grabbed my hand and led me off the dance floor, stopping behind the guest house. My back settled against the wood in the pitch black, far from the blinding white blobs of partygoers. Music pumped in the distance.

He leaned his arm against the wall above my head and, without a word, ran his knuckles against my cheek. We inhaled deeply from the brisk walk to the far side of the property and the charge between us. My choices were wrong, but the passion between us was real, and I knew the feelings were different than the romances in my past.

Matthew slid his hand around the nape of my neck and kissed me with an intensity that pulled me from every thought running through my overcrowded brain. He made his way to my neck, and I inhaled with pleasure.

His breath matched mine. He swallowed deep and rested his forehead against mine with his eyes closed. When they fluttered open, our eyes met, and smiles emerged as I traced his jawline. I laughed, and Matthew laughed with me.

"God, I have wanted to do that for so long."

My eyes shifted down. Matthew tested everything I thought I knew about myself and my marriage. Nothing would ever be the same. I was finally wide awake.

chapter
forty-four

Exiting through the side gate, we circumvented the crowds and endless goodbyes. Matthew laced his fingers with mine and walked with confidence. Lukas waited for us in the pebbled driveway.

"Let's go over to Long Beach, Lukey." Matthew revealed his drunken state, calling Lukas "Lukey." We all laughed.

We sat tense in the back seat, our fingers interlaced. The promise of that kiss hadn't faded, and spending time with Matthew away from the world captivated me. Matthew stroked my knuckles with his thumb, finally lifting my hand and tenderly kissing my palm. Within minutes, Lucas pulled into an empty lot. As Matthew helped me from the car, I looked into a sky curtained in ebony and spotted with glimmering late summer stars. As we meandered toward the narrow bay beach, the gentle water lapped against the earth, reminding me of summers by the lake as a kid. Before my sister had been diagnosed, we had spent hours racing from the beach to the lake, hurling our skinny bodies into the water as my mom hovered nearby.

I glanced at Matthew and understood not everyone has this opportunity, this gift of feeling a natural pull and connection with someone. Life careened forward after death, breakups, and misfortune, and if Matthew could be by my side throughout all the good and bad, the comfort I found with him would give me the strength I needed.

"You cold?" Matthew asked.

"Cold is not hearing from you."

"What was I supposed to do, Skylar? You sleep over, I make you breakfast, and all I can think about is wanting that morning to be my everyday routine. Our everyday together. But you get back in the car and go back to your husband. Did you ever think about how I feel? I would be with you every second of every day, but you're married, and I can't change that. When you get in that car and head uptown, I'm crushed. It takes me days to recover from the dream I create in my head of a life with you."

My frustration swirled, entangled with desire. "Why am I always drunk around you lately? This is not good. At all." I used the words to push us apart, even though all I wanted to do was mash my lips against his and climb on top of him in the sand. I pushed the want deeper, away from the surface.

Lukas jogged toward us with my phone outstretched in his hand. "Skylar, your phone is ringing."

What time was it? It must be Neil. I had to answer it. I didn't want to answer it. "Hello?"

"Hey, babe. How was the party? Thought I'd check in." Neil sounded sleepy.

His words cooled my fire for Matthew, allowing me better perspective and composure.

"Great. It was fun."

I walked along the sand away from Matthew. It felt wrong speaking to Neil in Matthew's presence. I didn't feel guilty, only awkward, and that concerned me.

"Are you back at the house?" he asked.

"Uh, no, not yet," I stammered. I marveled at Neil's ability to completely shelf our recent argument and the impending move. The relocation dominated my thoughts, yet Neil acted as if the topic was no longer an issue between us.

"Oh, okay. I'm beat. Catch you in the morning. What time will you be back?" Neil asked.

"Uh," I giggled, "I'm not sure yet."

"Are you drunk?" Neil asked.

"Maybe? A little, very little bit," I said, irritated by Neil's line of questioning.

"Sky, really? At a client's house?"

"I gotta go, Neil. I can't do this now. Goodnight." I pressed the red end-call button and hurled the phone across the beach. Matthew looked over with hurt in his eyes.

I looked at Matthew, cutting off the line of questions before they began. He lifted his palms to face me, shrugging his shoulders and implying, "I get it." He sat back on the sand and ran his hands down his face. For the first time, I saw my actions causing suffering to this man whom I adored, and my heart ached with his.

"I'm done talking about my husband. I'm here with you, and there's no place I'd rather be. I know things are complicated, but I can't help but feel lucky to have found such a deep connection with you."

"Come here." He wrapped his arms around mine, clasping my hand and placing them at my heart's center.

"So, tell me more about this booming business of yours. I'm impressed, Mrs. Pearce. I'm hearing good things."

"Are you stalking me, Mr. Cherning?"

"Hardly. You're a hot topic. Honest. Brad's been bragging about you all summer."

"Things are off to a good start. My career, that is." I dug my bare feet into the sand, concealing my toenails. Matthew sighed, and we sat in silence until he smoothed my hair behind my ears and looked into my eyes.

"It was getting too real, Sky, but tonight erased everything I was trying to avoid. You're my kryptonite. The pull is too strong. If I allowed things to continue, well, I knew where it was heading, and we can't. You know it's not an option for us. At least right now."

"I could have used a friend the past few months. It's been rough. I tried to hear your voice in those moments. The kiss was amazing, but it's your friendship, your advice, our ability to talk for hours about anything that I cherish the most."

"And? Could you hear my voice?"

"I could."

The moon was a mere shaving, giving the stars a leading role.

"It's been awful at home. I confronted Neil about his relocation, and he just simply doesn't understand. We've been arguing all the time. He disregards my career, my goals, and I'm not sure how much longer I can tolerate being in a marriage that lacks respect." Matthew listened with intent and empathy.

"I'm so sorry. I had no idea. I'm sorry I wasn't there for you. You know you have the strength to be your own woman."

"But we were friends, Matthew. You walked away from that."

"Skylar. Be real. You know we were never just friends. We may not have acted on it, but it's always been there. I depended on you, too. You understand me, and I feel safe in sharing all my feelings with you. How was that fair to me, or Neil?"

I shrugged when I couldn't find the words, and we sat silently as the waves rippled on the smooth rocks nearby.

"Seriously, Skylar, I hope you know what you've got. You're the real deal. Talent, beauty, goals, passion. Don't sell yourself short. You're incredibly capable. You deserve a lot. More than I think you are aware of, Skylar."

Involuntary tears filled my eyes as I faced a hopeless predicament. Although I didn't want to, it only seemed right to give Neil one last chance to save our marriage. I had to try with Neil so guilt about Matthew wouldn't consume me. The sun began to peek from beneath the horizon as we headed back to the car.

chapter
forty-five

On my return drive to Manhattan the next day, I secretly cursed Lauren and Brad and their damn white party. It would have been so much easier if I hadn't seen Matthew again. Avoiding my true feelings would be the only way through. I imagined a life without Matthew, and I imagined a life without Neil. Neither seemed like the right decision, and the shame of admitting my growing attachment to Matthew made an objective approach difficult. My phone whirred.

"Hey. You almost home?" Neil asked. Anxiety zipped in my chest.

"Yeah, maybe a half hour or so? What are you up to?" I buried the late-night phone call, attempting a fresh start with Neil.

"Just waiting for you. Thought we could grab lunch when you get back," he replied.

"Okay. When are you going to San Francisco.?" I asked.

"Monday. Should be back on the weekend."

"Labor Day? You need to be out there on the holiday?"

"I'll explain when I see you," he said and hung up the phone.

I turned the key to our apartment as my hands anxiously shook, wishing my nerves could be tamed. Neil's legs rested on the cocktail table, his face hidden behind the Sunday paper.

"Hey." I trudged in, lugging my duffle and hanging bag.

"Well, you look exhausted," Neil noted.

I withheld a response and darted for the bedroom, unpacking my bags. Neil soon followed.

"Fun party?" he asked from his coveted recliner.

"Yeah, it was. Hopefully, I'll get some good referrals."

"Toilet's leaking again. Can you deal with that this week? And we are all out of turkey and cheese, and milk, too, I think," Neil said.

Once again, we both avoided any conversation regarding moving. The shopping list and running toilet couldn't be further from my mind, and I knew I couldn't carry the burden of my conflicted feelings. I was in a tailspin and wished Neil understood, but we continued averting the tough conversation ahead.

I got the sense Neil assumed no conversation indicated my agreement, but that couldn't be further from the truth. I shied away from the topic as my internal conflict intensified. The thought of Neil and I splitting up over this scared me in a way that reminded me of my sister. It's the moment of knowing something in your gut yet refusing to accept it. I knew my sister's diagnosis, but I blocked out the facts in search of hope. I hoped for a better relationship with Neil, hoped for him to be a better husband, but my gut warned me of the truth.

"Yup. I'm on it." I continued unpacking my bags, gaining emotional strength for the tough conversation ahead. I pushed through the whirlwind of emotions in my heart. The pending move to California and Matthew's kiss cluttered my thoughts. Neil suggested an outdoor neighborhood cafe to enjoy the weather, and I knew it was time for me to speak up.

As we walked the few blocks toward the café, I reminded myself that Neil was my husband and that he deserved my focus right now despite my preoccupation with Matthew. Needing reminders for the obvious confirmed the state of my relationship with Neil.

"So, it seems Giotto is worried about the timing of their release date. They want me to fly to San Francisco tomorrow. I know it sucks we can't spend Labor Day together."

"When did you find out?" I asked.

"I think maybe Friday? Thursday? I can't remember. At least we have today. Did you know anyone at the party?"

"Not really. Just my guys, and a few others."

Lying was not a skill I pulled off well. But pretending life was fine with Neil had become a performance I delivered well. Thankfully, he changed the subject.

"Sky? You okay?" Neil asked.

"How could I be okay?" I whispered.

"It will be great, Skylar. San Francisco is a fantastic city. I'll have an unbelievable career there. Change is difficult, but this is the right move for us."

"My business is just getting started. I'm just gaining some footing." My voice cracked as I slid my hand out from under Neil's. I didn't want him touching my hand so soon after it held Matthew's. I wanted Matthew's touch lingering on my skin. I did my best to stay focused on Neil.

The grumpy waitress pounded the glassware on the table, shaking it on the uneven sidewalk. The flatware clanged, breaking the moment between Neil and me. Our lunch proceeded with a mundane conversation about Neil's trip and work projects. I floated above the conversation like a ghost listening in, removed as if someone else's life was being discussed. I found my courage and the words I had been searching for.

"Neil, I would never ask you to give up your career, and I don't understand how you could ask me to give up mine. You have no reservations about asking me to leave New York. It just seems like you're confident I'll go along with your master plan, and maybe I have in the past, but things are different now. I'm different now. Maybe that's what made us work in the past, but it doesn't anymore. I'm a business owner, an independent woman with a career, business contacts in New York, not to mention my family and friends." I felt the weight of the conversation lift from my head, yet it filled the air with tension.

"I don't know what you want me to say, Sky. I don't know what you expect me to do. Let's just try to get through this stuff with the apartment; then, we can figure out a way to set up your business in California. The real estate broker will come by at six on Tuesday. That work for you?"

I heard his words, but they bounced off my ears like a rubber super ball. A nod was all I could conjure. *"We can figure out a way to set up your business." He hasn't been interested in anything regarding my business while I figured everything out on my own. Now he plans on helping me?* I felt pulses of fury in my temples.

"Sky, you in there?" Neil's laughter trickled through his words, but his sense of humor didn't resonate.

"Not really. You're not even listening to me. I'm telling you how I feel. You're my husband. Don't you care how this move will affect me?" was all I could muster.

"It's going to be okay. Look at me." Neil took my face in his hands. "Lighten up. It's going to be okay. Trust me. San Francisco is a great city. I don't have a choice, so neither do you. We are in this already, so please do what you need to do to get on board."

I stared through Neil, struggling with a thousand storylines in my head. California, my business, my family, and Matthew. Each held substantial weight in my resistance to this non-negotiable move.

"Choice? You don't think I have a choice? Of course I do, Neil. Are you joking right now? Neil, I'm collapsing here, trying to make sense of what's happening between us, and you're just ignoring me in the equation. I don't know what's going to happen with us. Is my marriage ending? Is my life starting over in California? I'm trying to keep it together, but you're not helping at all. You're nowhere, Neil. You don't tell me about the move, and now you just assume I'm going without a conversation? I'm struggling here, trying to be a good wife and partner, trying to see things from your perspective, but you haven't given any thought about me. None." I sighed after the eruption as Neil stared at me in confusion.

"Skylar, you're being overly dramatic. I have a fantastic opportunity, and it happens to be in California. Most wives would consider themselves lucky to be in your shoes. I know it's not perfect, but I want you with me. I need you with me. Listen, seems like you need a little mental break from all this. Let's just get all the logistics worked out while I'm back at work in San Francisco this week, and we can revisit this conversation when I get back. I need you by my side through this, Skylar."

The six-block stroll back to our apartment was solemn. Neil reached for my hand and interlaced his fingers neatly with mine, but I swiftly pulled away, shoving my hand deep into my pocket. I felt his desire to smooth things over, yet I also felt the shards of a broken marriage.

chapter
forty-six

Sleep did not join my closed eyes that night. I lay awake yet motionless so as not to disturb Neil. Deep in the night, I noticed the illuminated voicemail icon on my cell phone. I slipped it into my hand and tiptoed into the bathroom.

"Hey, you. I could try to play it cool, but the truth is I can't stop thinking about you. Well, call me. It'd be great to hear your voice. Hope you're doing okay and still in New York."

I slid down the shower wall to the cold floor. The tips of my fingers were slow and deliberate when pressing the numbers. "Hi," I whispered.

"Skylar?" Matthew's hoarse voice soothed my pounding heart. I worked to hush my sobs.

"Hi."

"What's going on? What time is it?"

I locked the door and muffled my voice by running the shower.

"I don't know. I'm sorry. I shouldn't have called. I'm a mess. I have no idea what I'm doing. I guess I just needed you to be my friend right now and help me through this." I reached for a tissue.

"I'm here for you. Tell me what's going on?"

"I don't want to go. I don't want to leave. I can't do it."

"Take a deep breath and tell me what's happening."

"San Francisco is happening. Neil already has a real estate broker coming to the apartment."

"Skylar, tell him you don't want to go. What about your

friends, your business?" Matthew's voice lowered to a mumble as he added, "And me."

"I know, but he has a career. He can't just say he's not going."

"I wish I could take all this pain away. You don't deserve this. Did he ask you how you felt? Was there any conversation?"

"He doesn't hear me. He makes more money than I do, so I guess he figures we should follow his job. I don't know."

"You and I both know that money isn't the only factor in this decision. Moving across the country is a big deal, and so is not consulting your wife about a huge life change. Listen, it's four a.m. Can you hang on for an hour? I'll pick you up. We'll go for a run in the park."

I closed the valve on the shower and slithered back into bed. Neil's groggy head popped up, returning to a heavy snore within seconds. The smooth, solid gold band wrapping my ring finger became heavy. I slid it off, placing it on my bedside table. Maybe I could re-establish myself in California. Maybe Neil was right to assume his career should be prominent in our decision. I shoved my anger in the corner and worked to see his side, see the positives, and try to understand Neil.

Unrelenting fear wrestled my positivity to the ground. While many concerns twisted me in knots, discovering truths about Neil and my marriage alarmed me the most. Realizing my marriage wasn't based on respect or partnership shook me awake. I stared at the digital clock on my night table as the minutes passed like drips of water from a leaky faucet. My lonely wedding band grew cold without the warmth from my body. I wondered what Matthew was doing. Was he back asleep? Eating leftover Chinese? Wondering how to get rid of me and my drama?

When the red digitized numbers morphed into 4:45 a.m., I shimmied to Neil's side of the bed and whispered my plans for a morning run. I dutifully kissed his cheek, thinking only of leaving the apartment as soon as possible.

I stepped outside at exactly 5:00 a.m. Matthew's back faced me. The late August morning already had a chill in the air. I whistled to get his attention, and he swiveled on his Nikes as my feelings for him slammed into me. The peace I felt with him warmed me. He didn't need to say or do a thing, and neither did I. The chemical reaction happened regardless of where we were, the time of day, or the weather. It was just there.

"You look like you could use a hug," he said.

"A friendly hug, yes." I glanced over my shoulder, searching for nosy neighbors.

Matthew wrapped his arms around me, enveloping me. I closed my eyes as his hug seeped into my pores and burrowed to the center of my core. Matthew rested his chin on my head for a moment, replacing it with an elongated kiss on my head.

"We will figure this out," he whispered.

Tears swelled in my eyes and fell onto Matthew's shirt.

"Think you can keep up with me?" I broke the somber moment, forcing a smile.

We jogged into the park, pacing side by side. I convinced him to join me in squats, push-ups, and burpees when we arrived at Bethesda Fountain.

"So, you ready to spill?" he asked.

"It feels a little strange sharing details about my marital woes with you."

"Hey, I'm in this with you. I've always known you were married; this isn't new. If I haven't shown you already, I'm telling you now, I'm here for you. I know it's a little weird, given how we've crossed the line, but what we have is rooted in honesty and trust, and more than anything, friendship," he said grasping my hand and pulling my body to face him.

The only man that had ever been in my corner regardless of the circumstances was Johnny—not judging or controlling or correcting, just accepting me for who I was naturally. I took a few deep breaths.

"It's a mess," I began. "I didn't think my marriage would unravel like this. I guess I just thought we would never leave New York," I admitted.

"This was never a possibility when he took the job at Giotto?" Matthew asked.

"No, not that I was told. Now I'm questioning everything. I'm seeing things in Neil I never saw before. And then there's you. My feelings for you are clouding my thoughts, sidetracking me with shame and guilt that likely has nothing to do with my relationship with Neil."

"I don't want to complicate your life. I tried to stay away. I know I should stay away, but it's not that simple. You feel it, right? The pull?"

"Matthew, I'd have to be dead to not feel it. And it's wrong. But the messed-up part is I don't feel guilty. I don't know why. I'm a horrible person, a horrible wife, but it feels like you were put in my path for a reason. I don't need to pretend with you." I could barely look him in the eye as my raw honesty emerged.

Matthew embraced me with strength and tenderness. We remained still for what seemed like eternity with the world around us frozen.

"I know. That's what I love about you. You're just you. And it's enough for me, more than enough actually," he whispered.

chapter
forty-seven

The real estate broker made her way through our tiny apartment in less than ten minutes. My annoyance prevented me from escorting her through the three rooms. She could figure it out on her own. My anger about the situation fell her way, and I forced a hello that was gruff and uninviting.

"Well, that about does it." She was tentative, sensing my terse disposition. "I'll give you a call next week, and we can discuss timing. Sound good?"

"Yup." I shuffled to the door and opened it, avoiding eye contact with her.

My heart weighed heavy, and my deep inhalations provided zero relief. My soul was shattered at the reality of giving up my business, friends, and family. My girlfriends all listened patiently, but none of them had ever been married, and it was difficult for them to understand the consequences. Charlie asked what I would do if Neil and I were still dating, not married yet. My immediate response was stay in New York. No hesitation. But marriage was not dating. We had a life together, although lately it did seem like our lives were barely connected.

I wondered if Neil felt I was being selfish or unreasonable. I wondered if, in fact, I was. Replaying all the conversations in my head gave me clarity, and I immediately knew I had been nothing but reasonable and kind. Being true to myself and my own needs didn't make me selfish, but Neil had a way of portraying me as such in every conversation. I knew turning up my own voice would lead me in the right direction. I kept thinking of the loneliness in San Francisco—Neil working long hours and me struggling to get clients. I would have to spend money on advertising or marketing. The whirring in my mind never stopped while I struggled to focus on my current clients through my unrest.

Couples traipsed through our apartment, critiquing the molding and paint color.

"The current renter is an interior designer." I overheard the broker using my career as a selling point.

Although it was a rental unit, I had spent time transforming the space into a home for us. We had been responsible for paying for the improvements, but it had been worth it. The landlord had agreed to break our lease if we found a renter that would cover our remaining months. I suddenly appreciated the elaborate crown molding we'd added in the primary bedroom and the glass tile backsplash in the kitchen, which I had personally installed on a snowy weekend. Neil had watched as I mixed mud and grout. I had encouraged him to join me on the adventure, but he had simply replied, "Not my thing." The lukewarm feelings I once had about the uptown apartment were replaced with sadness at the prospect of abandoning my New York home.

The final viewings ended for the weekend, and I slid into bed, allowing the choked tears to fall.

"Sky? What do you feel like having for dinner?" Neil called.

I heaved a deep breath, wiped the tears, and cleared my congested throat. "I don't know. Whatever. Not that hungry," I called back.

Neil entered the bedroom with his eyes focused on a paper takeout menu.

"This new Chinese place looks good. We could go there too if you don't feel like staying home. We have been home all day," he commented.

More tears at the mention of Chinese food. I hated Chinese food. If I didn't speak up, I would suffer a lifetime of Chinese food in San Francisco.

"Neil," I whispered, "I don't think I can do this."

"What? Chinese? We should give it a try sometime. Doesn't have to be tonight."

"No. The move. I just can't." I barely got the words out amongst the tears.

"Aww, Sky. C'mon."

"You know I love you and want you to be successful, but don't you want me to be as well? I've worked so hard to get where I am today. All the schooling and entry-level jobs. And now, here I am where I never dreamed I would be. My name on the door. My accomplishment. I made all this happen." I cracked myself open. I hoped the uncomfortable vulnerability I shared with Neil would penetrate him, make him see life through my eyes.

"If I walk away from this opportunity, there may never be another one. You don't want me to blame you for that someday. I've worked too hard to walk away. I just can't," Neil admitted.

I closed my eyes, hoping the room would stop spinning, but instead, I thought about my sister's favorite stories. She'd loved the unexpected fates of the Greek goddesses and the compromising situations that were forced upon them. Debating whether the whirlpool vortex or snake-like hair with dog heads was scarier had kept us from thinking about the monster slowly killing her.

I'd searched for ways I could relieve her pain, and now I felt the same about Neil. I couldn't live with our marriage ending because of me. The survival of my marriage depended on my stepping back in my box, allowing Neil to soar at the expense of my own desires. But I also remembered the feeling of soaring. The feeling of lightness and courage paired with confidence as I built my own success. Reconciling these emotions seemed impossible. I was trapped by my sister's worst version of Scylla and Charybdis.

chapter
forty-eight

Brown cardboard boxes blocked the once-open space within the apartment. I fielded client calls while wrapping delicate items with the pages of an old *New York Times*, my fingertips blackened from the ink.

"No, I'll be back and forth until all my jobs are complete, don't worry. I'm very organized, so the days I am in town will be productive. Don't worry." I reassured clients as needed, which was often.

The silver picture frames displaying photos of Neil and I documented our life as a couple. Our first vacation together in the Berkshires; the first wedding we had attended together. I wrapped them in the science section of the newspaper. The simplicity of the past seemed far from the complexities of the moment. I hardly recognized the young girl in those photos.

Since meeting Neil, I had grown into a woman far from the eager-to-please girl I packed away in the boxes. Despite Neil's heavy weight thwarting my career, I rose to my potential with help from Johnny and Matthew. With Neil in San Francisco, I completed the packing on my own. I stored my anxiety and sadness deep inside, struggling through the days. I was able to clear the bookshelves before the phone rang again.

"This is Skylar."

"Hey." Matthew's voice was quiet. "I just hung up with Johnny. He said you're going. Is it true?"

My limbs grew heavy and loose. My teeth dug into my lower lip as thoughts of leaving everything and everyone I loved—including Matthew—twisted in my head.

"Skylar? Is it true?"

"It's true."

"Skylar, why are you doing this? I know you don't want to do this." Matthew verbalized the truth I had buried deep. It pricked tears from my eyes. I thought I had pushed my feelings far enough away that they would never return, but Matthew resurfaced the undeniable truth.

"I know, Matthew, but what can I do? He has a successful career. His earning power is greater than mine. I committed myself to him. He's my husband."

I fought with my sobs and lost.

"Is that what he told you? Those sound like his words, Skylar, not yours." Matthew's voice grew forceful from frustration.

"It's the truth," I replied.

It hit me that this was Neil's truth, not mine. I had been living for everyone else, yet I deserved a chance at living for myself. Could I look myself in the mirror if I succumbed to yet another sacrifice of myself for Neil? I thought of that girl suffocated in the picture frames who served everyone else's needs but her own. At times, I felt like another nameless, faceless woman sacrificing for all those she cared for around her.

My past choices had made me feel hollow from pouring myself into others. California was an empty destination for me. Neil's suggestion of having babies and forgetting my career affirmed what my inner voice screamed. I sank to the floor, curling into a ball in the corner of my apartment. I heaved tears without speaking.

"Is he in New York?" Matthew asked. I didn't lift my head, and my tears persisted.

"Skylar! Is he in New York?" Matthew raised his voice, waking me from my trance.

"No!" I yelled back.

Matthew's tone softened. "I'm coming over," he whispered.

I buried my face and my tears in my knees.

chapter
forty-nine

I huddled in the corner of our petite apartment and begged the agony of my uncertainty to evaporate. The internal voices grew louder as the conflict within me was forceful yet undecided.

I forced myself to envision a life in San Francisco. "Just go there for a moment," I kept telling myself, but I couldn't imagine it. I had been to Northern California as a child and recalled bits and pieces of the city. I could see Lombard Street behind my closed eyes and hanging onto the cable car with a queasy stomach, fearing I would fall off into the hilly streets. The reel of memories sped by in seconds simply because there were so few scenes.

I tried imagining Neil and I walking hand in hand in a stereotypical San Francisco neighborhood that I pulled from a scene in *Mrs. Doubtfire* or *Full House*. Neil and I sitting in that stupid car with John Stamos. It was ridiculous, but I couldn't laugh.

The knock on the door was slow and tentative. Delicate. I forced my limp body up to stand. My eyes were drenched, and I felt makeup dripping down my face. I couldn't be bothered with fixing my frazzled hair or pajama-like outfit. I remembered a time when I had calculated my appearance before seeing Matthew, but not today. I'd lost my energy for trivial matters. I pulled the door toward me and leaned on the edge as my head drooped down. I didn't want to see his eyes or smile. It hurt too much.

"Hey," he whispered.

The deep rasp in his voice sent a flurry of heat up through my chest and into my throat. I released the door and slumped into the sofa. The forced images of California had long gone. I reached for a pillow and buried my face in the softness as the waterworks unleashed.

"Skylar. Come here." Matthew replaced the pillow with his body.

We sat in an entangled lump, Matthew stroking my hair until my blubbering quieted.

"It's gonna be okay, Skylar. Just give it some time," Matthew said.

"How, Matthew? How?" My frustration injected my tone. "If I go, I lose myself, all I've worked for, friends and family, and pretty much all I've ever known, my whole support system. Everything."

"But not your husband. If you go, you get to keep Neil."

I sat back, and the stillness of the room was noticeable. Matthew's words felt thick and weighty. He was right. In a few words, he'd summed it up. Each time I was with him, I realized it was more than intense chemistry that stirred the molecules when we were together. And just like that, it was crystallized. The spinning thoughts were halted.

"Yes. That's it. I am essentially being asked to choose Neil or the entire rest of my life. That's the decision. I can have Neil or everything and everyone else in my life."

"Does he understand what he's asking of you?" Matthew asked.

I paused, contemplating our conversations. Had I been clear enough? Had I stuck up for myself and communicated effectively? Was I willing to throw my marriage away? The man I had thought would be by my side when my work was first featured in a magazine and when my brother got married. I had thought Neil was that man. But now, it was unclear. How could I follow a man whose expectations included giving up my life and my career for him?

"I don't think so, but you know his career is important for our financial security."

"Why do you sell yourself short? You're smart and capable and driven. I have never seen a woman so determined in my life. You're quiet about it, which is cool. You're not this powerful bull throwing your weight around. You're on your path with blinders on, and you are getting there. You can be financially successful, too. You can have it all, and you don't even know it. In some ways, that is beautiful and refreshing, but it's also insanely frustrating. You are incredibly special, Skylar. I wish you could see your potential, because I do. I see it. I see greatness for you. I see you larger than life and pushing your dreams over for bigger ones behind it. I want that for you. The power you hold is electric. If you recognize it, own it, you're limitless." Matthew paced the apartment as he spoke with dynamic gesturing hands.

Neil had dumped a heavy weight upon me, leaving me with a difficult decision that kept me paralyzed, fearful about my future. My dilemma grew knowing Matthew lit up my emotions and filled a desire I'd lacked for years. I stared at Matthew in silence, in awe.

"What?" he asked.

"I've never had anyone believe in me the way you do."

"Skylar, I'm sure your family, your siblings, they must have—"

"Of course they did, but with you, it feels different. There aren't expectations. You have nothing to gain from this. I feel that." A lone tear escaped the corner of my eye.

I hadn't made a final decision regarding the move, but I went through the motions and boxed our belongings, wondering if pretending I was moving would convince me to go. "Looks like we are ready to go." Neil kissed me on my head as he dropped his bags next to the front door. He strode to the kitchen, and I heard the crack of a beer bottle opening. Slumping into the sofa, he asked about my week.

"Fine," I said.

"Wrapping up all your loose ends?" he asked.

"Neil, I, I need to talk to you." One last effort to reveal my truth. "This move isn't the best idea for me, for us," I said. My heart throbbed, fueled by anxiety.

"What do you mean? I thought we decided. We've discussed this, Sky. It's the best chance at me having the successful career I've been working toward. I'm at the brink. It's normal for you to be scared and anxious. But I promise it will be okay. Maybe we just start our family a little earlier. You can focus on decorating a new home and raising a baby. You'll meet mommy friends. You'll make a life for yourself, I promise."

Neil spoke in a sweet, gentle voice as if I were a child. Anger floated up from my toes as he spoke. Family? Mommy friends? It was as if he had been blind for the past years, refusing to acknowledge my accomplishments. I felt physically dizzy from the complete disregard for me as an independent person. Matthew was right. Neil only saw me as a supporter of his dreams.

"Neil, I can't. I won't do this. I won't give up everything that makes me who I am for you. For your career. It's too much sacrifice for me."

"No one is asking you to give up who you are. I'm doing this for us. I'm working my ass off traveling across the country for us. For you. I just want you with me. We can't live on different coasts, Skylar. That's not going to work." Neil took my face in his hands. "It's going to be okay. Stop panicking. Everyone loves you. You'll have friends and business contacts in no time."

"Neil, I would be leaving everything in New York."

"No, you're not. You're not leaving everything. You have

me. That's all you need, Skylar. I'll be there for you."

"Really? You haven't been there for me at all lately. You were entirely disinterested when I started my own business. And while you're at work for thirteen hours a day, I won't have you. I may as well be in New York."

I could tell Neil wasn't listening to me. He heard me, but nothing penetrated. He didn't take me seriously. I knew the words I needed in this moment, but I couldn't get them across my lips. Words of anger, disappointment, and hurt rushed through my head. I closed my eyes and wished a telepathic message would force Neil to realize asking me to yield to his agenda at the expense of myself was outrageous.

The day of the move drew closer, and a darkness came over me, heavy and paralyzing. I didn't know how I would ever board that plane, abandoning everything that had meaning in my life. The denial shifted, and an agonizing throb invaded my chest.

chapter
fifty

Charlie organized a "see you soon" party, but I insisted she cancel it. I could barely lift my head. I felt as if I was drowning within a swarm of bees buzzing so loud I couldn't hear my own voice, much less anyone else's.

"I don't think I can go," I told Charlie.

"Have you ever thought about whether your marriage would survive if Neil stayed in New York?" Charlie asked.

"Maybe? I don't know. It seems to get harder every year. Lately, harder every day."

"Maybe you should give it a shot. Maybe six months. Then, if California is as awful as you think it will be, at least you can tell Neil, and yourself, you gave it a shot."

"My gut tells me this is a bad idea. It would be so much easier if I could just say, 'Yay! Let's do it! This is going to be great!' But I don't believe that. Not even a little. It's not just about the relocation, but it's clear he doesn't see me for who I truly am, and he certainly doesn't understand me. But I did make a commitment, and letting go is hard. He helped me when I was in such a dark moment in my life; I feel like I owe him something."

"Yeah, I understand that, but you don't owe him your life, Skylar."

The boxes and furniture had been transported across the country, and our apartment sat naked with only essential items. Neil spent the week in California and would stay until

I arrived. Giotto had given us a temporary apartment until we found a rental.

The week was filled with farewell dinners, coffees, and lunches. But every night after dinner, Matthew and I met for a drink at a quiet neighborhood bar downtown. I wanted, needed, to be with him.

"Are you staying?" It was his first question every night. He was joking, but not joking. I mustered a weak smile and slid onto the barstool next to him.

"I have no idea how I'm doing this. It's like I'm blocking it out."

"Five more days and the blocking will stop, Skylar. Can you see the next fifty years with him?" he asked.

"Wow. Way to get right to it."

"Listen, Sky, you will kill it anywhere. You're talented and personable. I know you can do this. I don't want you to go, but maybe it's for the best. I mean, what are we doing here? I can't walk away from you, but I can't have you either, so this torture is probably not healthy for either of us."

"I know," I whispered.

Matthew slid his hand over mine. There were no more words to say. Of all the people I interacted with each day—the guy at the coffee shop, the recurring faces on my daily subway, all the salespeople I met at work—why did I feel this with Matthew? I fought for my marriage every day, but Neil saw it as my duty, and in my heart, I knew I could never come to terms with his outrageous assumptions.

"I wish things were different," Matthew whispered to himself, but loud enough for me to hear. "I wish we could give this a chance."

I let my eyes peer deep, invading his soul and looking for answers.

"Me too."

"It's been so long, Skylar. I've dated, and I put myself out there, but you're different. There's something you do to me.

You make me feel like there's hope. As much as I try forgetting you, your face pops up in my dreams. When I have exciting news, like a new deal at work or my basketball team winning, I want to call you. I hold myself back." He put his face in his hands, as if the conversation hurt.

When it was time to go, I slid across the leather seats, and Lukas closed the door. I wondered if I could be comfortable having someone drive me throughout Manhattan. I had only known the subway and buses. Lukas navigated the narrow downtown streets with care. I rested my head back and gazed out the window.

"Hey," Matthew said. "Are you okay?"

"I don't know. I'm trying to be okay. I'm screwed either way, right? So may as well not destroy someone else's life in the process."

"You mean Neil?"

"Yes, Neil. I feel like I owe it to him to give this a shot. I would feel guilty if I didn't." Marriage was a contract with vows and commitments. I wrung my hands, wondering if I could reconcile abandoning those promises.

Matthew sat silently, but I could tell his mind was swarmed with thoughts and things he wanted to say but held back. I knew what he thought. I was selling myself short. Not giving myself a chance. Sacrificing myself for Neil. But isn't that part of marriage? Compromise and sacrifice. Everyone can't get their way.

Matthew leaned over and cupped my face in his hands, aligning his lips with mine. The kiss was soft and supple and long. So deliciously painful. It hurt. When Matthew pulled away, he nuzzled his nose with mine, and I saw tears brimming in his eyes.

"I wish it didn't have to be this way," he whispered.

chapter
fifty-one

"Tomorrow's the big day! You ready?" Neil was filled with enthusiasm. "I got the apartment ready to go. I've been running around so it will be ready when you arrive. It's been a lot with work, but it's all ready for you," he said with pride.

"Thanks."

"Are you all wrapped up with work?" he asked.

"Not at all. It's been challenging since I don't want to close my business. I'll need to make a few trips back east to finish up some projects," I explained.

"I have a lot to show you out here. You're going to love it. I know you'll be happy, even without your business. Maybe you could get a job with a designer like you did with Andrew," Neil said.

I didn't want to start over, and a slow heat from anger began around my neck. I had accomplished my goals in New York, goals no one other than Matthew had thought I would ever achieve.

The thrashing in my head and stomach escalated, reaching an unbearable level. If I were honest with myself, Neil and I had been spiraling down a drain for months. His travel to California and consuming career put me on the outside. Building my business had strengthened my voice, and although I hesitated to admit it, Matthew gave me strength.

I wanted to love my husband, but sacrificing New York cut away too much of who I was, who I wanted to be. The sharp ache of anxiety lived in my gut.

In a decisive moment, a peacefulness swept over me, removing angst and uncertainty like a bridled horse, thrashing about, finally released from constraints, free to run through forbidden fields, bucking and kicking with joy laced with resentment from the years of captivity. I was ready for a new beginning. A new beginning in New York.

"I'm not coming to California. The truth is, it's more than just the move and the sacrifices I would be making. It's us, our marriage. You don't understand me anymore. I've grown and changed. I'm not the naive young girl I once was. I want more for my life, my career, my relationships. We just don't make sense anymore." The boulders I carried broke into gravel, and the breath I'd held for months gave way to a deep inhale, and I finally had air in my lungs again.

"Skylar, this is stupid. We're fine; you're just being dramatic about the move. You may think you've grown, but this ridiculous behavior is completely in line with an immature girl." My fight disappeared. Nothing would be gained by an argument.

"There's nothing you can say to change my mind. And quite honestly, your response validates all my fears about moving and the truth about our marriage. I'm staying here in New York. I've made my decision."

"That's the most selfish thing I have ever heard. I thought marriage was unconditional love, but you're just selfish, Skylar."

"If loving myself and choosing my own aspirations over yours is selfish, then I guess you're right. I won't love and support you at the expense of myself, Neil. Our marriage has only been about my supporting you. You've never seriously supported my dreams. You never will. I'm choosing me, and your temper and name-calling won't change a thing. I. Choose. Me."

chapter
fifty-two

I had three phone calls to make.

First, I called Charlie. She offered me a place to stay, and I moved into her apartment. While my feet hung off her hard sofa, my thoughts quieted, and my sleep was uninterrupted for the first time in months.

My second call was to Johnny. When we met in his office, Johnny hugged me as I choked through the saga with Neil. I knew my next task of locating an affordable office space would pose its challenges in Manhattan, and it weighed on me, so I cut my visit with Johnny short.

"Thank you, Johnny. I am so grateful for your friendship. I could stay all day, but I'm off to find some cheap office space so I can get back to business."

"Office space? Skylar, you can work from here. Pick a desk, pick an office. Stay as long as you want, rent-free. I insist."

Tears collected in my eyes from the most generous offer I could never have anticipated. I simply hugged Johnny as tightly as I could.

"I assume that's a yes."

"It's a hell yes," I said.

Then, the third call.

"Hi. Can you meet me at the coffee shop near Johnny's office?"

"I'm on my way," Matthew said.

I sat in the red vinyl booth, fidgeting with the sugar packets. I saw him before he located me in the corner booth, and the grimace on his face filled me with guilt. He gave a limp wave as he strode towards me.

Matthew placed his face in his hands. "I don't know how to do this. I don't know how to say goodbye. I respect your choices and your marriage, but this is . . . horrible. I suppose you picked this coffee shop because you were saying goodbye to Johnny."

"Not exactly. As it turns out, we may be meeting here more often. This is my new neighborhood. I'll be working out of Johnny's office for a while. I'm staying, Matthew. I realized Neil and I weren't meant to be. This move, it just put it all in fast forward. I belong here, in New York."

At first, Mathew looked pale and stunned. After a moment of digesting my words, he slid next to me in the booth and wrapped his arms around me, hugging me tighter and tighter. I closed my eyes, melting into his embrace. He turned his head and kissed my neck, nuzzling closer.

"I have never wanted to love someone as much as I want to love you," he whispered.

"I feel the same. But let's take it slow. I want to do it right this time." But as I held him, I knew this was right. Neil and I could only work when I was broken. With Matthew, love didn't have an agenda. We could love each other from the most honest places in our hearts.

epilogue

"So, Skylar, tell us about your inspiration for this design."

The sun reflected off the building across the street, barely missing my eyes in the Condé Nast offices. As the months had passed, my creativity had flourished, feeding off Manhattan's dynamic energy, which filled me each day. Neil had soon agreed that a divorce was a practical decision, and my complete attention could finally zoom in on my future, including this feature article.

"Well, the location provides so much inspiration. It was easy to feed off the location and mission of the founders.

"The clients were wonderful to work with and were receptive to my ideas. If I were to choose one element, though, I would say the beach, Long Beach to be specific, provided a huge amount of inspiration."

An important call came in for the interviewer, and she excused herself for a moment.

"How am I doing?" I asked Matthew.

"Skylar, you're amazing. I'm in awe of you, and this journalist is in awe of your work. I overheard her saying she wants to increase the spread to four pages."

The urge to kiss Matthew surfaced, and I paused, intentionally taking notice of the moment. The love swirling inside my heart for Matthew, my pride growing from my dreams coming true after long hard work, and my first published design in a reputable design magazine brought a giddy smile across my face. The magazine editor returned and shooed Matthew out of the way.

"I'll happily get out of your way and grab some coffee for

the celebrity designer," he said.

I rubbed the bracelet charms dangling from my wrist. The familiar letters of my sister's initials slid between my fingers, and I knew she would be proud of me. I squeezed my shoulders back, feeling pride from my accomplishments. I turned toward Matthew, and even in the distance I could see his tender smile as I shared with the magazine editor my experience designing the pediatric oncology center. That's when I knew I really could have it all.

acknowledgments

The journey of writing a novel was not something I contemplated properly. I can recall my initial thrill with writing, seedlings planted in the eleventh grade. It's been many years since the arrangement of words began filling my brain and thoughts were reframed as sentences in my head. The learning curve was steeper than expected, but I'm thankful for all those who heaved me up the hill.

This story drifted in my head for years; one ordinary day in 2016, I opened my laptop and began writing. I felt my way through the process one inch at a time. There were many stops and starts over the years but my determination to complete this book never waned. There was much to learn and finding patience was challenging. I found ways around each roadblock, and there were many. Gotham Writers helped me around my first challenges and gifted me the most wonderful writing group, my rainbow writers, Anthony, Nikkay, Sapna, and Sonia. You have given me immense courage over the years. Without you, there is no *Renovation*. The struggle of not feeling I could complete this novel was lifted when I met my writing coach Kathy Dodson. Kathy did more than put red lines through my misshaped sentences; she understood the depth and meaning behind what could be seen as a light, enjoyable beach read. Thank you, Kathy, for your patience and emotional investment in a first-time author who needed much handholding through the process. I know you will give me the courage to complete my second novel.

My "why" in this world is and always has been my family. My three incredible daughters, Bailey, Gabrielle, and Remi, keep me young, focused on the things that truly matter in life, and always on my toes. Our meaningful relationship is my oxygen. To my parents Maxine and Howard, who have always been my bedrock, my cheerleaders, consistently unwavering in their commitment to my daughters and me. I thank you for providing me with a solid work ethic, which carried me through the grueling process of writing, editing, and publishing a novel. To my big sister, Caryn, who taught me how to be strong.

Family is not always defined by blood relation, but by those who sat with me through times of feast or famine—they were always at my table. My soul sisters, Stacy, Diana, Amy, Julie, Sari, Jamie, Michele, Cheryl, Kat, Lorin, Meryl and Jon. You've elevated me and kept me grounded with love and compassion.

In my opinion, a home is vacant without fur-filled sofas. I must thank my fur babies, Hercules, Ducky, and Benji, for warming my feet and keyboard over the years. Thank you for the companionship in what can be a very lonely process.

Eternal gratitude to my readers for taking time, the most precious of all commodities, to read my words. I am thrilled to share *Renovation* with the world, and I hope you can escape daily life while reading yet relate to Skylar's emotional journey. May we all be on a journey of renovating ourselves throughout our lives.

about atmosphere press

Founded in 2015, Atmosphere Press was built on the principles of Honesty, Transparency, Professionalism, Kindness, and Making Your Book Awesome. As an ethical and author-friendly hybrid press, we stay true to that founding mission today.

If you're a reader, enter our giveaway for a free book here:

SCAN TO ENTER
BOOK GIVEAWAY

If you're a writer, submit your manuscript for consideration here:

SCAN TO SUBMIT
MANUSCRIPT

And always feel free to visit Atmosphere Press and our authors online at atmospherepress.com. See you there soon!

about the author

Renovation is Leslie Abner's debut novel. Leslie graduated from Cornell University and pursued a career in Interior Design at The New York School of Interior Design Graduate School. Leslie founded LA Studio 23 years ago and currently works on both residential and commercial interior design projects. Beyond writing, she fills her time with raising her three daughters, enjoying outdoor activities and traveling.

Printed in the USA
CPSIA information can be obtained
at www.ICGtesting.com
LVHW041202161124
796821LV00037B/447